Salute to the

AIR FORCE

MEDICAL BRANCH

on the

75th Anniversary

Royal Canadian Air Force

Thanks
Harold Wright

Harold M. Wright
Lieutenant-Colonel, Retired

Published by
Harold M. Wright
1834 Louisiana Avenue, Ottawa, Ontario, Canada
K1H 6V1

Canadian Cataloguing in Publication Data

Wright, Harold M., 1920 -
Salute to the Air Force Medical Branch
on the 75th anniversary of the Royal Canadian Air Force

ISBN 0-9686588-0-6

1. Wright, Harold M. 1920
2. Biographical   Anthology
3. Historical - aviation medicine   Anecdotes. I Title

Preface

In 1997, on a visit to the RCAF Memorial Museum at Trenton Ontario, it was observed that there were not many artifacts to recognize the contributions of the RCAF Medical Branch to aviation. This was discussed with the Executive Director, who suggested that since visitors liked to view pictures and text, the Museum supported the idea of gathering and assembling material in the form of counter top albums. Such albums would recognize the accomplishments of Medical Branch members in aviation medicine, research and development, search and rescue and medical support to RCAF operations.

Air Marshal Robert Leckie, writing in *The Journal of the Canadian Medical Services* in November 1946 said,

> *"I would like to take this opportunity to express my personal appreciation to all Officers of the R.C.A.F. Medical Branch for the high standard of professional service which has been provided for the R.C.A.F., appreciating that it was only by the individual effort of each Officer that this was attained.*
> *The Medical Branch, through your efforts, has worked in complete co-ordination with the other branches of the R.C.A.F. in the rapid development of aerial warfare and played no small part toward the satisfactory outcome of the recent struggle. You have gained an admirable record in the field of aviation medical research and pioneering in many of its aspects."*

This book, which was produced from the material gathered for the Museum albums, tries to personalize the "individual efforts" of some of those referred to by A/M Leckie. It was decided to prepare it as a salute to the Royal Canadian Air Force Medical Branch and to Canadian Air Force medical personnel through a collection of biographic sketches specially prepared for this project. These sketches help to outline the contributions made by these individuals in support of the RCAF and Air Force operations. The material here collected has been gathered from many sources, mostly autobiographical. In most cases, their stories appear as they were written with some editing for consistentency in format. This album is not all inclusive. Rather, it is an attempt to recognize those who were willing to contribute and on whom data could be found. The editor apologizes for any omissions.

In the case of deceased or incapacitated persons, historical data was extracted from published sources or gathered from relatives and friends with first-hand knowledge of the person concerned. Because some photos are outdated, orders, decorations and medals attributed to an individuals may differ from those reflected in the medal ribbons shown in the accompanying photographs.

The biographies are grouped in chapters based on their principal accomplishments in the support of Air Force operations and titled, somewhat tongue-in-cheek, to indicate their "claim to fame." Chapter Title pages list these biographies in alphabetical order.

It is hoped that the reader will find enjoyment in reading of these many accomplishments and perhaps gain some insight into the role the RCAF Medical Branch played in the field of research, aviation medicine and medical support to the Air Force.

Harold M. Wright, Lieutenant-Colonel (retired)
Ottawa, Ontario
December 1999

FOREWORD

Canadian Air Force history in peace and war is covered in many volumes. In all cases, the emphasis on what generated success is the bravery and skill of aircrews. And, this is rightly so.

Some authors do indeed, give the much deserved credit due the ground crews for the vital part they played in keeping the aircraft serviceable, safe and ready for their crews. The part played by others behind the scenes, however, while equally essential, is seldom noted.

Without pressure-breathing, the "G" suit, aerospace preventive medicine, certain high altitude research and a myriad of other medical solutions, it is possible that many of today's high performance and high-altitude demands on the aircrew could not have become acceptable as early as they were. The part played by Canadian Air Force medical personnel in innovating and developing solutions to the challenges that faster aeroplanes and higher altitudes generated for aircrew, were the story told, should be a matter of national pride.

Around the world, "G" suits and pressure vests are standard equipment for fighter pilots. Both are Canadian Air Force Medical Branch inventions. The pioneer work done at the Institute of Aviation Medicine by our medics in all the fields of medicine as it affects aircrew attracted world wide attention. Its cooperation with NASA and later the Canadian Space Institute has honed the broad reputation of the Medical Branch even more.

The material which follows in this overdue book is a compilation of some of the history of the Air Force Medical Branch. Through the years, I was a beneficiary of the support provided by the personnel involved. When we rebuilt our Air Force in 1978 and created Air Command, we were presented the opportunity to tie the medics into the whole decision and operations process. This we did.

I can only add my admiration for what the medics have done to enhance further the unmatched reputation of Canada's Air Force. The RCAF excelled at every task it ever tackled. The Medical Branch helped make that possible.

Wm. K. "Bill" Carr
Air Marshal (retired)
December 1999

Acknowledgements

A good deal of support was provided in completing this project for which the author is profoundly grateful. First, there were those who contributed their stories for inclusion and those who helped develop biographical sketches for those unable to prepare their own. Then, there were those individuals who supported this project financially, without whose help this would have been an onerous personal financial burden. Grateful thanks are extended to the Department of National Defence, the National Archives of Canada, Canada Post Corporation, The Canadian Journal of Cardiology, Dalhousie University of Halifax Nova Scotia and to individuals who provided biographic material and photographs to illustrate the text.

Someone had to put all this text in type, proof-read the copy, design the layout and do a final manuscript edit. My thanks, therefore, to my wife, Dorothy for her patience and copy edit assistance, and to Janis and Randy Ray for their invaluable help in preparing the initial copy. I am deeply indebted to Charles King, whose story appears under *The Innkeepers,* for his advice, encouragement, editorial assistance and design of this book. Any errors or omissions, of course, are mine alone and I humbly apologize if these offend anyone.

Finally, I thank you, the reader, for taking the time to browse through these pages and reading of the efforts of members of the Medical Branch in helping the Royal Canadian Air Force accomplish its many military and humanitarian missions.

Harold Wright

TABLE OF CONTENTS

1. THE LEADERS

Medical Officers of Air Rank/General Rank

2. AVIATION MEDICINE PIONEERS

Research Scientists, Inventors and BioScience Specialists

2. AVIATION MEDICINE PIONEERS - Continued

3. THE FLIGHT SURGEONS

4. SEARCH & RESCUE MEDICS
Para-rescue MOs, Nurses & Medical Assistants

5. THE PHYSICIANS
Medical Officers - WW II and Post-War

6. THE NIGHTINGALES
Nursing Officers

7. THE INNKEEPERS
Medical Associate Officers (Health Care Administration)

CHAPTER 1

THE LEADERS

AIR RANK/GENERAL RANK
MEDICAL OFFICERS

- **Major-General J.J.S.G. "Benny" Benoit**
  The first Francophone Air Force Surgeon General; 41 years service in the Army, the RCAF and the Canadian Forces Medical Service.

- **Air Commodore George D. Caldbick**
  First recipient of the RCAF Flight Surgeon's badge.

- **Major-General Wendy A. Clay**
  First female pilot, Flight Surgeon and Surgeon General of the Canadian Forces.

- **Air Commodore A.A. Gordon Corbet**
  First Senior Medical Officer of the first hospital built under the British Commonwealth Air Training Plan at Uplands, Ontario and the first post-war Director General Medical Services (Air).

- **Major-General Robert W. Fassold**
  First RCAF de Havilland Comet aircraft pilot, later a doctor and Surgeon General.

- **Major-General Wilson G. "Bill" Leach**
  Winner of the McKee Trans-Canada Trophy for his contributions to aviation medicine, Surgeon General and Commander of Military Merit.

- **Major-General Pierre R. Morisset**
  Class valedictorian of medical class of 1971, accompanying physician for three royal tours; Surgeon General and Commander of Military Merit.

1

- **Major-General Donald G. M. Nelson**
  First Surgeon General to attend National Defence College.

- **Brigadier-General Harold Robinson**
  First Air Force specialist in ear, nose and throat, held a masters degree in health care administration.

- **Air Commodore R.W. Ryan**
  Australian born doctor from the Royal Air Force Medical Branch, loaned to the RCAF as an advisor during the formation of its Medical Branch.

- **Air Commodore James W. "Fred" Tice**
  In 1943, appointed first Director Medical Services (Air).

Joseph Jean S.G. Benoit
CStJ, CD, MD
Major-General

Joseph Jean Benoit, nicknamed "Benny," was born on 14 February 1932 in Rivière-du-Loup, Québec where he grew up and obtained his early education and completed high school, all in the French language. His logical choice of university for post-secondary education was Laval University in Québec City where he successfully completed a bachelor of arts degree program in 1950.

Postgraduate studies in medicine began in 1952 at this same University with the help of the Canadian Army. Officer Cadet Benoit was enrolled in the Canadian Officer Training Corps (COTC) in the Infantry Division. This led to a commission as a 2nd Lieutenant and attachment to the 2nd Battalion of the Royal 22nd Regiment, then located in the Federal Republic of Germany. Following Lieutenant Benoit's return from Germany, he was promoted to Captain and appointed an instructor with the COTC unit at Laval University.

In September 1956, while undergoing his final university year in medicine, Benoit transferred to the Royal Canadian Air Force. Regulations at this time required him to resign his commission as an Army Captain and be enrolled as a Pilot Officer with simultaneous promotion to Flying Officer. He was graduated from Laval University's Doctor of Medicine program in June 1958 and promoted to Flight Lieutenant.

On graduation, his first duty post, as a brand new RCAF

MGen J.J.S.G. Benoit

3

Medical Officer, was to one of the Pine-Tree Line radar stations at Parent, Québec. These radar sites were situated on hilltops in remote communities along the 50th parallel as part of the North American early warning system during the Cold War. A doctor, one or two nurses and medical assistants provided medical care to the Air Force members manning the radars and to their dependents living on the Station. For Flight Lieutenant Benoit, it was a "postgraduate" course in the school of hard knocks. As a new doctor, he had to rely a good deal on the support and advice of the physician from the community as he faced some very difficult medical and injury situations amongst the RCAF members and their families.

These stations were situated in the wilds and were seasonally plagued by swarms of black flies. The military approach to this environmental problem was multi-faceted. First, everyone was issued personal supplies of black fly repellent This had little effect, so households and worksites were issued with hand-operated vaporizers and a DDT solution. This helped a little, but was still not the answer. Then great foggers, towed by trucks were driven around the station, spraying an oily DDT fog over everything and everyone caught outdoors. When this didn't have the desired results, the Air Force flew over the station in a Douglas DC-3 Dakota, carrying barrels of the oil-DDT mixture and equipped for aerial spray. If the station was forewarned, children were brought into the house, laundry was removed from the lines and cars were put under cover, if possible.

Air Force Headquarters had an entomologist on staff who seemed to make the decision when to spray. This, it was learned, was based on the "black fly landing reports" supplied by stations along the Pine Tree Line. Station Commanders and the Senior Medical Officers (SMOs) were required to position airmen or airwomen at points around the station, seated with a one-foot square piece of Air Force blue material on their lap, counting the number of black flies that landed on the fabric in a given period. This information was dutifully recorded and sent by "priority" message to Headquarters by 1615 hrs daily. Since the "fly-count" on a piece of fabric did not always reflect the intensity of the fly infestation, the Station Commander and the SMO decided that when an aerial spray was needed, the fly-landing count would, mysteriously, show a dramatic increase over the previous day. When the fly

4

population tapered off, the count would, in like manner, drop to a low level. In this way, they got the spray they wanted when it was needed and were able to warn station personnel and their families to take the necessary precautions before the airplane arrived.

Finally, relief was in sight as F/L Benoit found his way to RCAF Station Rockcliffe. There he was assigned to the Station Hospital, which was to become Canadian Forces Hospital Rockcliffe. The staff of this hospital formed the nucleus of what was to become the new National Defence Medical Centre in Ottawa. This three-year posting added to his self-confidence and medical experience so that in 1962, he was selected to be Chief of Anaesthesiology at Canadian Forces Hospital Churchill, Manitoba. Two years of experience in anaesthesiology prepared him to continue his studies in that specialty, which he successfully completed at the University of Toronto between 1962 and 1964.

With the Royal College of Physicians certification in anaesthesiology on his resume, Squadron Leader Benoit was appointed Chief of Anaesthesiology at Canadian Forces Hospital Oromocto in New Brunswick. This general hospital was a joint venture between the civilian community of Oromocto and the Canadian Forces, sharing facilities and some staff. Military physicians were all members of the Oromocto General Hospital medical staff. This was a short appointment and Lieutenant-Colonel Benoit, after only one year in the job, and with a promotion, was appointed Chief of the Department of Anaesthesiology at Canadian Forces Hospital Halifax.

With a promotion to Colonel in 1974, Benoit was now ready for a command appointment to which he was assigned in Valcartier, Québec. He was Commandant of the Canadian Forces Hospital Valcartier and double-hatted as Chief of Anaesthesiology.

He brought his clinical and command experience to the National Defence Medical Centre in Ottawa in 1976 where he was appointed Chief of the Department of Anaesthesiology, a post he held for nine years. Benoit's promotion to Brigadier-General was announced in 1985 as he assumed command of the National Defence Medical Centre.

Four years later, in 1989, General Benoit assumed command of the newly formed Canadian Forces Hospital and Medical Supply System with headquarters in Ottawa. This short appointment led to his promotion to Major-

General in August of 1990 as he became Surgeon General, the first Air Force Francophone to hold this appointment.

He retired from the Canadian Forces Medical Services in January 1993, having completed 41 years service in the Army and RCAF. He is married to Claudette Poitras from Québec City and they have four children. Major-General Benoit remains active in the Defence Medical Association and spends his leisure time at his cottage, golfing or on holidays in Florida.

Summary of Achievements

Commander of the Most Venerable Order of the Hospital of St. John of Jerusalem (CStJ)
Canadian Forces Decoration (CD)
Jubilee Medal - Queen Elizabeth II
Queen's Honorary Physician (QHP)
Bachelor of Arts, Laval-1950 (BA)
Doctor of Medicine University of Laval-1958 (MD)
Certificate Royal College of Physicians Canada (CRCP C)
Certificate of Specialist in Province of Québec (Anaesthesia) (CSPQ)

GEORGE D. CALDBICK
OStJ, CD, MD
AIR COMMODORE

George D. **Caldbick** was born in Cobalt Ontario in 1910 where he received his early education before going on to Queen's University in Kingston Ontario for studies in medicine. He graduated from Queen's in 1937 and practised medicine from 1937 to 1940.

With the onset of war, Dr. Caldbick joined the Royal Canadian Army Medical Corps in June 1940 and transferred to the RCAF Medical Branch on its formation in November 1940. During the period 1941 to 1943, Flight Lieutenant (F/L) Caldbick was a Medical Officer at RCAF Stations in Moncton, New Brunswick and Summerside, Prince Edward Island.

George Caldbick went overseas to England in 1943. There he served with 426 (B) Squadron at Dishforth Yorks, that was then flying Vickers Wellington medium

A/C George D. Caldbick

bombers as part of No. 6 (RCAF) Bomber Group. Later he was posted to 408 (B) Squadron at Linton-on-Ouse Yorks, equipped with Avro Lancaster heavy bombers, as part of No. 5 Group. F/L Caldbick was repatriated in 1945 at the end of the war and was demobilized. He took this opportunity to continue his medical education and obtained a diploma in Public Health from the University of Toronto.

Dr. Caldbick re-enrolled in the RCAF in 1946. He was selected for further training and earned a certificate in Dermatology from Harvard

7

University. On 28 August 1962, he was the first of sixty-seven medical officers to be awarded the new Flight Surgeon's badge. This badge was originated by Group Captain Jack Wickett *(see Aviation Medicine Pioneers at Chapter 2),* Consultant in Aviation Medicine and Physiological Research on the staff of the Director General Medical Services (Air) [DGMS(Air)]. The badge, embroidered on woven cloth, displays a caduceus surrounded by a pair of upward pointing wings and topped by a crown. It is worn on the left breast of the uniform tunic.

George Caldbick spent several years on the staff of DGMS(Air) in increasingly senior ranks and appointments, culminating in that of Deputy Director General Medical Services in the newly formed Canadian Forces Medical Services with the rank of Air Commodore. He retired from the RCAF in 1965. A two-year post-retirement appointment with the Defence Research Board was followed by a four-year stint as a consultant with the Department of Veterans Affairs. Dr. Caldbick retired a third time in 1971 and remained in Ottawa until his death in 1987.

Summary of Achievements
Officer of the Most Venerable Order of the Hospital of St. John of Jerusalem (OStJ)
Canadian Forces Decoration (CD)
Defence Medal
Canadian Volunteer Service Medal and clasp
War Medal
Coronation Medal Queen Elizabeth II
Queen's Honorary Physician (QHP)
Doctor of Medicine Queen's University - 1937 (MD)
Diploma American Board of Dermatology (DABD)

WENDY A. CLAY
CMM, OSTJ, CD, MD
MAJOR-GENERAL

Wendy A. Clay was born in Fort St. John, British Columbia on 27 September 1942. She enrolled in the Royal Canadian Navy in the Medical Officer Training Plan and completed her studies in medicine at the University of British Columbia and an internship at the Toronto General Hospital in 1968.

Captain Clay's first duty post was to Canadian Forces Base Trenton, where she was an anomaly as a female medical officer. Trenton was also the Command Headquarters for Air Transport Command with Major-General Chester Hull as Officer Commanding. General Hull was more than a little disturbed when the wife of one of the airmen complained to him on a Monday morning that her husband had been taken to the hospital over the week-end with a fractured leg. There was no doctor on duty, she said, and her husband had been seen by one of the nurses who x-rayed the leg, set the fracture and put a cast on it! The Commander was quickly informed that he had Captain Wendy Clay on his hospital staff and, as a physician, she had given the corporal the best medical care available. With the gender confusion cleared, Doctor Clay was quickly accepted into the life of the Air Base. She was the first woman to qualify as a Flight Surgeon, during the course of which she flew in a Canadair CL-41

MGen Wendy A. Clay

Tutor jet training aircraft. This convinced her to take up flying and she enrolled in a pilot training program with the Trenton Flying Club. Successfully completing the course, Wendy received her pilot's wings and subsequently a commercial pilot's licence in 1970.

With a promotion in 1970, Major Clay was soon on her way to Canadian Forces Base (CFB) Moose Jaw Saskatchewan as Base Surgeon. CFB Moose Jaw is a jet training base and the home of the Snowbirds, the Air Force flying demonstration squadron. Her interest in flying and aviation medicine continued to grow, so she underwent basic pilot training in 1972.

Major Clay in a Tutor jet cockpit.

The following year, Major Clay was posted to Training Command Headquarters (TCHQ) in Winnipeg Manitoba. This headquarters later became Air Command in a Forces reorganization and Major Clay remained with the new Headquarters as Staff Officer Aviation Medicine until 1977. During this period, she completed a six-month advanced aviation medicine course in

Farnborough England, and returned to Moose Jaw for advanced flying training in 1974, becoming the first woman in the Canadian Forces to complete flying training to wings standard on the Tutor aircraft.

This was her proudest accomplishment. Major Clay flew the Tutor jet, the same as used by the Canadian Armed Forces Snowbirds, and took training identical to that of her male counterparts, including formation flying, instrument flying, night flying, and aerobatics. On 30 August 1974, she graduated with five male members of her course in advanced pilot training. By graduation day she had logged approximately 230 hours in a Tutor jet, as well as 247 hours in academic training. The Chief of Staff for Canadian Forces Training Command, Brigadier-General L.V. Johnson pinned on her Air Force pilot's wings while her father Mr. Lawrence Clay of Terrace BC looked on proudly.

More challenging work beckoned as newly promoted Lieutenant-Colonel (LCol) Clay moved on to join the staff of the Canadian Forces Institute of Environmental Medicine, a part of the Defence and Civil Institute of Environmental Medicine in Toronto in 1977. Here she assumed the duties of Director Medical Assessment and Training Division. In her three-year tour, LCol Clay squeezed in a six-month tour of duty with the Canadian United Nations contingent to the Middle East where she served in Egypt.

In 1980, LCol Clay was enrolled at the University of Toronto where she successfully completed studies leading to a Master of Health Science degree and certification in Community Medicine by the Royal College of Physicians and Surgeons (Canada). This was followed by a promotion to Colonel in 1982 and a new appointment on the Surgeon General's staff as Director of Preventive Medicine. This four-year tour came to an end in 1986 when Colonel Clay moved to Air Command Headquarters in Winnipeg as Command Surgeon, an appointment she held until 1989.

It was time to move again in July 1989 as Brigadier-General Clay returned to Ottawa to command the National Defence Medical Centre (NDMC). She held the appointment of Commandant of NDMC until 1992 when she was appointed Deputy Surgeon General at National Defence Headquarters Ottawa. The next two years were preparatory for General Clay's final appointment. In September 1994, with a promotion to Major-General, Wendy Clay was

11

appointed Surgeon General of the Canadian Forces and senior member of the Canadian Forces Medical Service. General Clay was the first woman to hold the rank of Major-General and the first to be appointed Surgeon General. The next four years were times of great stress and anxiety as the Canadian Forces down-sized and reorganized. General Clay had to accept the fact that her own appointment would be down-graded to that of Director General with a drop in rank for the next incumbent to Brigadier-General. In November 1995, Major-General Clay received an honorary Doctor of Science degree from the University of British Columbia and, the following month, was made a Commander of the Order of Military Merit.

Among the many guests at General Clay's retirement dinner in 1998, was Canadian astronaut Dr. David Williams, who had just returned from a mission in space. General Clay had been privileged to attend Dr. Williams' launch at the Kennedy Space Centre in Florida and invited him to her retirement dinner. Dr. Williams presented General Clay with a set of wings, suitably framed, that he had taken with him into space.

Major-General Clay is retired and lives in Ottawa but plans to return to British Columbia eventually.

Summary of Achievements:
Commander Order of Military Merit (CMM)
Officer of the Most Venerable Order of the Hospital of St. John of Jerusalem (OStJ)
Canadian Forces Decoration (CD)
United Nations Emergency Force Medal
Confederation of Canada Medal - 125th Anniversary
Doctor of Medicine University of British Columbia 1967 (MD)
Queen's Honorary Physician (QHP)
Diploma, Aviation Medicine (D Av Med)
Master Health Sciences (MH SC)(Toronto)
Fellow, Royal College of Physicians Canada (FRCPC)
Commun Med – Community Medicine Administrative
Doctor of Science (Hon - U BC)

A.A. GORDON CORBET
OSTJ, CD, MD
AIR COMMODORE

Gordon Corbet was born in Saint John, New Brunswick on 9 February 1906 where he received his early education. Following high school, Corbet went on to McGill University in Montreal and received a Bachelor of Arts degree in 1927 and Doctor of Medicine and Master of Surgery in 1932. After interning he went into private practice, specializing in pediatrics in Saint John, New Brunswick. There, he also joined the militia in 1935 as a Captain in the Royal Canadian Army Medical Corps.

On the outbreak of war in 1939, he was placed on active duty with his unit, No. 14 Field Ambulance. On 14 September 1939 he was appointed Medical Officer of No. 118 Squadron RCAF, the Air Force having no medical branch of its own at the time. In August of 1940 Corbet was promoted to Major and when the RCAF Medical Branch formed, in November 1940, he was transferred to it with change in rank title to Squadron Leader.

His next assignment was to No. 2 Service Flying Training School in Uplands, Ontario, but he was later transferred to Eastern Air Command Headquarters at Halifax, Nova Scotia in May 1941. Four years later he was appointed Director of Medical Services at the RCAF overseas headquarters in London, England.

Group Captain Corbet returned to Ottawa at the end of

A/C A.A. Gordon Corbet

1945 and in March 1946 he was appointed Director of Medical Services for the RCAF. In 1953, he was appointed Honorary Physician to the Queen. Corbet was promoted once more to Air Commodore and became Director General Medical Services (Air), an appointment he held until unification of the Forces. His outstanding achievements in the field of aviation medicine, in which he was a certified specialist, were recognized in 1960 when he was awarded the Theodore K. Lyster Award.

He retired early in 1961 and remained in Ottawa until his death on 4 December 1965.

Summary of Achievements
Officer Brother of the Most Venerable Order of the Hospital of St. John of Jerusalem (OStJ)
Efficiency Decoration (ED)
Canadian Forces Decoration (CD)
Czechoslovakian Medal of Merit
Canadian Volunteer Service Medal
War Medal 1939 - 1945—with Oak Leaf
Coronation Medal - King George VI
Coronation Medal - Queen Elizabeth II
Queen's Honorary Physician (QHP)
Doctor of Medicine McGill University-1932 (MD)
Theodore K. Lyster Award - Aviation Medicine

Note
Air Commodore Corbet's tunic was found in a local flea market. It was purchased by a former RCAF Medical Officer and it has been extensively restored for display in the museum.

ROBERT W. FASSOLD
OStJ, CD, MD
MAJOR-GENERAL

Robert W. Fassold, known to his friends as "Bob," was born in London, Ontario on 10 June, 1933 where he received his early education and post-secondary education. He attended the University of Western Ontario where he earned the degree of Bachelor of Science with honors in Biology in 1955. He joined the Royal Canadian Air Force (Auxiliary) in 1956.

Pilot Officer Fassold, who held a short-service commission, was sponsored for an 18-month pilot training program by 420 (Aux) Squadron, London Ontario. This squadron was disbanded just as Bob was completing his basic flying training on the Harvard aircraft at #2 Flying Training School at Moose Jaw Saskatchewan. His advanced pilot training was completed on the twin-engine North American B-25 Mitchell at #1 Advanced Flying School at Saskatoon, Saskatchewan. Flying Officer Fassold transferred to the Regular Force when he received his wings in 1957 and served with 2 Air Observer School at RCAF Station Winnipeg, Manitoba and then with 412 (VIP) Transport

MGen Robert W. Fassold

Squadron at RCAF Station Uplands Ontario. 412 Squadron's role was the transport of very important persons and it was equipped with the de Havilland Comet jet transport along with other passenger carrying aircraft.

In 1963, Squadron Leader Fassold returned to the University of Western Ontario in London where undertook studies in medicine under the Military

Medical Training Plan (MMTP). Bob graduated in 1967, the first under the MMTP and interned at Scarborough General Hospital.

Following his internship, Major Fassold was appointed Base Surgeon at Canadian Forces Base Trenton,Ontario where he also served as Flight Surgeon until 1971. In a postgraduate program at the University of Toronto, Major Fassold earned a Diploma in Public Health. This was followed by a year at the United States Air Force School of Aerospace Medicine, Brooks Air Force Base in San Antonio, Texas. These studies and residency earned Major Fassold certification by the American Board of Preventive Medicine as a specialist in aerospace and occupational medicine in 1973.

His new qualifications made him well suited for his next assignment on the staff of the Surgeon General in the Directorate of Preventive Medicine in Ottawa, Ontario, where Fassold served for the next two years. In July 1974, after one year as a section head, he was promoted to Lieutenant-Colonel (LCol) and appointed Acting Director of Preventive Medicine. One year later, in 1975, he joined the staff of the newly formed Air Command Headquarters in Winnipeg as a charter member. LCol Fassold was appointed Staff Officer Medical Operations.

In July 1977, newly promoted Colonel Fassold was named Commanding Officer of the Canadian Forces Environmental Medicine Establishment and Deputy Chief of the Defence and Civil Institute of Environmental Medicine in Toronto, where he also served as acting chief for more than one year.

Another promotion to Brigadier-General in July 1980 brought with it a new assignment as Deputy Surgeon General, National Defence Headquarters. On 9 September 1985 he was promoted Major-General and appointed Surgeon General.

General Fassold maintained his qualifications as a military pilot throughout his medical career and in addition, has held a civilian airline transport pilot licence since 1965. He has accumulated more than 9,000 flying hours on over forty types of aircraft, single and multi-engine, fixed and rotary wing, on wheels, skids, skis and floats.

With thirty-two years of military service, General Fassold left the Canadian Forces in 1988 to form a consultancy in Aerospace and Occupational Medicine with his major clients being the Canadian Space Agency and Canada

Post Corporation, a service he continues to provide. In addition, in 1995 he purchased an ex-RCAF de Havilland DHC-1 Chipmunk, a two-seat training aircraft, which he operates commercially, providing pilot training and passenger rides, including those at Canada's National Aviation Museum in Ottawa.

For many years, General Fassold has been an executive of the Aerospace Medical Association and served as its president in 1986-1987.

Bob Fassold is an Officer of The Most Venerable Order of the Hospital of St. John of Jerusalem.

Summary of Achievements
Officer of the Most Venerable Order of the Hospital of St. John of Jerusalem (OStJ)
Canadian Forces Decoration (CD)
Queen's Honorary Physician (QHP)
Bachelor of Science in Biology, University of Western Ontario - 1955 (B Sc)
Doctor of Medicine University of Western Ontario - 1968 (MD)
Diploma of Public Health (DPH)
American Board of Aviation Medicine (AB Av M)
American Board of Occupational Medicine (ABOM)

Notes:
Flight Lieutenant Fassold was the first RCAF pilot to qualify on the de Havilland Comet, a jet passenger aircraft that was flown on trans-Atlantic scheduled flights by the RCAF. He was the first aircrew member to train under the Aircrew Medical Training Plan. He remains active in the United States Aerospace Medical Association and is currently chairman of the Space Life Sciences Advisory Committee of the Canadian Space Agency.

Along with Lieutenant-General Larry Ashley, Commander of Air Command, General Fasssold took the last run on the old human centrifuge of the Defence and Civil Institute of Environmental Medicine at 1107 Avenue Road Toronto before it was dismantled. A new modern centrifuge has since been erected for continued research and training at Downsview.

WILSON GEORGE LEACH
CMM, CStJ, CD, MD
MAJOR-GENERAL

Wilson George Leach, known to his colleagues as "Bill," was born at Chalk River, Ontario on 28 September 1923. His schooling was interrupted in 1940 when he took a job with the Canadian Pacific Railway Company as a car-checker. In 1942, Bill enlisted in the Royal Canadian Air Force and was trained as a pilot. He received his wings and a commission as a Pilot Officer (P/O) the following year. P/O Leach was then assigned duties as a flight instructor at RCAF flying training stations until war's end.

A desire to become a medical doctor resulted in his returning to high school at Pembroke, Ontario to complete his Grade 13 examinations before accepting his veterans credits to assist him with higher education. In 1946 he was admitted to the University of Western Ontario at London in the general science course and two years later qualified for the medical program. During these initial years he supplemented his veteran's benefits by working during the summer months in the Canadian National Railways shops at London as a laborer and plumber's helper.

MGen Wilson George Leach

An interest in wound-healing techniques caused him to return to the RCAF Reserve in 1949 as a Flying Officer (F/O). For the next two summers he worked as a technical assistant in work on animal experiments to develop techniques in wound healing. F/O Leach accepted a permanent commission in the RCAF prior to graduating in Arts and Medicine in 1952.

18

His junior internship was completed at Victoria Hospital London after which he spent an additional year of postgraduate training at the University of Western Ontario, studying biophysics. In 1954 he was posted to the RCAF Institute of Aviation Medicine at Toronto, Ontario where he worked for the next twelve years.

As project officer in the respiratory physiology section, Squadron Leader Leach progressed through various departments until he was promoted to Wing Commander in 1961 and appointed Officer Commanding the Flying Personnel Medical Establishment. His work was primarily directed towards the protection of aircrew from the hazards of their hostile environment. This included such things as research on oxygen equipment, escape devices, survival equipment, the man-machine interface and performance under adverse environmental conditions.

With the evolution of the Avro CF-105 Arrow fighter aircraft, a great deal of work was devoted to the development of partial breathing equipment to counteract the effects of loss of cabin pressure at extremely high altitudes. Out of these experiments, techniques and procedures were devised for rapid decompression trials to be conducted in the high altitude decompression chamber. This chamber, which can simulate conditions at very high altitudes, was used to produce the effects of a sudden loss of pressurization similar to that which might occur if a pressurized aircraft at high altitude suffered equipment failure or a rupture of the aircraft's fuselage. The experiments included trials with both RCAF and civilian flying personnel.

In 1960 he was awarded the McKee Trophy for his contributions to manned flight through medical research and the Canada Decoration for service to the military. The report of this award read as follows:

"In 1960 The Trans-Canada McKee Trophy was awarded to Wing Commander W.G. Leach of Toronto. W/C Leach won the award in recognition of his contribution to the cause of Canadian aviation through his research in the field of high altitude physiology and for the courage and devotion to duty he displayed in conducting this research.

The McKee Trophy, which dates back to 1927, is presented each year for meritorious services in advancement of Canadian aviation. Emphasis is placed on performance throughout the year rather than on a single brilliant exploit, and special consideration is given to the application of aircraft and aviation equipment to new and useful purposes.

The trophy was donated by the late Dalzell McKee of Pittsburgh, a wealthy aviation enthusiast who made the first Trans-Canada flight by seaplane in 1926. Mr. McKee established the trophy in recognition of the welcome and assistance given him by the RCAF during his flight.

W/C Leach served in the RCAF as a flying instructor during the Second World War and left the service at the end of the war to enter medical school. On completion of his medical training, he rejoined the RCAF and served at RCAF Station London, Ont., before being transferred to the RCAF Institute of Aviation Medicine in Toronto in 1954.

For a number of years W/C Leach has conducted specialized research into the effects of anoxia and explosive decompression in high altitude aircraft, with emphasis on these problems as applicable to the new generation of turbo-prop and jet passenger aircraft which are being introduced into airline and military service throughout the world. The results of this research have received national and international acclaim, and have provided a base for further research in many countries. His work has also resulted in improved airline and military crew training techniques and the design of new oxygen equipment.

During his research work, Leach continually exposed himself to explosive decompression and periods of anoxia at high atmospheric altitudes despite the fact that no observations had ever been made which recorded the effects of such exposure. The personal courage he displayed in the pursuit of his research was beyond the call of duty, and has resulted in greater safety for people the world over who fly in high altitude aircraft."

In 1966, he was posted to the Surgeon General's staff where, as a Group Captain, he was appointed Director of Medical Staffing and Training. He held this appointment until 1969, when he enrolled in the one-year program at the National Defence College at Kingston, Ontario.

On completion of the National Defence College course, he was promoted to the rank of Brigadier-General in July 1970 and appointed Deputy Surgeon General (Operations), a position which later was renamed Deputy Surgeon General.

A further honour was bestowed on General Leach in 1973 when he was inducted into the Canadian Aviation Hall of Fame with the following citation:

"The dedication of his skills to the science of space medicine has resulted in outstanding benefit to Canadian Aviation."

Another promotion on 15 March 1976 to Major-General was announced as General Leach assumed his new appointment as Surgeon General. This was effected on 1 April 1976. General Leach was made a Commander of the Order of Military Merit 11 December 1978.

General Leach relinquished the appointment of Surgeon General 31 July 1980 on retirement from the Canadian Forces.

Summary of Achievements

Commander of the Order of Military Merit (CMM)
Commander of the Most Venerable Order of the Hospital of St. John of Jerusalem (CStJ)
Canadian Forces Decoration (CD)
Canadian Volunteer Service Medal
War Medal 1939 - 1945
Jubilee Medal - Queen Elizabeth II
Queen's Honorary Physician, (QHP)
National Defence College, 1970 (a course no longer given)
Bachelor of Arts University of Western Ontario (BA)
Doctor of Medicine University of Western Ontario (MD)
Post graduate course in biophysics, 1953 - 1954
McKee Trophy Winner, 1960
Member of Canadian Aviation Hall of Fame - 1973

PIERRE R. MORISSET
CMM, CSTJ, CD, MD
MAJOR-GENERAL

Pierre Morisset was born in Sudbury, Ontario in 1943. At the age of 18, he enrolled in the Royal Canadian Air Force under the Regular Officer Training Plan as an Officer Cadet and obtained a Bachelor of Arts (Pre-Med) degree from the University of Ottawa. Pilot Officer Morisset underwent pilot training and received his wings. His first tour of duty was at RCAF Station Centralia, Ontario where he was employed as a flight instructor.

Flight Lieutenant Morisset applied and was accepted for the Military Medical Training Plan and obtained his degree in medicine in 1971. Major Morisset was the Base Surgeon at Canadian Forces Base (CFB) Ottawa and, as a Lieutenant-Colonel, the Base Surgeon at CFB Lahr Germany and Command Flight Surgeon for the Canadian Forces in Europe.

Colonel Morisset returned to university in 1979 and obtained a master's degree in Health Administration from the University of Ottawa. He received the Robert

MGen Pierre R. Morisset

Woods Johnson (Johnston and Johnston Award), being considered the student "most likely to succeed as a Health Administrator." On graduation, he was appointed Director of Medical Operations and Training at National Defence Headquarters (NDHQ) in Ottawa for a tour of duty before being appointed Command Surgeon Canadian Forces Europe.

While Command Surgeon, Morisset was appointed director of a NATO multi-national exercise called Gruener Landfrosh (Green Frog). This was an extensive exercise of medical troops that would support any NATO operation on the Continent. It was held every two years somewhere in Germany and was reportedly the largest military medical exercise held anywhere in the world. Colonel Morisset was justifiably proud, as a Canadian Air Force Medical Officer, to have directed this exercise.

Colonel Morisset was selected to attend the National Defence College in Kingston in 1987 after which he was promoted to Brigadier-General and appointed Deputy Surgeon General in July 1988. During his National Defence College course, he was elected course senior, the only Medical Officer to hold that appointment. General Morisset earned one more promotion to Major-General in 1992 as he was appointed Surgeon General at NDHQ. At age 49, he was the youngest officer to hold this post.

Active in sports such as hockey, track and field and squash, Pierre Morisset was captain of the track and field team while at the University of Ottawa. He held the Ontario/Québec conference record in triple jump. He

Flying Officer Morisset entering a T-33 cockpit

was both a player and patron of squash in the early 1990s. General Officers were encouraged to participate and promote the sport in the Canadian Forces. He participated actively, both as a patron and player, attaining championship status. He was made a Commander of the Order of Military Merit on 19 May 1994.

During his career as a Medical Officer, he was the accompanying physician for three royal tours: Prince Charles in 1975; Queen Elizabeth in 1976 (Olympics); and Queen Elizabeth in 1982 on her visit to Canada for the repatriation of the Constitution. He was also personal physician to His Excellency, Governor General Ramon Hnatyshyn during his tenure.

Morisset has twice been a guest lecturer at the Inter-Agency Institute of Federal Health Care Executives, a United States event.

General Morisset is a collector of antiques, mostly early Canadian furniture and Canadian glass. Fly-fishing is another hobby.

For the last twenty years, Pierre Morisset has been restoring hand-hewn log buildings. To date he has done four, three of which are "La Cabane" and the fourth is a barn used to dry lumber from trees that he cuts. He and his family are extremely proud of this work and expect that it will be designated heritage property in time.

Since he retired as Surgeon General, he worked as Medical Director at Buckingham Hospital in Québec. In August 1998 he retired from this post and is concentrating on his sawmill business, which includes a drying kiln.

Pierre Morisset is extremely content in retirement. He is married to Jeannine Chamberlain of Kirkland Lake Ontario. They have a daughter and a son.

Summary of Achievements

Commander of the Order of Military Merit. (CMM)
Commander of the Most Venerable Order of the Hospital of St. John of Jerusalem (CStJ)
Canadian Forces Decoration (CD)
Special Service Medal NATO
Queen's Honorary Physician (QHP)
Medical Doctor, University of Ottawa, 1971 - class valedictorian (MD)
Bachelor of Arts, University of Ottawa, 1963 (BA)
Masters of Health Administration, University of Ottawa, 1981 (MHA)
National Defence College, 1988

DONALD G.M. NELSON
CStJ, CD, MD
MAJOR-GENERAL

Donald Nelson, born in Toronto, Ontario in June 1914, received his early education in Guelph, Ontario and graduated in medicine from the University of Toronto in 1939. This was followed by an internship at St. Michael's Hospital, Toronto just in time for him to join the Army.

In June 1940 he enrolled in the Royal Canadian Army Medical Corps and, in November of that year, he transferred to the newly formed Royal Canadian Air Force Medical Branch. Flight Lieutenant Nelson served as a Medical Officer at various RCAF stations in Canada until 1945.

In 1945 he was appointed President of the RCAF Medical Board located in London, England, and in 1946 he returned to Canada with the rank of Squadron Leader and an appointment as Senior Medical Officer at RCAF Station

MGen Donald G.M. Nelson

Hospital Rockcliffe, Ontario. Squadron Leader Nelson took time out from his military duties in 1947 to undertake studies in Public Health at the University of Toronto. This two-year program led to a diploma in Public Health granted in 1948. He then returned to his former position of Senior Medical Officer at RCAF Station Hospital Rockcliffe as a Wing Commander.

In August 1952, with another promotion, Group Captain (G/C) Nelson was appointed Deputy Director of Medical Services for the RCAF on the staff of the Director General Medical Services (Air) at Air Force Headquarters, Ottawa where he served until 1956.

Selected to attend the National Defence College in Kingston, Ontario,

G/C Nelson completed the program in July 1957 and assumed command of the RCAF Institute of Aviation Medicine in Toronto. Four years later, in 1961, Nelson was posted to London, England where he was appointed Medical Liaison Officer at the Canadian Joint Staff.

He joined the staff of the newly formed Canadian Forces Medical Service Headquarters in Ottawa in 1964 with the rank of Air Commodore and was appointed Deputy Surgeon General (Professional). Four years in this appointment led to another promotion to Major-General and the position of Surgeon General of the Canadian Armed Forces in 1968. General Nelson was named an Honorary Physician to Her Majesty Queen Elizabeth II in 1964 and up-graded to Honorary Surgeon to Her Majesty Queen Elizabeth II in 1968.

In 1955 Nelson was made a Fellow of the Aerospace Medical Association. In 1970 he was named President-elect and in 1971 became president of the Association. He was also a Fellow of the American Public Health Association, with certification in Preventive Medicine (Aviation Medicine). In 1962 he was elected to the International Academy of Aviation and Space Medicine. He was a member of the Canadian Medical Association and the Ontario Medical Association.

In 1957 he was admitted to The Most Venerable Order of the Hospital of St. John of Jerusalem in the grade of Serving Brother, and was subsequently promoted to the grade of Officer in 1965 and to Commander in 1969.

He was the first RCAF Major-General Medical Services. He died in 1989.

Summary of Achievements

Commander of the Most Venerable Order of the Hospital of St. John of Jerusalem (CStJ)
Canadian Forces Decoration (CD)
Canadian Volunteer Service Medal
War Medal 1939 – 1945
Korean Medal 1951 – 1953
United Nations Service Medal, Korea
Coronation Medal Queen Elizabeth II
Centennial Medal
Queen's Honorary Physician (QHP)
Queen's Honorary Surgeon (QHS)
Diploma, Public Health (DPH)
Fellow Aerospace Medical Association (FAMA)
Medical Doctor (MD)
National Defence College

HAROLD ROBINSON
OStJ, CD, MD
BRIGADIER-GENERAL

Harold **Robinson** was born in London, Ontario in 1924 where he received his early education. His military career began with a tour of duty with the Royal Canadian Air Force, Supplementary Reserve. Pilot Officer Robinson underwent pilot training and received his wings before completing this service in 1945. In 1949, in the final year of his studies in medicine at the University of Western Ontario, Robinson re-enrolled in the RCAF in the Medical Officer list. In 1951, Flight Lieutenant Robinson was assigned to RCAF Station St-Hubert, Québec as Senior Medical Officer.

Squadron Leader Robinson served two tours of duty as Senior Medical Officer at 3 Fighter Wing, Zweibrucken, Germany, the first from 1953 to 1955 and the second from 1965 to 1968. It was at this point that he was promoted to Wing Commander and appointed Regional Surgeon at 1 Air Division, Metz, France. He then returned to Canada as a Colonel in 1969 to become Director Medical Treatment Services on the staff of the Surgeon General at Canadian Forces Headquarters in Ottawa.

BGen Harold Robinson

Colonel Robinson completed postgraduate studies in otorhinolaryngology, the medical specialty in ear, nose and throat, at the University of Toronto. It is believed that he was the first RCAF specialist in ENT.

In 1975 Robinson obtained a masters degree in health administration from the University of Ottawa. He is also a Queen's Honorary Physician and an Officer of the Most Venerable Order of Hospital of St. John of Jerusalem.

Brigadier-General Robinson was Commandant of the National Defence Medical Centre in Ottawa when he retired to Windermere, Ontario after thirty-two years of military service.

Summary of Achievements

Officer of the Most Venerable Order of the Hospital of St. John of Jerusalem (OStJ)
Canadian Forces Decoration (CD)
Canadian Volunteer Service Medal
War Medal 1939 – 1945
Canadian Centennial Medal
Doctor of Medicine University of Western Ontario (MD)
Queens Honorary Physician (QHP)
Masters Hospital Administration (MHA)
Fellow of the Royal of Surgeons Canada – Otolaryngology (FRCSC.OTOL)

R.W. RYAN
MD
AIR COMMODORE

R.W. Ryan, whose first name is not known, was born in Australia, 26 May 1888. Ryan was a graduate of Melbourne University Medical School where, in 1913, he was granted the degrees of MB (Bachelor of Medicine) and BS (Bachelor of Science).

During World War I, he was a Captain Medical Officer in the Royal Army Medical Corps, but attached to the Royal Flying Corps. In 1918 he was demobilized with the rank of Captain and later the same year joined the newly formed Royal Air Force Medical Service as a Flight Lieutenant.

In 1940 he was loaned to the RCAF to act as Special Advisor during the formation of the RCAF Medical Branch. On completion of this work he was appointed Director of Medical Services (Air) and served in this capacity with rank of Air Commodore until his recall to the United Kingdom, 15 September 1943.

A/C R.W. Ryan

On return to England he was placed in charge of the RAF Central Medical Establishment, London. On his retirement from the RAF in April 1945, he was appointed to the Health Department of the Allied Control Commission, Germany.

Note

No other information is known.

Summary of Achievements

Bachelor of Medicine, Bachelor of Science (MB BS) Doctor of Medicine
Melbourne University Medical School, 1913 (MD)

His orders, decorations and medals cannot be identified.

JAMES W. TICE
CBE, ED, MB
AIR COMMODORE

James W. Tice, known by his colleagues as "Fred," was born in Madoc, Ontario on 29 June 1898, . He entered the University of Toronto in 1916 and graduated with a Bachelor of Medicine degree in 1921.

Dr. Tice had a private practice in Hamilton in 1923, and joined the militia as a Medical Officer. Captain Tice served in No. 5 Field Ambulance from 1923 to 1935. In 1935 he was appointed Medical Officer in Charge in No. 19 (later 119 Bomber) Squadron, RCAF, an auxiliary unit. At that time neither the Royal Canadian Navy nor the Royal Canadian Air Force had their own medical service; the Royal Canadian Army Medical Corps (RCAMC) provided these services to all arms.

A/C James W. "Fred" Tice

Because of his service with 119 Squadron RCAF, Lieutenant-Colonel Tice was appointed to RCAF Headquarters on the outbreak of war. He was ahead of most RCAMC medical officers in the field of aviation medicine. For the rest of his service career he remained a member of the headquarters staff although he went overseas on temporary duty on several occasions. On 15 February 1943 he was appointed Director of Medical Services (Air), and a fortnight later was promoted Air Commodore. In June 1945, he was made a Commander of the Order of the British Empire and in March 1946, Air Commodore Tice retired and returned to his medical practice in Hamilton. In 1943 he was appointed Honorary Physician to the Queen.

Summary of Achievements
Commander, Order of British Empire (CBE)
Efficiency Decoration (ED)
Defence Medal
Canadian Volunteer Service Medal
War Medal 1939 – 45
Bachelor of Medicine (MB)
Queen's Honorary Physician (QHP)

CHAPTER 2

AVIATION MEDICINE PIONEERS

**RESEARCH SCIENTISTS,
INVENTORS & BIOSCIENCE
SPECIALISTS**

- **Group Captain Brock R. Brown**

   The first post-war Commanding Officer of the RCAF Institute of
   Aviation Medicine.

- **Group Captain Bonar Coles**

   A war-time doctor who remained in the service and later became a
   specialist in aviation medicine.

- **Flight Lieutenant James A. Firth**

   A war-time pilot and later a specialist in safety equipment who, at
   age 64, flew in a CF-18B Hornet.

- **Group Captain Wilbur R. Franks**

   The inventor of the anti-G flying suit. A DND Aeromedical
   Training building was named in his honor.

- **Commander Gary Gray**

   A medical officer with 28 years of dedicated service in aero-space
   medicine.

- **Group Captain G. Edward Hall**
  The first commanding officer of the RCAF Institute of Aviation Medicine; later Dean of Medicine of the University of Western Ontario and later President of UWO for 20 years.

- **Group Captain Hugh B. Hay.**
  A WW II navigator and pilot awarded the Distinguished Service Order and Distinguished Flying Cross; made109 operational flights; post-war doctor who became the Commanding Officer of the RCAF Institute of Aviation Medicine.

- **Flight Lieutenant Roy E. Longard**
  A war-time pilot who won the British Empire Medal. He became a Bioscience Officer.

- **Wing Commander Romney H. Lowry**
  A war-time pilot; later a doctor who specialized in aviation medical research.

- **Wing Commander George W. Manning**
  A cardiologist who studied over 350,000 aircrew electrocardiographs received from RCAF Stations in Canada and overseas between 1947 and 1986.

- **Group Captain James H. Murray**
  A war-time navigator shot down over Denmark on his 13th trip who returned to England to complete a full tour of operations. Later as a doctor returned to have the mayor of the Danish town give him the keys to the city.

- **Group Captain Thomas Jenner Powell**
  A doctor who served in the Indian Army - Indian Medical Service and later in the RCAF at IAM; had a keen interest in aviation medicine.

- **Master Warrant Officer Fred G. Routledge**
  An RAF veteran who served at the IAM as a Safety Equipment Technician and then as an Aeromed Technician, volunteered for aircraft seat ejection tests at ground level for capture in a net!

- **Major Douglas Soper**
  A war time navigator; bio-scientist at IAM; Aide de Camp for three Lieutenant-Governors of Ontario; post-retirement attorney.

- **Sergeant Edison "Ed" D. Stairs**

  An Aeromed Technician later a Bioscience Technician with twenty-two years of experience, training and assisting in research.

- **Wing Commander Chester B. Stewart**

  An associate of Sir Frederick Banting in aviation medicine research; post- retirement Dean of Medicine at Dalhousie University and later awarded the Order of Canada and four honorary degrees.

- **Wing Commander Roy A. Stubbs**

  A war-time pilot; graduated in 1950 in physics and mathematics; chief scientist at Defence and Civil Institute of Environmental Medicine; designed the deepest research diving facility in the world.

- **Flight Lieutenant Vincent J. Tremaine**

  An airman who logged over 3000 runs as an observer on the human centrifuge.

- **Squadron Leader O. Harold Warwick**

  An early researcher in the effects of high altitude on aircrew and on the oxygen systems and equipment to permit them to fly in this environment.

- **Group Captain John Wickett**

  A pre-war pilot, shot down in a de Haviland Mosquito in WWII and taken priosoner of war; post-war physician and one of the pioneers of aviation medicine who was a consultant on cockpit instrumentation for the Avro CF-105 Arrow.

- **Colonel A. Colin Yelland**

  A medical officer who conducted research in aviation medicine and served seven years as the Deputy Chief of Defence and Civil Institute of Environmental Medicine.

BROCK R. BROWN
SBSTJ, CD, MD
GROUP CAPTAIN

Brock Brown was born in Toronto, Ontario where he received his early education. He attended the University of Toronto and attained a Bachelor of Science degree and then a Medical Degree in 1930.

While in private practice in Toronto, he taught at St. Michael's Hospital in Toronto and worked at the Banting Institute with doctors Sir Frederic Banting and Charles Best. Doctor and Mrs. Brown became close personal friends of the Bantings.

Dr. Brown was quite an accomplished artist. He produced many caricatures and jokes for his school journal and illustrated a number of medical books during the depression to make ends meet. Throughout his life, art was an immensely satisfying pastime and he worked in such mediums as oils, clay, plaster and wood. He was part of the team that worked with Wing Commander W.R. Franks in the development of the first anti-G suit. He also contributed his expertise to the team in Houston, Texas in charge of the first U.S. space flight.

G/C Brock R. Brown

Brown also did some postgraduate training at the Leahy Clinic in Boston.

In 1941, he joined the RCAF and served as a medical officer at # 1 Air Observer School, Malton and it was there that he became interested in flying. His log book shows him flying in Avro Ansons, de Havilland Tiger Moths and Noorduyn Norseman, first as a medical observer and later in air sickness tests. Between April 1942 and February 1944 he had 122 day-hours and three night-flying hours.

While stationed at Malton, Ontario, he led a party of four, searching for a downed Anson aircraft. The search party was equipped with snowshoes and fur-lined jackets as they scoured the country on foot. It is believed they were successful in finding the aircraft.

In 1944 he went overseas and served at # 3 Personnel Reception Centre, Bournemouth, England until he returned to Canada.

On his return in 1946, he was posted to the RCAF Institute of Aviation Medicine in Toronto and served there until 1951. He enjoyed his time at the Institute as he was fond of flying and the problems associated with it. As time permitted he flew in the Anson MK IV aircraft, testing personal flying equipment. His log book shows him flying in a Boeing B-29 Superfortress in 1947. Although no other entries are recorded in his log book, it is known he made many unrecorded trips.

In 1947 he was granted permission to wear the USAF Flight Surgeon's Wing on graduation from USAF School of Aviation Medicine at Brooks Air Force Base in San Antonio, Texas. This he considered a great privilege.

His next posting was to RCAF Training Command at Trenton, Ontario as the Staff Officer Medical Services, a position he held for two years.

From Trenton he went to Harvard University for postgraduate training earning a Masters degree in Industrial Hygiene in 1954.

His studies at Harvard were followed by a short stint as the Senior Medical Officer, commanding the RCAF Station Hospital Rockcliffe, Ontario. Six months later he joined the Director General Medical Services (Air) staff at Air Force Headquarters in Ottawa. He served there as Director of Medical Services until he retired in 1959.

On retirement, he became the Senior Treatment Officer for the Ottawa District of the Department of Veterans Affairs, retiring in 1970. He died at the National Defence Medical Centre in October 1974.

Summary of Achievements

Serving Brother of the Most Venerable Order of the Hospital of St. John of Jerusalem (SBStJ)

Canadian Forces Decoration (CD)

Canadian Volunteer Service Medal

War Medal, 1939 - 1945

Queen Elizabeth II Coronation Medal

Bachelor of Science Medicine, University of Toronto (BSC MED)

Doctor of Medicine, University of Toronto - 1930 (MD)

Fellow of American College of Physical Medicine in Aviation Medicine

Master of Industrial Hygiene, Harvard FACPM (MIH - AV MED) -

Diploma in American Board - Aviation Medicine - 1947 (DAB AV MED)

USAF Flight Surgeon's Wing

Note

Brock Brown's son, Peter, helped with these biographical notes and it is as complete as can be remembered. Peter, who died since the start of this project, recalls going to the Toronto railroad station with his mother to meet his father returning from overseas and calling out to every air force officer with the greeting, "Hello, Dad!" He had never met his father and did not know the difference!

BONAR COLES
SBStJ, CD, MD
GROUP CAPTAIN

Bonar Coles was born in Clarence, Ontario and got his early education in Woodbridge and Weston, Ontario. In the late 1920's, he took undergraduate Geology at McMaster College in Toronto. He graduated in medicine from the University of Toronto in 1935. The Geology courses must have been useful as Bonar spent a number of summers and one winter staking claims and prospecting for gold in the northern Ontario bush, which put him through medical school during the depression.

After joining the RCAF in 1939, he was stationed at the Institute of Aviation Medicine in Toronto. This was followed by service at the Canadian Joint Staff in London, England. On his return from overseas, he was assigned to No. 1 Air Command Headquarters, Trenton, Ontario as the Principal Medical Officer.

From September 1951 to September 1954, Coles was the Commanding Officer of the Institute of Aviation Medicine, Toronto. From 1954 until his retirement in 1960, he was the Staff Officer

G/C Bonar Coles

Medical Services at Air Defence Command Headquarters at St-Hubert, Québec.

He returned to the family farm in Woodbridge, Ontario in 1960, but continued work with the Department of Veterans Affairs as Medical Officer of Pensions at Sunnybrook Hospital until final retirement in 1968. He passed away in the winter of 1975.

Summary of Achievements

Serving Brother of the Most Venerable Order of the Hospital of St. John of Jerusalem (SBStJ)
Canadian Forces Decoration (CD)
Doctor of Medicine, University of Toronto, 1935 (MD)
Diploma in Public Health (DPH)
American Board of Preventive Medicine (AB Prev Med)
American Board of Aviation Medicine (AB Av Med)

Note
This incomplete information has been obtained from several sources. Mrs. Coles, now in her 90s, is supportive of museums. Earlier she donated several artefacts to The Royal Canadian Military Institute and was pleased with this tribute to her late husband.

JAMES A. FIRTH
CD
FLIGHT LIEUTENANT

James Firth was born in Campbelltown, New Brunswick on 10 January 1920. Little is known of his early schooling; his story seems to begin with enrolment in the RCAF in October 1940.

As a newly enrolled airman, sometimes known as an "erk," R73199 Aircraftman 2nd Class (AC2) Firth, J.A. paid his dues with basic training at No. 1 Manning Pool and security guard duties at No. 1 Bombing and Gunnery School at Jarvis, Ontario. Finally selected for pilot training, Leading Aircraftman (LAC) Firth graduated as a pilot candidate from No. 1 Initial Training School in Toronto, Ontario in 1941. This was followed by flight training at No. 10 Elementary Flying Training School at Mount Hope near Hamilton, Ontario, a British Commonwealth Air Training Plan (BACTP) training station. Elementary training was given on the Fleet Finch, a single engine biplane, on which Firth earned his wings. This was followed by more advanced training on the North American Harvard aircraft at No. 2 Service Flying Training School at Uplands, Ontario.

F/L James A. Firth

Graduating with a "Distinguished Pass" earned Firth a commission as a Pilot Officer (P/O), a new service number, J6837, an elevation from an erk to a "sprog" as newly commissioned pilot officers were known. There was little delay in transferring P/O Firth to England and onto operational flying training on Spitfires, from which he graduated at the top of his class. Over time, Firth would serve with 411 RCAF Squadron (Spitfires) and 116 Royal Air Force Squadron flying Hurricanes. There were also secret operations on Westland Lysanders. These short-take-off-and-landing (STOL) type aircraft were often used to fly Allied agents into and out of occupied Europe.

At the end of the war, Flight Lieutenant Firth continued to serve in England on duties related to the RCAF repatriation programs. This involved the inspection of accommodation and vessels to be used to house and transport returning airmen. It even involved the accommodation and transportation for Canadian War brides on their way to join their new husbands in Canada.

Firth was demobilized in 1947, but returned to the RCAF in 1954 as a Medical Associate Officer (Bioscience). He was trained as an aeromedical training officer at the RCAF Institute of Aviation Medicine from November 1954 to May 1955, During this time, Firth worked in the hypobaric chamber on experiments being conducted at a simulated altitude of 65,000 feet to assess and prove the potential of high altitude partial pressure garmentry and all associated life support equipment, such as `G' valves, oxygen, regulators, pressure gravity valves, pressure breathing helmet and oxygen mask. All of this prototype equipment was being developed for the crews of the Avro CF-105 Arrow by Wing Commander W.G. Leach *(see The Leaders)* and Dr. Fred Sunahara.

Firth also assisted Guardite Corporation (USA) to set up a hypobaric chamber and subsequently organized their aviation medicine unit. He was involved in the acceptance trials of the Guardite high altitude hypobaric chamber, confirmed the safety of chamber by being the first subject to ascend to 43,000 feet simulated altitude. He was also the first to undergo a rapid decompression in the parasite hypobaric chamber from 25,000 feet to ground level. These chamber combinations were designed to demonstrate the effects of explosive decompression such as would occur if a pressurized aircraft's canopy was damaged by accident or enemy action.

In 1955, Flight Lieutenant Firth moved on to RCAF Station Cold Lake, Alberta to run the Aviation Medicine Unit at that location. He was Officer-in-Charge of a number of Aeromed Technicians, who participated in hypobaric chamber operations and conducted periodic maintenance to ensure maximum

43

operational safety. As part of these duties, he was required to lecture in aviation medicine subjects, aircraft oxygen systems, escape equipment, ejection seats and survival seat kits to all aircrew personnel. As a secondary duty, Firth helped organize, and set up volunteer ground search and rescue teams to participate on many occasions of aircraft accidents. During this time, F/L Firth graduated from the USAF physiological training officer course at Maxwell Air University located at Gunter Air Force Base, Alabama in June 1956. He also completed the instructors course at the RCAF Survival Training School in December 1956.

From 1959 to 1963, Jim served on the staff of the Surgeon General under Group Captain J.C. Wickett. He was co-author with Wing Commander Ken Hobbs of the *Aeromedical Handbook for RCAF Aircrew.*

From 1963 to 1969, Jim served in Europe with the 1 Air Division's Aviation Medicine Centre at 3 (Fighter) Wing Zweibrucken, Germany. This facility was subsequently moved to Lahr, Germany with the reorganization of Canadian Forces Europe and Captain Firth coordinated this move. In 1965, he graduated from the sea survival course at the RAF School of Combat Survival and Rescue in Plymouth, England and later helped to establish the RCAF Sea Survival School at the Air Weapons Unit at Decimommanu Sardinia in 1965. Canadian and other NATO fighter squadrons in Europe rotated through Decimonnanu for live-firing training over the Mediterranean

In February 1974, Jim joined the public service and served at the Defence and Civil Institute of Environmental Medicine (DCIEM), first as head of the safety systems section and later as technical advisor to the Director of the Medical Life Support Division. Jim retired from the public service in 1989. Firth is credited with work on the inventions of the partial pressure Jerkin developed at DCIEM. He worked on the Phoenix Program between 1977-1981 and received recognition by the DCIEM Phoenix Award. Phoenix was a program to prove that aircrew of pressurized high performance fighter aircraft, flying above 65,000 feet could survive explosive rapid decompression (canopy loss/canopy strike by enemy fire), wearing a pressure breathing oro/nasal oxygen mask/partial pressure jerkin/"G" suit combination. This work was connected to the acquisition of new fighter aircraft (NFA), the CF-18 Hornet. Survival seat packs for crews of these aircraft were also developed at this time.

Over the course of his military career, Firth was involved in numerous

44

aircraft crash investigations and in several life-saving incidents, particularly in sea-rescue training. He was also privileged, at age 64, to participate in a simulated air combat flight in CF-18 B on 19 April 1984.

Summary of Achievements

Canadian Forces Decoration (CD)
1939 - 1945 Star
Aircrew Europe Star
Defence Medal
Canadian Volunteer Service Medal with Clasp
War Medal 1939 - 1945
Special Service Medal - Nato
Silver Medal (Canada) 1987 (Awarded by the Government of Canada for thirty-five years of dedicated service).
National Defence Chief of Research and Development (CRAD) Meritorious Service Award 1983 "For an exceptional and distinguished contribution to the effectiveness and efficiency of the public service."
DCIEM Phoenix Award, "In recognition of his contribution to the Phoenix New Fighter Aircraft Experimental Program 1977 - 1980".
Society of Aerospace and Flight Equipment (SAFE) Award 1985, "For an outstanding contribution in the field of safety."

WILBUR ROUNDING FRANKS
OBE, MD
GROUP CAPTAIN

Wilbur Rounding Franks was born in Weston, Ontario on 4 March 1901. Descended from an old United Empire Loyalist family, he moved to Western Canada as a small boy with his parents, Mr. and Mrs. J.T. Franks, and received his elementary and secondary education in Regina, Saskatchewan.

Franks graduated from the University of Toronto in 1924, with a Bachelor of Arts degree and a Master's Degree in Physiology in 1925. Three years later he graduated with a Bachelor of Medicine degree. Dr. Franks then took a rotating internship at the Toronto General Hospital and carried out research projects for Dr. Frederick Banting. During 1930-1931, while on a sabbatical, he undertook postgraduate studies at the University of Zurich and the University of Munich in Germany.

On his return to Canada in September 1931 he resumed his career as a research associate with the Banting and Best Department of

W/C Wilbur R. Franks invested with the Order of the British Empire

Medical Research at the University of Toronto, specializing in cancer research. Prior to his enlistment in the RCAF, he was an associate professor at the Department of Medical Research, University of Toronto, and a close colleague of Sir Frederick Banting. Data on the anti-G suit's construction and performance was one of the secrets Sir Frederick was carrying to Britain when he was killed in a crash of a Lockheed Hudson near Musgrave Harbour in Newfoundland in February 1941.

During the period of 1939 - 1941, Dr. Franks performed medical research for the Department of National Defence with Major Sir Frederick Banting and because of the highly secret nature of his work, he was commissioned a Lieutenant in the Royal Canadian Army Medical Corps. When the Royal Canadian Air Force formed its own medical branch in November 1940, he was transferred to the RCAF with the rank of Flight Lieutenant.

Franks now began active medical research into solving the problems related to pilot blackouts from acceleration in manoeuvres with high gravitational (G) forces. During his cancer research experiments in 1938, he had discovered that he could prevent small test tubes from breaking during acceleration in the centrifuge by immersing them in water. He correctly concluded that similar immersion should protect pilots

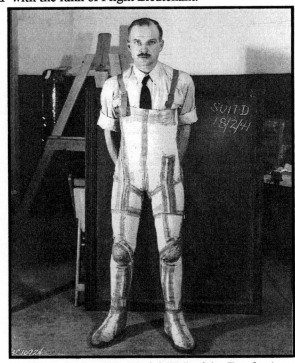

W/C Franks wearing Model "D" of the Franks Anti-Gravity Suit - February 1941

subject to high acceleration and deceleration forces. He designed a protective suit, made of durable non-stretch fabric, containing water-filled bladders. This suit, which was fitted over the legs and abdomen of the wearer, automatically exerted counter pressure by hydrostatic force during high-G loadings. Wearing the Franks Flying Suit during tests, he was the first person to be successfully protected from radial acceleration in an aircraft. *(See the anecdotes related by Wilbur's son Hugh further in this narrative.)*

During this time, he was instrumental in procuring facilities for the RCAF No. 1 Clinical Investigation Unit at 1107 Avenue Road in Toronto. As early as 1939, he had sketched out the fundamental design for a man-rated centrifuge.

In March 1941, Franks went to RCAF Headquarters in London, England and served at the RAF Physiological Laboratory at Farnborough, Hampshire. He also served at the Air Fighter Development Unit, RAF Fighter Command at Duxford and with the Royal Navy Fleet Air Arm in connection with the further development and introduction of the Franks Flying Suit. This was the first anti-G suit to be used operationally anywhere in the world.

Squadron Leader Franks returned to Canada in 1943 and served as Director of the Investigation Section of RCAF Headquarters Directorate of Medical Services in Ottawa until 1945. That appointment was followed by attachment to the RCAF Institute of Aviation Medical Research Council, Ottawa, correlating the work of both civilian and military research projects being carried out in Canada.

On 1 January 1944, Squadron Leader Wilbur Rounding Franks, while at No. 1 Clinical Investigation Unit, was awarded the Order of the British Empire for his contributions to the advancement of aerospace medicine. The citation read:

> *"This officer, who has done outstanding work in medical research, has been the instigator of blackout experiments which, after numerous exasperating disappointments, ingenious experimental procedures and operational trials in various places and altitudes, has been developed for use in tactical operations. This development has been an outstanding contribution to the war effort and has been made available only after many very real risks subjected to by this officer."*

(See also the RCAF Public Relations Press Release of 9 December 1944 in the notes at the end of this narrative.)

Wing Commander Franks retired from the RCAF in 1946, but retained his association with the Air Force in the capacity of its scientific advisor in aviation medicine with the RCAF Institute of Aviation Medicine. He also returned to the Banting and Best Department of Medical Research to continue his cancer research. He retired from that department in 1969.

Dr. Franks was awarded the Legion of Merit by the President of the United States of America in 1946. The Aerospace Medical Association awarded him the Theodore C. Lyster Award in 1948, for "outstanding research in aerospace medicine" and the Eric Liljencrantz Award in 1962, for "outstanding research in the problems of acceleration and altitude." He was made a fellow of the Aerospace Medical Association (1950), the Canadian Aeronautics and Space Institute (1960), and an Honorary Fellow the Ontario Medical Association (1985). He was appointed an Honorary Physician to the Queen in 1966 and Honorary President of the Canadian Society of Aviation Medicine in 1974.

Dr. Franks' Anti-G Suit illustrated on one of a 1986 commemorative series of postage stamps on Canadian technical achievements.
(Courtesy Canada Post Corporation.)

Franks was nominated for, but not awarded the McKee Trans-Canada Trophy in 1956. The citation, written by the Director General Medical Services (Air), Air Commodore A.A.G. Corbet, read:

> *"As early as 1938, he became involved in the medical problems of aviation, when Sir Frederick Banting reorganized his department of medical research in preparation for war. Dr. Franks became interested in*

49

the physiological problems associated with acceleration. He, along with others, was instrumental in the design and construction of the human accelerator which was the first research machine of this type to be used by the allies.

As an outcome of research on this machine and in actual flight, Dr. Franks designed an anti-G suit known as the "Franks' Flying Suit." This was used effectively in actual combat in the late stages of the war.

Following the war, he became a scientific advisor to the RCAF and in this capacity he was intimately connected with both the development and teaching carried on at the Institute of Aviation Medicine.

The Anti-G suit was gradually modified into a more practical garment and then at Dr. Franks' suggestion was combined with the pressure breathing waistcoat to form a very effective garment for short term protection of pilots at very high altitudes.

For the past few years he has been investigating actively the hypothesis that a combination of several minimal stresses, such as hypoglycemia, hypoxia, hyperventilation, acceleration, fatigue, etc. summate to get pilots into physiological difficulty while flying high performance aircraft. The evaluation of his theory leads to the identification of the physiologically important sources of stress and then naturally to means of control, protection from or removal of the stress. The theory has gained considerable credence both here and in the USA and Group Captain Franks has assisted in the planning and direction of a similar program being conducted at the USAF School of Aviation Medicine. The first published work on this subject was given at the AGARD* meeting last spring in Brussels.

For nearly 20 years, G/C Franks has been closely associated with aviation in Canada, and has flown many thousands of hours. He is recognized as the authority in aviation medicine by most of the leaders in aircraft design and construction in Canada. He is widely regarded by experts in the U.S. aviation field and throughout the world by specialists in the field of aviation medicine.

In 1956 he received international recognition for a brilliant piece of research work on the chemistry of body-tissue metabolism under reduced oxygen tensions. The significance of this highly technical procedure is that crash investigators will now have information available to them as to the oxygen status of the pilot prior to his death. Many heretofore unexplained fatal crashes can now be definitely credited to defective oxygen supply. This has far reaching implications in the flight safety field both in military and civilian aviation.

The details of the actual chemical test are not available but it is based on the detection and estimation of lactic acid in brain tissue. As lactic acid production increases under conditions of low oxygen tension, it will be seen that the diagnosis of hypoxia may be made quantitatively with accuracy at postmortems.

It should be noted, however, that it has been difficult to single out any one special achievement or any one year of particular brilliance. Dr. Franks has been a constant contributor over the years to the newly formed but rapidly growing specialty of aviation medicine."

*AGARD - NATO Advisory Group on Aerospace Research and Development

In 1984, he was awarded the highest Canadian award for technical achievement in aerospace, namely the J.A.D. McCurdy Award presented by the Canadian Aeronautics and Space Institute. He was elected a member of Canada's Aviation Hall of Fame in 1983, with the following citation:

"His invention of the Franks Flying Suit and the Human Centrifuge, which have been accepted throughout the aerospace industry, and his significant contributions to research in aerospace medicine, have been of outstanding benefit to Canadian aviation."

The G-suit has indeed stood the test of time, for without it, the astronauts flying the space shuttle could not function through the high decelerative forces on re-entry into the earth's atmosphere. It is important that we should be able to remind future generations of how this most important tool in the exploration of space was invented at the University of Toronto by Dr. Franks.

His wife Ruth, a psychiatrist, served in the Royal Canadian Army Medical Corps during WWII and predeceased him. He had twin sons, William a physician and Hugh a financial consultant.

Wilbur Franks died at Sunnybrook Medical Centre in Toronto on 4 January 1986.

Summary of Achievements

Order of British Empire (OBE)
Defence Medal
Canadian Volunteer Service Medal
War Medal, 1939 - 1945
Queen's Honorary Physician (QHP)
Officer of The Legion of Merit - USA

Notes
Royal Canadian Air Force Directorate of Public Relations
Press Release No. 4891—9 December 1944.

Ottawa – Details of one of the best-kept secrets of the war – The Franks Flying Suit – which eliminates blackout in high-speed flying, were released from RCAF Headquarters today. Invented in 1939 by W/C Wilbur R. Franks, OBE, formerly of the University of Toronto, the suit has been in restricted operational use off British and US aircraft carriers since 1942.

Developed by the RCAF and the Banting Institute, University of Toronto, the "FFS," as it is known in secret air force documents, prevents "blackout" in fighter pilots, thus giving allied air forces a tremendous tactical advantage in swirling dogfights miles up in the sky. Safeguarded against the "blackout" hazard, allied fighter pilots can turn faster than their adversaries and get on their tails.

"Blackout" is an air force term for temporary blindness, sometimes leading to unconsciousness, caused by the action of centrifugal force on the pilots of fast-maneuvering aircraft. Abrupt changes of direction at high speeds greatly increase this effect, known in air force medical circles as "G." Without the Franks flying suit (FFS), many pilots "blackout" at five "G" – or five times the normal pull of gravity at the earth's surface. With the suit, vision and consciousness remain unimpaired.

At "7G" a 150-pound pilot weighs more than half a ton and his four-ton fighter is heavier than a Lancaster bomber. His blood grows heavy as iron and "pools" in his feet and legs, where his heart can't pump it into the brain.

By an ingenious adaptation of a scientific principle hit upon by Dr. Franks back in 1938, the "FFS" provides pressure against the pilot's body which automatically compensates for the internal forces set up by increased "G." Columns of fluid such as air or water are contained in a rubber skeleton lining and held comfortably close to the pilot's body from ankles to chest by non-stretchable fabric. When sharp turns at high speeds build up "G" in the pilot's blood stream, a corresponding force from the suit balances pressure inside and out and permits the normal flow of blood to his brain. Since W/C Franks tested his first suit back in 1940, more than 250 modifications have been made. Now, as manufactured for the British Ministry of Aircraft Production, it comes in seven standard sizes and by lacing devices and specially constructed zippers invented by Dr. Franks and his associates, fits every size and build like a flexible, skin-tight suit of underwear. Its skeleton construction permits the body to breathe and it can be kept open until the pilot is ready to go aloft. Then it is zipped tight and the suit filled with air or water.

When the suit first was put in operational use, its efficacy already had been demonstrated in mimic dogfights by the RCAF, and by hundreds of tests on Dr. Franks and his Banting Institute associates on a specially developed giant "whirligig" at Toronto.

Its first war test came in 1942, when carrier-based fighter planes of the British Fleet Air Arm speedily swept aside enemy opposition at Oran, in French North Africa.

For his part in the invention of the anti-blackout suit and for other developments in the field of aviation medicine, Wing Commander Franks was created an Officer of the Order of the British Empire in the 1944 New Year's Honors List.

In 1986, a building dedicated to aeromedical training was opened in Winnipeg and named the Wilbur Rounding Franks Aeromedical Training Building. At the official opening, colleagues were asked to relate anecdotes of their service with Dr. Franks. Some of these follow.

From Major (Retired) D. Soper

Major Soper was in Aircrew in World War II and after university returned to the RCAF, serving as a bioscience officer at DCIEM.

Reference the request for stories, etc. that can be used at the dedication ceremonies of the "W/C WR Franks Building," I'm sure you will receive many submissions relating to this wonderful man who was one of the founders of aviation medicine.

During my time in the CFMS, I was a biosciences officer employed at various times at the RCAF Institute of Aviation Medicine (IAM) in Toronto, the RAF Institute of Aviation Medicine at Farnborough and at the Surgeon General's HQ. Although I was never directly involved with any of Dr. Franks' projects (e.g. causes and pathology of accidents, acceleration, etc.), I was indirectly associated with him over the years when he was consultant to the RCAF and to the IAM in particular.

I first reported in uniform to the RCAF IAM in June 1952. On my first day, as part of my indoctrination, I was taken on a tour of the Avenue Road site. Before WW II, this area was home to the Eglinton Hunt Club whose buildings had been converted for military purposes. The facilities were really quite splendid even if they were hidden in an array of huts, shacks, horse stables, etc; I do not remember any dog kennels. The research facilities included the human accelerator on which Dr. Franks had conducted his research in developing the anti-G suit. There was a "tropical" room and a "cold" room, and a "high altitude chamber." It was an exciting place to work as the Korean War was being waged in the midst of the Cold War. NATO was just getting up steam.

I was taken on this tour by S/L (later G/C) Jack Wickett who helped rebuild the IAM (after its demise following WW II) by personally recruiting many of the doctors and scientists (me included). As we walked between the buildings, we approached a smallish man nattily attired in civilian clothes. Jack Wickett whispered to me, "Here comes W/C Franks of G-suit fame. Give him a salute and make him feel good." As we passed him left shoulder to left shoulder, I saluted Bill Franks and he returned it with his nearer arm, that is, with his left arm! I think that was the only time we ever exchanged salutes.

Dr. Franks had a warm and casual manner and didn't stand on ceremony. He was always very friendly and addressed each of us respectfully with the endearing Scottish term of "laddie." I cannot recall him ever calling me by my name; it was always "laddie."

The contributions made by Dr. Franks to aviation medicine were recognized during WW II when he was made an Officer of the Order of the British Empire on 3 January 1944. After the war, the USA appointed him an Officer of the Legion of Merit on 2 November 1946.

Dr. Franks was very modest about these awards and his achievements; it was a long time before I became aware of these honours. He was referred to simply as W.R. Franks, M.D. and I never saw any reference to his OBE. I attended many formal dinners in Canada and USA when Dr. Franks was present and I never saw him wear any insignia, decorations or medals. That was his way. He was a delightful person whom we all admired and respected greatly.

In the 1950s and '60s, the RCAF often sent a substantial delegation to the annual meetings of the Aerospace Medical Association, which were held in different cities in the USA. Delegates from Air Force Headquarters, Command Headquarteres and the IAM would be "directed" to attend. Often, an RCAF aircraft would be routed to and from the meetings to provide the most economical transportation. On occasion, Dr. Franks would accompany the delegation. There was always a lot to do at these meetings, e.g. presenting papers, manning the RCAF display, committee work, attending sessions, etc. It was all very fatiguing so for relaxation at the end of the day, the delegation would gather together for dinner and a few drinks.

On this occasion, the selected nightclub had a floorshow which included exotic dancers. The costumes of the dancers were adorned with three tassels, each in a strategic location. As the dancers shimmied and shook, the tassels were made to rotate. One damsel was able to cause the upper two tassels to rotate in opposite directions! Former flyers in the delegation, keeping their minds strictly on professional matters, had visions of aircraft equipped with counter-rotating propellers. Dr. Franks was even more professional in his appreciation. He wrote the appropriate mathematical equation on the tablecloth, estimated the rate of rotation, diameter of the circle, mass, etc. and calculated the G-force involved. All of which shows how business and pleasure can be interdependent.

From Colonel (Retired) R. Cunningham
(Colonel Cunningham was a Technical Assistant Medical and a Bioscience Officer, who retired as the Director of Medical Resources on the Surgeon General's staff)

As for anecdotes about Wilbur, I do not recall anything that would not be a matter of record by now, with all the brains you have been picking, certainly nothing directly related to aviation medicine or aeromedical training. We all know stories about his rather casual acquaintanceship with the real world and needing his good wife to see that he had money in his pocket as he set out to attend a meeting away from home.

I'm not sure who was there back in the early sixties when someone erased his precious blackboard on which he filed his ideas and thoughts. He was astounded at the thought of losing all that information, but then the enlarged photograph of the blackboard in its full detail, which had been taken prior to the dastardly deed, was trotted out to his immense relief and to the enjoyment of the perpetrators.

You will recall that his desk tended to be overloaded. I still chuckle when remembering the day a second top was installed, sitting on legs on the old top, giving him a fresh surface to work or to store papers on.

On a different note, I won't forget him coming in one morning about 1962 having read of John Land's work in reproducing colour from a black and white slide. Typically, he was excited by this idea which he admitted seemed to have no relevance to anything we were doing but stirred his imagination. Nothing would do but to try to replicate Land's work as described in the journal he had at hand. The details are long gone, but separated views of the subject were taken using filters and black and white film. When the slides were later projected, with one image superimposed on the other we saw faint colour. We did not pursue that small project but when I think back to it, I am struck by how it reflects the insatiable curiosity of our friend. He was apt to take an interest in things I would walk by and never notice. "Laddie," he would say, you should keep your eyes open. I wonder how many heavenly mysteries he had explored by now.

From Colonel (Retired) Jim Murray

(Dr. Jim Murray was a former Commanding Officer of the of Institute Aviation Medicine and subsequently the Defence and Civil Institute of Environmental Medicine)

Working with Wilbur Franks was an exciting experience. His approach to a problem was so refreshing! In spite of his great knowledge and training, his favourite phrase was, "Let us not be too clever." He proceeded step by step to satisfy himself that everything was consistent with the parts.

Wilbur had a sincere concern for Aircrew and would go to any lengths to see that they received the consideration they deserved from "the system." His approach to accident investigations embodied sympathy for the victim while at the same time a determination to extract the last detail of information that might help prevent a recurrence.

Combined with all of the above was his enthusiastic enjoyment of a party. Especially noteworthy was his participation in conviviality at the Aerospace Medical Association Meetings. At one meeting in Denver, Colorado he was escorted to his hotel by the local police from the airport. On a previous visit to Denver with the Aerospace Medical Association he had been detained by the police when his exuberance had attracted their attention - to the embarrassment of all concerned.

He was tremendously devoted to the memory of Sir Frederick Banting and the Banting Institute. They had earlier shared their concern about the approaching World War II and the need for aeromedical support. I have a vivid recollection of his description of a rally he attended in Munich while on postgraduate studies in Germany. The rally was addressed by Adolph Hitler and he was profoundly impressed with the way Hitler controlled and inflamed the crowd of over 50,000 - he felt that a confrontation was inevitable.

It is certainly fitting that the Canadian Forces Aeromedical Training

Building should be named after Wilbur Franks. Thanks for giving me the opportunity to add these recollections to the ceremony dedicating this building.

From W/C (Retired) Roy Stubbs

(W/C Stubbs was in Aircrew in WW II and after the war was a bioscience officer at DCIEM until his retirement)

During the years from 1950 to 1965, I worked closely with Dr. Franks in research and development at the RCAF Institute of Aviation Medicine in the following fields:

- motion sickness
- protective headgear and clothing
- ejection seats
- pneumatic anti-G suits and control valves
- oxygen systems
- pressure clothing

There were many incidents and stories about Dr. Franks during these years. The following are two of my favourites.   During the early war years, when Franks had developed the Franks Flying Suit, a water-filled anti-G suit, it was considered so important to Fighter Command in the United Kingdom that the hard-pressed RAF shipped a Hurricane from the front-line to test the Franks Flying Suit in Toronto. It was in the spring of the year 1941 and photos of the aircraft with Franks and its pilot were taken with snow still on the ground at the airfield. After the war, an American contested Franks' patent rights for the flying suit and a court action was held in the USA at which Franks was requested to testify with regard to the vital dates of the testing of the suit. Since these dates were not well-defined, the court judge asked Franks to clarify the date since there was snow on the ground in the photos and asked, "When does the snow melt in Toronto?" Franks replied, "Your Honour, when the ambient temperature rises above 32 degrees Fahrenheit."

Another story is told from the aeromedical annual meeting held in Holland in the late 1950s. Franks arrived the day before the meeting and met with Surgeon Commander John Rawlins (later Sir John and Surgeon Admiral of the Royal Navy) to have a night on the town. After a heavy evening, at the last bar, the bill arrived. Franks and Rawlins refused to pay on the grounds that they were grossly overcharged. The police were called and they still refused to pay, but offered what they considered to be the correct amount. They spent the night in the local jail.

The next evening at the official opening of the aeromedical meeting, the welcoming address was given by the mayor of the city who concluded his remarks by granting Dr. Franks the freedom of the city with thanks for his research. Dr. Franks replied, "This award would have been most useful last night."

From: Major General (Retired) R.W. Fassold

(Robert W. Fassold is a pilot and physician, who was Commanding Officer of the Defence and Civil Institute of Environmental Medicine and a former Surgeon General)

The most visual memory many of us have of Wilbur was from one of his lectures to flight surgeons on protective equipment, I think, or it might have been on impact forces. Whatever the subject, Wilbur, standing behind one of those big old wooden lecterns at the front of the classroom, would be delivering his lesson to varying degrees of attention when he would suddenly stop talking and pull out from inside the lectern one of the RCAF white jet helmets of the day and plunk it quickly on his head.

Then, still in silence and just as quickly, he would pull out a large carpenter's hammer and give himself two or three resounding whacks on the head to the astonishment of a now fully alert class! He was of course illustrating the impact absorbing capabilities of the helmet and the lecture would then continue as though nothing unusual had happened.

From Squadron Leader (Retired) J. Tunney

(Joe Tunney was a former Clerk Medical and Medical Associate Officer at the RCAF Institute of Aviation Medicine.)

Gentlemen of the Air Force. In the 1946 - 1953 post-war era Dr. W.R. Franks was a frequent guest speaker at the School of Aviation Medicine. On one occasion he was scheduled to address a class of pilot trainees undergoing testing at the Initial Training School. Unknown to Dr. Franks it was the first day for summer uniform wear, i.e. no jackets, no ties, open neck shirts.

Dr. Franks entered the air-conditioned classroom dressed in suit, shirt and tie, but when the students arose, all he could see were open neck shirts. He said "The King may call you gentlemen of the Air Force, and when you dress like gentlemen, I will return." He promptly left the classroom. He returned two days later. Without doubt, this acceptance of his high standards was due to the high esteem in which he was held by the Staff of the Initial Training School and the respect for his knowledge and expertise in the field of aviation medicine.

Bus Ride. Dr. Franks retired from the RCAF at the end of WW II, but continued to work as a civilian consultant at the Institute of Aviation Medicine. It was customary for his wife to pick him up in the car at the end of most working days. She would have the security guard in the guardhouse call down to Dr. Franks' office to tell him she had arrived, and then she would return to her car and read until he was ready to leave. The wait was frequently one or two hours, but she would patiently wait for him. On one such occasion, some two hours or so after the telephone call, he walked out past the guardhouse, crossed Avenue Road and boarded a just arriving bus. The bus then proceeded south on Avenue Road.

Mrs. Franks saw him in her rear-view mirror and honked her horn, but when he got on the bus, she followed it to the next stoplight. Dr. Franks was sitting on the bus beside an open window, with one elbow resting on the window ledge, deep in thought and pre-occupied as usual. Mrs. Franks pulled alongside the open window and repeatedly honked her horn. When he realized the car was his, he got off the bus and according to Mrs. Franks said "Well, hello dear, what are you doing up this way."

Long Holiday. In 1953 I was commissioned from the ranks and transferred from the Institute of Aviation Medicine (IAM) to the RCAF Medical Selection Unit at London Ontario. Some three years later, in 1956 I had an opportunity to drop into the IAM. When I saw Dr. Franks his greeting was "Hello Laddie, did you have a good holiday," as if I had been gone only for a few days.

Train Ride. Mrs. Franks loved to tell the story about Bill on the train ride to Ottawa in mid-1943. Mrs. Franks was an Honorary Lieutenant-Colonel Consultant in Psychiatry to the Canadian Women's Army Corps. She and W/C W.R. Franks were both due to attend meetings in Ottawa at National Defence

Headquarters on the same day, so they decided to pool their tickets and get a bedroom on the train from Toronto to Ottawa.

On arrival at the Toronto Union Station, the porter took their luggage and they proceeded to the club car on the train. They were both in uniform, LCol Franks in her army uniform and W/C Franks in his RCAF uniform.

When it came time to retire they both left the club car and with LCol Franks leading, proceeded to the bedroom car. But as they began to enter the bedroom the porter barred W/C Franks from entering. Despite all his protestations, the porter would not let him enter. W/C Franks spluttered, "But we are married." The porter replied that since the start of the war he had heard that excuse thousands of times. W/C Franks pleaded with his wife to explain the circumstances to the porter, but all she did was smile sweetly as she closed the bedroom door. W/C Franks spent the entire night in the smoking car with the porter. Mrs. Franks later claimed it was the best night of uninterrupted sleep she had enjoyed for a long time.

Case Study. The wife of Dr. W.R. Franks was also a well-known doctor and psychiatrist in the Toronto area. At a social gathering I attended I recall her saying, in jest, that one of the reasons she married Bill was so that she would have a full time case study at hand.

From Hugh Franks, son of Wilbur R. Franks

At the unveiling of the commemorative plaque at the old Institute of Aviation site on Avenue Road in Toronto on 3 October 1998, Hugh Franks, the son of Wilbur R. Franks, related two anecdotes from his father's early days of research on the anti-G suit. He revealed that the first anti-G suit was really two condoms and went on to tell how it was tested. Dr. Franks placed a little laboratory white mouse in a condom, secured it around the mouse's neck, then placed the first condom inside another partially filled with water and secured that to make it water tight. The little mouse, encased in two condoms, was then twirled about to increase G forces. When the mouse was found fully conscious at the end of the experiment, Dr. Franks knew he was on to something that would work.

His next attempt to test a primitive anti-G suit was on himself. He donned the rubber contraption that had water-filled bladders strategically placed to

61

compress the lower limbs and body trunk. Seated in the front seat of a Fleet Finch (a two-seat, single-engine primary flight training aircraft), he instructed the pilot, on reaching a reasonable altitude, to dive the aircraft to it's physical limits and then pull out sharply. The pilot did this, but on recovering from the dive the aircraft wobbled about the air for a few minutes before resuming normal flight.

"Doc!" screamed the pilot, "I blacked out!" Dr. Franks who knew nothing about flying an aircraft was not only unconcerned, he was jubilant. "Well, I didn't!" he exclaimed.

From Group Captain T.J. Powell
(Group Captain Powell was a former Commanding Officer of the Institute of Aviation Medicine and a colleague of Dr. Franks.)

I knew Wilbur Franks from 1953 to 1959 when I was at the IAM in Toronto. He was a brilliant man. His intellect was second to none and he would often break off in a conversation for some reason and start again, using the same words three or four days later.

His wife, Dr. Ruth Franks, was a psychiatrist. They had both studied in Austria. She was a charming lady who was very much in love with Wilbur. She understood his foibles. I remember an evening at the IAM Officers Mess with my wife. Dr. Ruth was also leaving and she looked into the anteroom where the party was going on. Wilbur was having a marvelous time dancing. Dr. Ruth turned to us and said, "You know, if I hadn't been married to him, I could have certified him years ago".

Wilbur certainly had his peculiarities. I cannot remember the sergeant's name who told me this story about looking after Wilbur. A young Erk, an Acey-Deucy, who had been appointed to look after Wilbur's comings and goings and needs said to the sergeant one day "Dr. Franks is crazy." "Oh, no, no, no," replied the sergeant, he's just a little peculiar at times but he's not crazy." A few days later the AC2 said "Sergeant, he is crazy. I just heard him on the phone. He said to the operator "Get me Dr. Franks." The young man may have never learned that there were two doctor Franks, Ruth and Willbur.

On one of our trips, when we were having a party, Wilbur said, "You know, alcohol is Gods' gift to man. If it hadn't been, then putting fruit juice out in the sun for a few days and producing alcohol would never have happened".

I want to give you the true story of the Denver Colorado meeting and the troubles Dr. Frank's had there. I cannot quite remember the year but it would be around 1955. There were a number of us from the IAM and we had all been having a party in a nightclub in Denver, which closed quite early at midnight or earlier. Bill Franks and G/C John Young decided to go to a nightclub some miles outside the city. So they started out in a taxi that was stopped for speeding. They all got out and tried to persuade the sheriff not to charge the taxi-driver as they had told him to hurry up. Bill wanted to know the badge number of the sheriff so he just lifted it up so he could see it better. The next thing he knew he was in handcuffs and in the back seat of the sheriff's car. John Young returned to the hotel and went out early next morning with a lawyer to make bond arrangements. The arresting sheriff was asked if he was going to charge Wilbur Franks and he said "Oh no. He's too dumb". So the lawyer, John Young and Wilbur came back and I saw them enter the hotel. It wasn't until later that I got the full story. There has been a number of stories about the arrest but this is the true story.

While in Denver, we were all getting up somewhat early and I went down to the coffee shop and was going to sit with Bill for breakfast but he said "No. No. Busy". There he was, writing away. At 9 a.m., he delivered a paper which he had written in that coffee shop. It was a brilliant exposition of a new method of recording G-Forces by scintillations produced when sharp, gravelly things would scratch against a film. I cannot remember the utilization of this idea but he certainly was brilliant.

Bill was a wonderful travelling companion. I had the honour of going on a three-week tour of RCAF and USAF stations in Europe with Wilbur in 1957 when I was commanding the IAM because (G/C) Don Nelson *(see The Leaders)* had gone to the National Defence College. We arrived in Paris about 11 p.m., having driven from Metz, France where the Headquarters of RCAF Europe was located. We got into the hotel and I started to go to bed when Wilbur came into my room and said "Laddie, what are you doing? This is Paris!" So we went and saw Paris. I'm afraid we were a rather sorry pair at the opening of the AGARD (NATO Advisory Group on Aerospace Research and Development) meeting at the Palais de Chaillot the next morning but it had been a good night. The almost ten days we spent in Paris were wonderful days and full of much fun and friendship. One of his sons had a girlfriend who was studying at the Sorbonne and Wilbur decided that he should take her to lunch. He asked where she would like to go. She said there was a restaurant in the Bois de Boulogne which she had heard was very nice and would like to go there. Bill asked me to come along with him. So the three of us went to this lovely restaurant on a beautiful day and had a nice lunch; nothing spectacular. It was the only time I have ever seen Wilbur discomposed was when he was presented with the bill. I glanced at it and it was for seventy-five dollars or its equivalent—an absolutely unheard of amount in those days for lunch.

But, nothing less, I helped him out with the bill and I do remember the three salads we had were small lettuce leaves soaked in oil and vinegar and cost the equivalent of about six dollars. I would not advise anyone to go to the restaurant in the Bois de Boulogne if they haven't a pocketful of money.

At an Aeromedical Association Meeting in San Antonio Texas, there was a small nightclub that Bill and three or four IAM officers went to one evening. The proprietor came to the table and Bill asked him to join us. Suddenly, Bill said, pointing to me, "Meet Bugsy Powell from Chicago. I think he would like to take over your club." The proprietor, not the least abashed, immediately drew his gun from a shoulder holster, placed it on the table saying, " I would be very glad to discuss this with you." We finally got out of this predicament and went elsewhere. Bill was fun.

I think this is the end of my reminiscences about Bill but he was a great help to me in my work at the IAM in charge of the Central Medical Establishment, which looked after aircrews medical problems, and was the final arbiter of such problems.

Dr. Franks liked a good party and always looked forward to the Institute's Annual Christmas Party. Some say it didn't start until he arrived.

GARY W. GRAY
OMM, CD, MD
COMMANDER

Gary **Gray** was born in Palmerston, Ontario and got his early education there. In 1968 he graduated from McGill University in Montreal, Québec with a degree in medicine. In 1976 he obtained a Ph.D. in altitude physiology and in 1978, he completed specialty training in Internal Medicine at the University of Toronto.

His military training included the Flight Surgeon's course and the Field Ambulance course. His Canadian Forces career was primarily in Aerospace Medicine at the Canadian Forces Institute of Environmental Medicine (CFIEM) later to become the Defence and Civil Institute of Environmental Medicine (DCIEM). His early career was research-oriented, investigating hypoxia and altitude illness in the altitude chamber and at the altitude research station on Mount Logan, British Columbia.

Cdr Gary Gray

Although Gray originally enrolled in the RCAF, his rank was Captain in the Canadian Armed Forces as dictated by the 1967 White Paper on unification of the Forces. He took a voluntary release in 1986 after 21 year's service, then re-enrolled in 1991 and went on to complete 28 years service in 1998. When he re-enrolled, he joined the "Sea Element," denoting a preference for service in the Navy, but he did not go to sea except for a sea-trial for a motion-sickness study.

Later, he returned to clinical medicine and helped to develop the aircrew medical selection process and the aircrew consultation service at DCIEM into

65

a world-class facility available to both military and civilian aircrew, which is also used for selection and ongoing screening of the Canadian astronauts. He was instrumental in initiating an advanced Aerospace Medicine program at the University of Toronto.

For his outstanding work in Aviation Medicine he was awarded the Order of Military Merit. He spent virtually all his career at the Institute of Aviation Medicine, the Canadian Forces Institute of Environmental Medicine and the Defence and Civil Institute of Environmental Medicine where he continues to work as a consultant.

Summary of Achievements

Order of Military Merit (OMM)
Canadian Forces Decoration (CD)
Silver Jubilee - Queen Elizabeth II
Doctor of Medicine, McGill University - 1968 (MD, CM)
Doctor of Philosophy, Toronto - 1976 (PhD)
Fellow of the Royal College of Physicians of Canada - 1978 (FRCPC)
Lecturer in Medicine, University of Toronto
Consultant in Medicine, Medical Assessment Section, Defence and Civil Institute of Environmental Medicine

GEORGE E. HALL
AFC, ED, MD
GROUP CAPTAIN

George Hall was born 10 October 1907 in Lindsay, Ontario and received his early education in the local public schools. On graduation from the Lindsay Collegiate Institute and in keeping with his desire to be a farmer, he attended the Ontario Agricultural College (OAC) in Guelph, Ontario from which he graduated in 1929 with the degree of Bachelor of Scientific Agriculture. George Hall continued his studies at the University of Toronto from which he received a Masters degree in Scientific Agriculture in 1931, Doctor of Medicine in 1935 and Doctor of Philosophy in 1936.

G/C George E. Hall

While he was a student in Toronto, Hall studied for a time in England and Belgium. In 1935, he joined the University of Toronto's Department of Medical Research as a research associate at the Banting Institute and rose to the rank of professor by 1939. Dr. Hall's researches included metabolic and nutritional problems, embolism of the lungs and coronary thrombosis. His scientific studies led to his election as a Fellow of the Royal Society of Canada in 1944. During his life, Hall received five honorary Doctor of Laws degrees, as well as many other awards.

Dr. Hall had a long association with the militia prior to the beginning of WW II in 1939. As a student at OAC, he served with the 29th Field Battery of the Royal Canadian Artillery. Later, in Toronto, he served with the Governor General's Horse Guards. In 1938, he transferred to a field ambulance unit of the Royal Canadian Army Medical Corps (RCAMC). At that time, the

RCAMC was responsible for providing medical services to the Royal Canadian Air Force (RCAF). Hall realized that the RCAF needed its own medical service, especially in view of the particular needs and requirements of aircrew and he was a leader in the drive to establish the RCAF Medical Branch.

At the outbreak of hostilities in 1939, Hall entered the active force of the RCAF where his administrative, medical and scientific skills were put to good use. He was instrumental in persuading RCAF HQ to build a research building on the grounds of No. 1 Initial Training School (the old Eglinton Hunt Club at 1107 Avenue Road in Toronto). This building housed No. 1 Clinical Investigation Unit (C.I.U.), which was devoted to the study of aviation medicine. Hall was Commanding Officer of No. 1 C.I.U. from 1941-1944.

No. 1 C.I.U. was the forerunner of the RCAF Institute of Aviation Medicine, which is now the Defence and Civil Institute of Environmental Medicine located at Downsview in Toronto. Later he was Director of Aviation Medical Research at Air Force Headquarters Ottawa, where he supervised the projects carried out at No. 1 C.I.U. (Toronto) and at No. 2 C.I.U. (Regina). Ophthalmologic research was carried out at McGill University in Montreal. A high altitude training unit, called the Flying Personnel Medical Establishment, was operating at Halifax, Nova Scotia, and an air-sea rescue research unit was formed at Sea Island, British Columbia.

In his research work for the RCAF, Group Captain Hall took part, as much as he possibly could, in actual service flying. On 9 January 1943, G/C Hall was awarded the Air Force Cross, a rare distinction for a non-flying officer. Hall's contributions were also recognized by the USA with the award of the Legion of Merit in the grade of Officer on 23 November 1946.

At the end of WW II, Dr. Hall became Head of Medicine at the University of Western Ontario (UWO). On 1 July 1947, he became President of UWO and served in that capacity until 1967.

Dr. Hall maintained an active interest in the medical problems of the armed forces and served on the Canadian Forces Medical Council of which he was chairman, 1962-1967. George Hall died on 11 February 1972 at the age of 64. He is buried in Woodland Cemetery in London, Ontario.

Summary of Achievements

Air Force Cross (AFC)
Efficiency Decoration (ED)
Defence Medal
Officer Legion of Merit - U.S.A.
Canadian Volunteer Service Medal
War Medal 1939 - 1945
Medical Doctor (MD)
Doctor of Philosophy (Ph D)
Doctor of Science (DSc)
Doctor of Laws (LL. D)
Fellow Royal Society of Canada (FRSC)
Note: This biographical sketch was prepared by Major (retired) D. Soper.

HUGH B. HAY
DSO, DFC, MD
GROUP CAPTAIN

Hugh B. Hay was born in Edmundston, New Brunswick on 26 February 1916. Little is known of his early childhood and education. His story begins at the age of 24 when he left McGill University Medical School in Montreal, Québec to enlist in the RCAF on 20 September 1940.

Hay was selected for pilot training, but did not do well. He was re-selected for navigation training and despite his disappointment at not getting his first choice, he excelled in his second.

Throughout 1940 to mid -1941, Pilot Officer Hay was trained in basic and advanced air navigation, air gunnery and communications in preparation for squadron service. He was soon in action as a navigator in a variety of bombers. As early as November 1942, he earned his first decoration, a Distinguished Flying Cross (DFC). Pilot Officer Hay's citation reads as follows:

G/C Hugh B. Hay

"Pilot officer Hay as navigator has participated in some outstanding attacks on enemy targets and brought back some highly successful photographs. Undoubtedly, a large measure of the excellent results obtained are due to the exceptional navigation skill displayed by P/O Hay. He has shown a great devotion to duty."

Flying Officer (F/O) Hay's distinguished service continued unabated as he racked up more operations as a navigator on the de Havilland Mosquito bomber. On 29 August 1944, F/O Hay was awarded the Distinguished Service Order, a rare accomplishment for a holder of the DFC. The citation read:

"This officer has participated in a very large number of sorties involving attacks on a wide variety of enemy targets. He has invariably displayed a high standard of courage and resolution. He has rendered much loyal and devoted service."

In late 1944, using the clout he had earned through his courageous and distinguished flying service, he convinced his superiors that he should at last be allowed to take pilot training. He returned to Canada and commenced training at 1 Initial Training School (ITS) in Toronto. On graduation, he placed Leading Aircraftman Propellers on his Flight Lieutenant's uniform. This insignia, usually placed on tunics of Aircraftmen 2nd Class (AC2) on graduation from ITS, was meant to poke fun at the system that had withheld his pilot training for so long; he was the only officer, and a well-decorated one at that, on his course of Aircraftmen. Needless to say, the Commanding Officer was not amused.

On completion of ITS, F/L Hay went on to Elementary Flying School and earned his pilot's wings. At the end of the war F/L Hay was a staff pilot at RCAF Station Trenton, Ontario and qualified on the de Havilland Vampire, a jet aircraft then in service in the RCAF. Because Hay had completed three years of the medical program at McGill University before enlisting, he was transferred to the RCAF Institute of Aviation Medicine (IAM) in Toronto. During a visit to the IAM by the Chief of the Air Staff, Air Marshal Robert Leckie, a request was made to have the RCAF subsidize the completion of Hay's medical training. This was granted and he completed his medical education and received his degree in Medicine from the University of Western Ontario in 1949.

Squadron Leader Hay was next assigned to the Medical Liaison Staff in London, England and subsequently posted as Staff Officer Medical Services at Air Transport Command. Subsequent promotions brought Group Captain (G/C) Hay the assignment as Commanding Officer of the RCAF Institute of Aviation Medicine for the period August 1961 to September 1965.

G/C Hay obtained a degree in Public Health at Harvard and was certified

71

in the specialty of aviation medicine by the Canadian Forces Medical Council.

Notes
From Flight Lieutenant H. Terry Goodwin DFC, DFM
Hugh Hay's pilot for his third tour who recalls Hay as follows.

"I met Hugh—but his family and family friends call him Burn—at Marham in England when we were posted to the Mosquito Conversion Unit in December 1943. We were posted to 692 Squadron at Graveley, west of Cambridge, as one of the original de Havilland Mosquito crews. I had seen Hugh out of the corner of my eye at 61 Squadron at Syerston on Lancasters but had not talked to him. At that time he had finished his second tour. A bomber squadron tour consisted of thirty operational flights over enemy territory. He had done one tour on Handley Page Hamptons and the second on Bristol Manchesters and Avro Lancasters.

He and his pilot, Peter Casement, were part of Bomber Command that had been sent to help Coastal Command in the Battle of the Atlantic. They were on their first sortie when the following adventure occurred. Normally, Coastal Command pilots would see one German submarine during their entire tour. But on their very first trip, Hugh and Peter not only saw one but sank it. Hugh did the bombing. The first two depth charges straddled the sub and this was captured on film. The next two overshot and the camera failed to capture this. The third pair of bombs again straddled the sub and the pictures showed the submarine crew in the water, having abandoned their sinking U-Boat.

When they returned, the Royal Navy just would not believe it. They took them to Portsmouth and grilled them for four days. Finally Peter and Hugh gave up and told them to forget the whole thing, they had not really seen the sub. Then the Navy said "But what about the pictures? Where are your depth charges?" Only then did the Navy believed them.

Hugh had credit for sixty-three operational trips when he joined me and then did forty-six more. He got the Distinguished Service Order while flying with me when we laid mines in the Kiel Canal in May 1944 just before D-Day. One source remembered him saying that he had one hundred and nine trips and was about to go on his next trip. A senior RAF officer overheard the comment and forbade him from making any more operational flights saying: "You're finished."

After he finished on Lancasters he became an Oboe controller. Oboe was the code name given to a highly secret radio navigation system. It was used to direct bombers from a control site in England to targets as far away as the Ruhr Valley in Germany.

This gallant officer was a navigator, pilot and a doctor in the RCAF and the only person to have achieved this outstanding feat. He died at he National Defence Medical Centre in Ottawa Ontario on 27 September 1979.

Summary of Achievements

Distinguished Service Order (DSO)
Distinguished Flying Cross (DFC)
Canadian Forces Decoration (CD)
1939 – 1945 Star
Aircrew Europe Star with Clasp
France and Germany Star
Defence Medal
Canadian Volunteer Service Medal
Operations Wing and Bars
Bachelor of Science (B Sc)
Medical Doctor, University of Western Ontario, 1949 (MD)
Diploma of Public Health, Harvard (DPM)

ROY EDWARD LONGARD
BEM, CD
FLIGHT LIEUTENANT

Roy Edward Longard joined the RCAF in October 1941 at Halifax, Nova Scotia. Longard received his pilot's wings at the Service Flying Training School at Calgary, Alberta in May 1942, following pilot selection and training in Brandon, Manitoba; Regina, Saskatchewan; and Vancouver, British Columbia. Flying training completed, he was posted to Halifax, Nova Scotia for overseas duty in England.

Trans-Atlantic travel by sea in wartime was not swift. Travelling in a slow moving convoy of ninety-seven ships took twenty-eight days on the Atlantic and seven days in Iceland. Several ships were sunk by submarines in the western approaches, and what remained of the convoy, docked in Scotland after a thirty-five-day voyage. This was followed by another long journey by rail to reach the south of England only to be put back on another train to return to Scotland to Kinloss. No. 19 Operatonal Training Unit (OTU) was located there and it provided conversion training to prepare pilots to fly heavy bombers. The training aircraft was the Armstrong Whitworth Whitley, a twin-engined bomber of 1935 vintage that had been the mainstay of the RAF's bomber fleet in the opening days of the war, but was now obsolescent and used only for training and low-level operations.

F/L Roy E. Longard

Finally, a posting to an operational unit, No. 51 Squadron Dishforth, Yorkshire in 4 Group of Bomber Command put Flight Sergeant (F/Sgt) Longard on operational bombing raids over Europe and eventually to secret operations in the Middle East and the Mediterranean. On some of these flights,

74

their payload was secret service agents and equipment to be dropped over Yugoslavia. The flight would continue to Kabrit in Egypt and then return to the island of Malta to repeat the operation.

On Longard's return to England, his squadron was assigned to maritime patrol duties, flying out of Chivenon in Devon as part of No. 19 Coastal Command. These were long flights over the Bay of Biscay and west over the Atlantic, searching for U-Boats. On one such patrol, on 29 July 1942, at about two hundred miles southwest of Ireland, the aircraft engines caught fire and the plane crash landed into the sea. The crew, some with injuries, managed to get out and inflate their dinghies, but they were in forty-foot seas in the tail end of a hurricane. Air Gunner Sergeant MacDonald of Toronto, who had been seriously injured in the crash with fractures to his pelvis and spine, died after several hours in the dinghy. The remainder of the crew was picked up by a Polish destroyer after drifting for nearly thirty-five hours. They were taken ashore at Clovalley Devon, transferred to a local hospital and eventually taken to a military hospital in the Midlands for twelve-weeks of recuperation.

This brought F/S Longard's tour of operations to a close and he was was posted back to Canada in December 1942, arriving in Halifax on Christmas morning.

The Queen's New Year's list of 1943 published in *The London Gazette* records that F/S Roy Edward Longard was awarded the British Empire Medal Military Division effective 1 January 1943.

Drawing on Roy Longard's wartime experience, he was posted to No. 1 Clinical Investigation Unit in Toronto in April 1943 to work with Squadron Leader Bright and Squadron Leader Whillans. They were developing new survival equipment - rations, dinghies and survival gear. As a part of this work, Longard was required to field test the gear with winter survival trials in the wilds of Ontario. Roy also helped to produce a one-hour, aircraft crash, survival film, depicting summer, fall and winter survival techniques.

In 1946, as the RCAF started to reduce its strength to its peace-time needs, those selected to remain in the regular force were required to take a lower rank. This was called "R" day or reversion day. Longard reverted to the rank of Warrant Officer Second Class (W/O 2) and became member of the regular force.

In 1948, with a promotion to W/O 1 and having attained the highest qualification level in his trade, Longard was made a trade examiner for Aeromedical Technicians.

In 1950, Longard attended the Health Physics Technician's course at Randolph Air Force Base at San Antonio, Texas. This course taught atomic radiation detection. He subsequently became an instructor at the School of Aviation Medicine at the RCAF Institute of Aviation Medicine in Toronto.

Roy was commissioned April 1958 and with the rank of Flying Officer (F/O) was posted to RCAF Station McDonald, Manitoba as the AeroMed Training Officer and as a member of Station Flight Safety Committee. F/O Longard was responsible for training aircrew candidates in oxygen equipment and other safety equipment during their flying training program. Longard held similar posts at RCAF Station Portage la Prairie, Manitoba in 1959, at RCAF Station Chatham, New Brunswick in 1962, and Canadian Forces Base Shearwater, Nova Scotia in 1966. In May 1965, Flight Lieutenant (F/L) Longard graduated from the Physiological Training Officer course for Allied Medical Officers given at Brooks Air Force Base in San Antonio, Texas.

F/L Longard had a continuing interest in Air Cadets and in the RCAF Association. While in New Brunswick, he was the Air Cadet Liaison Officer No. 349 Squadron and Liaison Officer No. 255 Wing RCAF Association Campbellton, New Brunswick.

Roy Longard retired in August 1968 after a distinguished career and twenty-seven years of dedicated service.

Summary of Achievements

British Empire Medal (BEM)
Canadian Forces Decoration (CD)
1939 - 1945 Star
Aircrew Europe Star with Atlantic Clasp
Africa Star
Canadian Volunteer Service Medal and Clasp
War Medal 1939 - 1945
Operations Wing

ROMNEY H. LOWRY
AFC, CD, MD
WING COMMANDER

Romney Lowry, like so many young men at the outbreak of war in 1939, rushed to enlist in the Royal Canadian Air Force in his home town of Toronto, Ontario. He was barely 19, having been born in 1920 when WWI was still a vivid memory.

Lowry was a good flyer and, after earning his pilot's wings, he was kept on as a flight instructor. He served in this role at RCAF Stations in Calgary Alberta; Dauphin, Manitoba; and Hagersville, Ontario. Flying Officer Lowry's persistence finally prevailed and he was finally transferred to No. 6 (BR) Squadron at Alliford Bay, British Columbia. This bomber reconnaissance squadron was flying Consolidated PBY5 Catalinas flying boats and PBY5A Canso amphibian aircraft.

Squadron Leader Lowry's leadership qualities were clearly demonstrated and he was given command of 4 (BR) Squadron at RCAF Station Ucluelet, British Columbia. This squadron flew PBY5A Cansos, the amphibious version of the Catalina, on anti-submarine patrols. His one year as Squadron Commander (30 September 1943 - 31 October 1944) added lustre to his career with the award of the Air Force Cross on 3 November 1944.

W/C Romney H. Lowry

Wing Commander (W/C) Lowry was demobilized in 1945 and he returned to school to undergo medical training. He rejoined the RCAF in 1948 as a Flight Lieutenant Medical Officer for duty at the RCAF Institute of

Aviation Medicine (IAM) in Toronto. Promoted to Squadron Leader, Lowry remained at the IAM from 1948 until 1953, except for a brief period of duty in Korea in 1950. He was the first Flight Surgeon to arrive in Seoul, the Korean capital, to aid the wounded and was awarded the Air Medal USA for Korean Operations.

Following Wing Commander Lowry's return from Korea, he was enrolled at the John Hopkins University in the U.S. for postgraduate studies from 1953 to 1957.

From 1957 until retirement he served at several appointments. He was always interested in aviation medicine and served as the superintendent of the Defence Research Medical Laboratory, later designated the Defence and Civil Institute of Environmental Medicine from 1971 - 1978.

Summary of Achievements

Air Force Cross (AFC)
Defence Medal
Canadian Volunteer Service Medal
War Medal 1939 – 1945
Canadian Korean Medal
United Nations Service Medal – Korea
Air Medal - USA

Note

Romney Lowry is deceased and efforts to locate his next of kin or relatives have been fruitless. The details in this summary have been prepared from various documents with apologies for any errors and omissions.

GEORGE W. MANNING, MD
WING COMMANDER

O ne of the hazards of having an ardor for research is that it may lead to areas on the periphery of the central focus of a lifetime of work. This happened to George W. Manning whose career began in biology and physiology, moved to medicine and thence to aviation medicine, but ended in four decades of outstanding contributions to practice, teaching, and research in cardiology.

It all began in the heady milieu of Sir Frederick Banting's laboratory where attention had turned from diabetes to coronary artery disease, silicosis, asphyxia, and other conditions needing illumination. The prescient Banting had begun research in the problems of aviation before World War II, but advent of the war drastically increased it and it was to envelop Manning for the next five years.

Born in Toronto in 1911, the only child of a railway man who later went into the hat business, Manning decided in high school that he would be a doctor. He enrolled in the University of Toronto in 1931, taking the honors course in biological and medical sciences. He graduated with a BA in 1935 and was appointed research assistant in the Banting Institute, completing his MA there in 1937. This period was spent in research on coronary artery disease, which was published in the *Canadian Medical Association Journal,*

W/C George W. Manning

79

(1937) with G.E. Hall and F.G. Banting under the title *Vagus Stimulation and the Production of Myocardial Damage*. He then proceeded to study medicine and received his MD in 1940.

Manning interned for three months at St. Michael's Hospital in Toronto and then requested release to return to the Banting Institute, which was now fully engaged in aviation research associated with the war. He registered for Ph.D. studies, but completion of this was to be deferred until 1948. The Banting group was studying urgent problems such as motion sickness and the effect of altitude on peripheral and night vision. In 1940, Manning joined the Royal Canadian Air Force and was placed in charge of No. 2 Clinical Investigation Unit in Regina, Saskatchewan.

In 1943, he was transferred to a British research station in England, working on pressure breathing jackets and oxygen masks. Later he was sent to Belfast, Ireland to work with (later Sir) Henry Barcroft on anoxic collapse. Nearly forty full reports were authored or co-authored by Manning during his years with the Air Force. At the end of hostilities in 1945, he returned to Canada and was offered an appointment in the faculty of medicine at the University of Western Ontario (London) subject to further studies in cardiology. There followed a year as a senior intern at Toronto General Hospital and then an additional year or more as a Nuffield Fellow in Britain.

In civilian Britain, Manning became a member of the Heart Unit of London Hospital in Whitechapel which, as the world's first, was founded by Sir James Mackenzie (1853-1925) who was followed by Sir John Parkinson and Dr. William Evans.

This was a period when bedside cardiology was at its peak and new developments such as cardiac catheterization and phono-cardiography were beginning to be introduced. Parkinson and Evans and their heart unit had a profound effect on Manning and were to determine the creation of his own heart unit when he returned to Canada in 1947. He then completed his Ph.D. at the University of Toronto and moved to his new post at the University of Western Ontario (UWO).

As agreed when he was still in the Air Force, Manning became the second full-time faculty member at UWO and continued full time for twenty-five years at Victoria Hospital and after that for an additional sixteen years when a

80

university hospital was built in London. During the earlier years he rose from fellow to full professor and to chief of cardiology in both hospitals and acquired fellowship in the Canadian Royal College and the American Colleges of Physicians and Cardiology. In 1948 he established the first specialized cardiac care unit in Canada and saw it grow from one tiny basement room with a staff of two to one of the largest and best equipped in Canada with a large staff of cardiologists and technicians. Among other achievements, the unit has become Canada's leading center for cardiac transplantation and for the surgical and medical treatment of arrhythmias.

Manning's consuming interest had been electrocardiography. During the years 1947-1986, he received all the electrocardiograms from RCAF stations in Canada and overseas. His heart unit served as the ECG laboratory for the RCAF and by 1986 he had received over 350,000 tracings. This was of great value to the Air Force but, in addition, was the source of numerous papers of significance to clinical cardiologists. In 1965, he developed a vectorcardiograph capable of recording three spatial loops from the same cardiac cycle. Although discussed at several scientific meetings, it was eventually abandoned when other diagnostic procedures in cardiology rendered it less useful.

In addition to dozens of unpublished reports and addresses, Manning published more than a hundred papers and edited three books—one on electrical activity of the heart, one on atherosclerosis, and a privately printed two-volume book entitled *Banting, Insulin and Aviation Medical Research*. Keenly interested in medical history, he has also written *A Forty Year History of the Department of Medicine, 1945-1985*, published by the University of Western Ontario and a History of the *Royal Canadian Air Force Electrocardiographic Program, 1939-1986*, published by The Queen's Printer, Ottawa, for the Defence and Civilian Institute of Environmental Medicine at Downsview, Ontario.

Like so many talented leaders in medicine, Manning has spread his mantle widely. He has served innumerable organizations and has been honored by many. Science, cardiology, and aviation have not consumed him entirely. During the "Dirty Thirties" he helped put himself through school by teaching the piano and he also formed an orchestra through which he met his wife.

81

Married in 1940, they had three children and four grandchildren. He died 2 October 1992 while this profile was being prepared by Dr. Robert E. Beamish. Published with permission of the *Canadian Journal of Cardiology*.

Summary of Achievements

Canadian Volunteer Service Medal
War Medal, 1939-1945

Note 1.
George Manning was a founding member of the Ontario and Canadian Heart Foundations and has received its Distinguished Service Award. The Civil Aviation Medical Association made him an Honorary Life Member and gave him the Award of Service in 1982, while the Institute of Aviation Medicine conferred the Award of Merit in 1979. He was also awarded the W.R.Franks Merit of Service to Aviation Medicine Medal in 1984. He is a Life Member of the American College of Cardiology and is the only Canadian to have served as its Vice President. His university made him Professor Emeritus on his retirement.

Note 2.
Air Force doctors did not often go on parade during WW II, however the one time George Manning did he forgot the command and instead of saying, "By the left, Quick March!" he turned around to the formation he was leading and said "Follow me!"

James Hamilton Murray
CD, MD
Colonel

James Murray was born 21 January 1923 in Detroit, Michigan, but spent his youth in London, Ontario where he got his early education. He was not yet twenty when he joined the Royal Canadian Air Force in 1942.

Jim qualified as a navigator at #1 Air Navigation School Malton, Ontario, received his wings and a commission as a Pilot Officer (P/O) in April 1943 before proceeding overseas. P/O Murray was posted to the Royal Air Force and assigned to 43 Squadron in 4 Group of Bomber Command. The Squadron was flying the Handley-Page Halifax II, a four-engine heavy bomber, which at that time had been retired from assignments to main targets as it could not reach a high enough altitude over the target. Therefore, the squadron was assigned minelaying duties, which

G/C James H. Murray

were done at low level, over the Baltic Sea. On his 13th trip, his aircraft was shot down over waters near Denmark. Murray parachuted out of the burning aircraft and landed in the water a few hundred yards from shore. He had to quickly get out of his waterfilled boots, inflate his flotation vest, called a Mae West, and swim ashore. The inflatable vest was named after Mae West, a voluptuous blond actress because it approximated Miss West's well-endowed bosom when inflated. He was fortunate to get to a house near the shore, where the friendly occupants gave him dry clothing and hid him in the woods until the German search died down.

Later, with the help of the Danish underground, he made his way to Copenhagen and was joined by two others from his crew who had also been lucky. The rest of the crew was listed as missing. The Danes got him across the Kattegat Straight to Sweden, a neutral country. From Sweden, the British Consul arranged for him, and other crew survivors, to fly to Britain in the bomb bay of a de Havilland Mosquito bomber that was being operated out of Stockholm as a commercial British Overseas Airway Company flight solely to transport diplomatic mail.

Following a furlough in Canada, he returned to Britain and joined a Canadian crew with 428 Squadron in 6 (RCAF) Group of Bomber Command. 428 Squadron flew, at various times, Vickers Wellingtons, Handley-Page Halifax bombers and Avro Lancaster bombers. Flight Lieutenant Murray completed his second tour with 428 Squadron and returned to Canada for demobilization. He landed in Halifax, Nova Scotia the day after the VE Day riot in that city, and received phenomenal administrative support to get out of town as soon as possible. Uniformed members were not welcome on that day in Halifax following a mass riot of military personnel in the area.

On return to civilian life he returned to the University of Western Ontario in London, Ontario and was accepted in the veterans' class in the medical school. This class consisted of one hundred veterans, the largest class Western had ever graduated up to that time! Following his internship at the Victoria Hospital in London, Murray re-enrolled in the RCAF and served as a General Duty Medical Officer at RCAF Station Aylmer, Ontario, then operating as the principal Manning Depot for the Air Force and at RCAF Station St-Jean, Québec.

Squadron Leader Murray's wartime experience and medical training were put to much better use when, in 1953, he was posted as an instructor to the RCAF Institute of Aviation Medicine in Toronto, Ontario until 1957. Murray spent the academic year 1957-58 acquiring a Master's degree in Public Health from Harvard University, graduating cum laude.

His new degree and a promotion to Wing Commander were quickly put to work as Murray was appointed Command Flight Surgeon for Air Defence

Command in St-Hubert, Québec. From 1960 to 1962, he was responsible for aviation medicine and preventive medicine for a command of 15,000 personnel spread out all over Canada from coast to coast and into the far North.

A further promotion to Group Captain (G/C), gave Murray additional responsibilities as Command Surgeon 1 Air Division Europe at Metz, France. The Division comprised 25,000 service and dependent personnel located at four bases in France and Germany that operated their own hospitals, and personnel at remote sites in other North Atlantic Treaty Organization (NATO) countries. In addition to these onerous duties, G/C Murray managed to qualify during this time for a Diploma in Public Health from the American Board of Preventive Medicine and a Fellowship in Public Health from the American College of Preventive Medicine, both in 1962.

On his return from Europe, G/C Murray was selected to attend the University of Toronto in a two-year program, leading to a Diploma in Hospital Administration. The internship year of this program, 1966, was spent at the Hospital for Sick Children as an Administrative Resident.

G/C Murray now assumed command of the RCAF Institute of Aviation Medicine in Toronto in 1966 and became involved in many research projects, the results of which were published in peer review journals. These included such subjects as;

    a. the effects of hypoxia on the neurons of the central nervous system,

    b. anatomical stresses caused by ballistic ejection seats,

    c. epidemiological study of an outbreak of epidemic diarrhea, and

    d. many aspects of quality control in hospital and clinical institutions.

Summary of Achievements

Canadian Forces Decoration (CD)
1939 – 1945 Star
France and Germany Star
Defence Medal
Canadian Volunteer Service Medal
War Medal 1939 – 1945
Special Services Medal NATO

Operations Wing and Bar
Doctor of Medicine, University of Western Ontario 1950 (MD)
Master of Public Health (Harvard) (MPH)
Fellow American College of Physical Medicine (FACPM)
Diploma, Hospital Administration [DHA – (Toronto)]
Diplomate, American Board of Preventive Medicine (DABPM)

Awards
University of Western Ontario – Entrance Scholarship for highest marks in mathematics and science - 1940.
Alpha Omega Alpha Honour Medical Society - Elected from University of Western Ontario - 1949.
Harvard University M.P.H. (cum laude)
University of Toronto, G. Harvey Agnew Award for highest standing in Hospital Administration 1965
Fellow, Aerospace Medical Association – awarded for work in aviation medicine research, development and practice -1968.

Note
In the 60s while stationed in Europe he contacted the mayor of the city of Maribo on the Island of Lolland seeking information on the scene of his ditching in the sea. The mayor invited him to visit and along with the town councillors granted him the keys to the city. He was put in touch with the farmer who hid him from the Germans.

THOMAS JENNER "JAY" POWELL
CD, MD
GROUP CAPTAIN

THOMAS Jenner "Jay" Powell was born in Nantwich, England on 14 November 1913 and, at the age of 29, came to Canada. He studied biology and medicine and then medical sciences at the University of Toronto, receiving a Bachelor of Arts degree with honors in 1936 and a Doctor of Medicine (MD) in 1939. He interned at the Vancouver General Hospital in Vancouver, British Columbia from 1939 to 1940 where he met and married Margaret Marion Hamilton.

He was commissioned in the Indian Medical Service in July 1940 and served for several years on the Northwest Frontier where he commanded the 8th Indian Field Ambulance and raised it to war establishment. He also served in the Middle East as Commanding Officer of the 13th Indian General Hospital in Aden in what was then a British Protectorate and is now the People's Democratic Republic of Yemen.

When the Indian Medical Service was disbanded in 1947, he resigned his commission as a

G/C T.J. "Jay" Powell

Lieutenant-Colonel in the Indian army and returned to Canada in January 1948 to join the Royal Canadian Air Force as a Medical Officer in its Medical Branch. After a few months as the Senior Medical Officer (SMO) at RCAF Station Greenwood, Nova Scotia, Squadron Leader Powell went to RCAF Station Trenton, Ontario as SMO and remained there for four years until he

87

was promoted to Wing Commander (W/C).

W/C Powell's interest in aviation medicine resulted in his being sent to the RAF Institute of Aviation Medicine in Farnborough, England for a year of study. This earned him his Flight Surgeon's wings and prepared him to take on the task of commanding the Central Medical Establishment of the RCAF Institute of Aviation Medicine in Toronto, Ontario in 1953. Powell was subsequently certified by the American Board of Preventive Medicine in 1955.

W/C Powell served a tour as Commanding Officer of the Institute of Aviation before leaving for another year of study at the School of Aviation Medicine at the US Naval Air Station in Pensacola, Florida in 1958.

On his return from his studies in the U.S. in 1959, W/C Powell was assigned to the Medical Selection Board at RCAF Station Centralia, Ontario as its Officer Commanding. The Board examined and selected candidates for aircrew training in the RCAF. He performed this role until July 1960.

Jay Powell was keenly interested in aviation medicine and had international recognition. He authored several articles published in various scientific journals, including Aviation, Space and Environmental Medicine.

From July 1960 to July 1963, W/C Powell served at Air Defence Command St-Hubert, Québec in two appointments. The first as deputy to the Staff Officer Medical Services (SOMS) and then, with a promotion to Group Captain (G/C), in the senior position.

His next assignment, from July 1963 to June 1964, was to the staff of the Director General Medical Services (Air) at Air Force Headquarters Ottawa where G/C Powell was Director of Medical Plans and Requirements. This short posting was followed by another short tour, this time as the Medical Liaison Officer at the Canadian Joint Staff in London, England. He served in this post from June 1964 to August 1965.

On his return to Canada in August 1965, G/C Powell assumed command of the Canadian Forces Hospital (CFH) Kingston, a position he held until his retirement from the RCAF in May 1966. CFH Kingston, a definitive care hospital, was not only responsible for the medical and surgical care of the military for a large area of Ontario, it was also charged with the care of penitentiary inmates who required surgical and medical hospital care. For this reason, the hospital had been built with secure wards to house patients from

Kingston Penitentiary, Joyceville Medium Security Facility and the Women's Penitentiary at Kingston Ontario.

After leaving the RCAF, Dr. Powell worked as a Pension Medical Examiner for the Canadian Pension Commission. He retired from this work in August 1984 after eighteen years.

Margaret, his wife of forty-four years, died tragically of a stroke while on their first post-retirement holiday in Portugal on 12 October 1984. Their only child Jennifer and son-in-law, Leonel Molina-Irias, continued to live in the family home with Jay after their mother's death. Jay Powell died in Ottawa on 21 January 1999 at the age of 85.

Jennifer remembers her life as an Air Force "brat" with affection, living on Air Force stations and in Permanent Married Quarters. In particular, she remembers living, for a time, in what was designed as the nurses' wing of the Station Hospital in Trenton, Ontario.

Summary of Achievements

Canadian Forces Decoration (CD)
1939 - 1945 Star
Defence Medal
War Medal 1939 - 1945
Bachelor of Arts (Honors) University of Toronto, Trinity College, 1936 (BA)
Doctor of Medicine, University of Toronto, 1939 (MD)
Fellow in Aerospace Medicine - Aerospace Medical Association
Fellow of American College of Physical Rehabilitation Medicine (FACPRM)
Associate Fellow Canadian Aeronautics and Space Institute
Life Member British Medical Association

Note 1
While stationed in England he met G/C Douglas Bader the RAF war ace who was on a book signing tour promoting his book *Reach For The Sky*. His daughter has donated this signed copy to the Air Museum.

Note 2

From Charles King, Major (Retired)

Charles King, relates the personal experience he had with Squadron Leader T.J. Powell that is indicative of the support and loyalty he gave to airmen in his command.

Leading Aircraftman (LAC) King was the medical records clerk at RCAF Station Hospital Trenton in early 1950 and was planning to be married later that year. A message arrived, posting King to London, Ontario. Without a car and little or no money for rail travel, this would have put more than a serious crimp in the wedding plans. S/L Powell called LAC King to his office, explained the posting message and asked his wishes regarding the move. When he learned of the personal inconvenience this would cause, he advised King to try to find someone on the Station of the same trade who might like a posting to London. LAC King, considering the worst case scenario, asked, "What happens if I can't find someone who wants to take the posting." Powell replied, "In that case, we'll admit you to hospital on any pretext and keep you there until they're tired of waiting for you and post someone else."

King found someone and the posting was changed, allowing his wedding plans to go forward. It also reaffirmed his confidence in the support he could expect from his officers in the RCAF. This had a profound effect on his attitude to juniors throughout his service after he, himself, was commissioned.

FRED G. ROUTLEDGE, CD
MASTER WARRANT OFFICER

Fred Routledge's early history is sketchy, but it is known that, as a young man in England, he worked in the garment industry. This civilian employment is what directed him into the safety equipment trade of the Royal Air Force (RAF) where much of its equipment, such as parachutes, webbing and packs were fabric. Fred served with the RAF in Great Britain during WWII and with 211 Squadron RAF in India in what is now Bangladesh. His war-time experience with the RAF in safety equipment work is what made him such a valuable asset to the Royal Canadian Air Force.

Aircrew members of the RCAF, with whom he had worked during the war, were influential in getting him to immigrate to Canada in 1947. He joined the RCAF in 1948 as a Leading Aircraftman (LAC) Safety Systems Technician and was posted to RCAF Station Summerside, Prince Edward Island to the Air Navigation School. Fred was soon promoted to Corporal and posted to 400 Squadron in Toronto in 1951.

Soon after arriving in Toronto he was asked to assist Squadron Leader (S/L) Romney Lowry *(see W/C R.M. Lowry elsewhere in this chapter)* to fabricate special garments for injured aircrew. This

MWO Fred G. Routledge

led to further work with S/L Lowry and S/L Jaworski on a dropable medical kit, capable of being dropped from an aircraft without sustaining damage to its contents. Fred's work so impressed Lowry and Jaworski that a transfer was arranged to get him on the staff of the RCAF Institute of Aviation Medicine on a permanent basis. Fred was to re-activate the wartime "Fabric Section" of the Institute. Routleldge's skills were so valuable to the development of new flying personnel safety and survival equipment that his trade was changed from Safety Systems Technician to Aeromedical Technician and eventually to Bioscience Technician.

Routledge helped develop ejection seat emergency survival packs, pressure breathing equipment, partial pressure suits and vests, Anti "G" Suits and various functional and survival clothing and equipment. His twenty-eight years service in the RAF, RCAF and Canadian Forces Medical Services were devoted to developing and perfecting protective and survival garments and equipment for aircrew. Master Warrant Officer (MWO) Routledge's devotion to duty went beyond the normal bounds when he volunteered to be ejected from an aircraft seat at ground level as part of a trial on safety equipment. The explosive shells in the aircraft's ejection seat drove the seat and occupant into the air to a height of fifty feet and Fred was captured in a safety net. This was not without some risk. MWO Fred Routledge brought his Air Force career to an end when he retired in 1970 at the compulsory retirement age of fifty.

Summary of Achievements

Canadian Forces Decoration (CD)
1939 - 1945 Star
Burma Star
Defence Medal
War Medal, 1939 - 1945
Canadian Centennial Medal

Douglas Soper
SBStJ, CD, BSc, LLB
Major

Douglas Soper was born in Essex, Ontario on 2 May 1924. He was educated in London, Ontario, and upon graduation from London Central Collegiate Institute, he enlisted in the RCAF as aircrew on 4 May 1942. He graduated as an air navigator from No. 1 Air Observers' School (Malton) in February 1943 and served overseas in the United Kingdom and in North Africa. He completed a tour of operations on Vickers Wellington bombers with No. 425 Alouette Squadron before returning to Canada in February 1945. He was demobilized from the RCAF in May 1945 with the rank of Flying Officer.

Douglas Soper graduated from the University of Western Ontario with the degree Bachelor of Science in Honours Biology in 1949 and he was awarded the University Gold Medal for Zoology. While at university, Douglas served in the Canadian Army (Reserve), 7th Medium Regiment of the Royal Canadian Artillery, and qualified as an Artillery Officer with the rank of Lieutenant.

After postgraduate studies in Biophysics, he joined the RCAF Regular Force in August 1951 and served at the RCAF Institute of

Maj Douglas Soper

Aviation Medicine (IAM) at Toronto as a Medical Associate Officer (Bioscience). He was employed in the Biochemistry Lab at IAM from 1952 to 1953 on two major projects: (1) Desalination of sea water using semi-permeable membranes; (2) post-mortem tissue analysis for carbon monoxide. This latter project was to help determine if an aircraft crash fatality might have been caused by exposure to carbon monoxide in the cockpit.

From 1953-1955, he worked in the Physics Lab on: (1) A comparison of the RCAF Hygrometer and the Alnor Dewpointer to measure water content in aviator's breathing oxygen; (2) the development of guard ring calorimeters and the Copper Man to measure insulation properties of fabrics and clothing systems. From 1955 to 1959, Douglas worked in the Environmental Lab on: (1) Flight tests of a transparent windscreen developed to permit escape of the rear occupant of the Avro CF-100 Canuck; (2) evaluation of the cockpit environment of the Avro CF-105 Arrow; (3) design and development of air ventilated suits for use with partial pressure suits at high altitude.

In April 1959, Douglas was transferred to England as a member of Canadian Joint Staff (London) and was employed on research duties at the Climatic Laboratory at the RAF Institute of Aviation Medicine, Farnborough. He was involved in three main studies: (1) Sweat gland fatigue; (2) acclimatization of fish filleters' hands in ice cold seawater; (3) study of the ML Partial Pressure Helmet for use with pressure suits at high altitude.

He returned from England in August 1961 for a second tour of duty at the IAM where his duties included: (1) Evaluation of an oximeter for use by aircrew as a monitor to detect hypoxia; (2) development and evaluation of aircrew clothing and related equipment; (3) development and evaluation of aircrew protective helmets.

He was Deputy Officer Commanding the Operational Medical Establishment at IAM, 1965-1967. In May 1967, he was transferred to the Surgeon Generals' Staff, CFHQ, Ottawa as Executive Assistant to the Surgeon General. He was acting Director of Bioscience from February 1968 to July 1968 when he joined the staff of the Directorate of Preventive Medicine (DPMed). He served as DPMed 3 until he retired from the RCAF, 13 May 1971, and took up an appointment with the Defence Research Board.

In addition to these duties, Douglas represented the Surgeon General and/or the Commanding Officer Canadian Forces Institute of Environmental Medicine at international and national meetings, such as the Commonwealth Defence Conferences on Clothing and General Equipment in UK (1961), Australia (1965) and Kenya (1969). He was Canadian member of the Human Factors Committee of the Air Standardization and Coordinating Committee.

He was also a member of a number of Defence Research Board Panels.

Douglas Soper was Aide-de-Camp to three Lieutenant Governors of Ontario from 1954-1969. They were: (1) The Honourable Louis P. Breithaupt; (2) The Honourable J. Keillor Mackay; and (3) The Honourable W. Earl Rowe.

Summary of Achievements

Serving Brother of the Most Venerable Order of the Hospital of St. John of Jerusalem (SBStJ)

Canadian Forces Decoration (CD)

1939 -1945 Star

Italy Star

Defence Medal

Canadian Volunteer Service Medal and Clasp

War Medal 1939 - 1945

Special Service Medal NATO

Canadian Centennial Medal

Operations Wing

Bachelor of Science, Honors Biology (BSc)

University Gold Medal for Zoology

Bachelor of Law (LL.B)

Notes

In 1968, the Royal Canadian Life Saving Society awarded him the M.G. Griffiths Award for bravery.

Douglas retired from government service in 1979.

Douglas and Marjorie were married in 1945 and have four daughters and four grandchildren.

On retirement he returned to London Ontario and earned his law degree.

He enjoys retirement and spends time Scottish dancing and travelling.

Edison "Ed" D. Stairs
SBStJ, CD
Sergeant

Edison Stairs, originally from Saint John, New Brunswick, joined the Royal Canadian Air Force in 1943 as soon as he was old enough to be enrolled. His aptitude for telegraphy was recognized during his early months at the Manning Depot in Toronto, so he was trained in this field, specifically to intercept coded Japanese radio transmissions.

In 1945, at the end of the war, Ed was demobilized and returned to school to study entomology at the University of New Brunswick in Fredericton and worked for a time in this field.

When the RCAF reopened recruiting, Stairs re-enrolled in 1949. His

Sgt Ed D. Stairs in "G" suit, entering the human accelerator, assisted by Flight Sergeant Vince Tremaine (see p. 107).

civilian studies and experience directed him into medical research and training,

96

so he was placed in the Aeromedical Technician trade (AeromedTech). His first posting was to the RCAF Institute of Aviation Medicine in Toronto, Ontario. Here, he was involved in decompression chamber activities as an observer and operator. The decompression chamber is a large, steel, two-room tank, lying on its side, used for assessing and training aircrew on the effects of high altitude flying. It was also used to test oxygen systems and other equipment intended for use in aircraft at high altitudes and to simulate explosive decompression.

Stairs also learned a good deal about the human accelerator, sometimes called the human centrifuge, acting as the observer as candidates were spun around to simulate various degrees of gravity or "G" created by centrifugal force. This machine was used to develop and test the anti-G suit devised by Group Captain Wilbur Franks *(see Franks elsewhere in this chapter)*. On two such accelerator runs on which Stairs was the observer, pilots were exposed to 9 G and 9½ G forces, approaching the limits of human endurance.

Another of the machines at the Institute was used to study motion sickness. Ed worked with the research team on these studies in which the candidate was rotated in many directions simultaneously to create the middle-ear disturbance that leads to motion sickness. As part of his training, Stairs was sent off to Edmonton, Alberta to take the Northern Survival Course. Students on this course learned to survive outdoors in Arctic temperatures, using winter survival gear and rations, some developed at the Institute of Aviation Medicine.

In 1954, his skills as an Aeromed Tech now well rounded out, Sergeant Stairs was appointed Non-Commissioned Officer In Charge (NCO i/c) of the high altitude decompression chamber at RCAF Station Chatham, New Brunswick. This unit was tasked with indoctrination and training of aircrew throughout New Brunswick and Nova Scotia, including the Navy's pilots from Shearwater, Nova Scotia.

Stairs continued this work until 1958 when he was transferred to 4000 Air Reserve Medical Unit in Vancouver, British Columbia. This Medical Unit was tasked with assessing the medical fitness of all aircrew and ground crew applicants from the Western provinces and for making recommendations as to their selection.

Aircrew training in Winnipeg was on the increase and in 1962 Stairs was transferred to RCAF Station Winnipeg, Manitoba to operate the decompression chamber there. Along with the indoctrination and training on oxygen and safety equipment in the chamber, Sgt Stairs' staff also provided electrocardiograpic (ECG) services for the base. All aircrew were routinely given ECG examinations as part of their annual medical assessment *(see George W. Manning elsewhere in this chapter)*. Sgt Stairs' role was expanded in 1963 when he took charge of the first Field Aeromedical Training Unit in Winnipeg to provide high altitude indoctrination (HAI) to flying personnel at RCAF Station Gimli, RCAF Station Portage La Prairie, RCAF Station Moose Jaw, as well as RCAF Station Winnipeg. Stairs led a team of eight non-commissioned officers to provide HAI lectures and training at these Stations and at the Air Navigation School in Winnipeg. Sgt Stairs conducted this highly successful program until 1966 when he was recalled to the Institute of Aviation Medicine in Toronto.

Ed was now able to pass on the many lessons he had learned during his years in the field as he coordinated training for new Bioscience Technicians, as the Aeromed Technician trade was now called. He also helped write the trade training standards for this new trade as part of a board chaired by the Surgeon General's staff.

Sgt Stairs retired from the Canadian Forces Medical Service in 1974 and established a home in Cobden, Ontario.

Summary of Achievements

Serving Brother of the Most Venerable Order of the Hospital of St. John of Jerusalem (SBStJ)
Canadian Forces Decoration (CD)
War Medal – 1939 – 1945

CHESTER B. STEWART
OC, MD
WING COMMANDER

C hester Stewart was born in Norboro, Prince Edward Island on 17 December 1910. He received his early education at Norboro and attended Prince of Wales College in Charlottetown, a Normal School, where in 1928 he acquired a First Class Teaching Certificate. He left his teaching career while Vice-Principal of Kensington High School in Prince Edward Island and returned to Prince of Wales College to complete his degree. This prepared him for admission to Dalhousie University in Halifax, Nova Scotia for pre-medical training and medical school in 1933. By taking extra classes and doing research with Dr. Donald Mainland, professor of anatomy, he earned his Bachelor of Science (Med) degree in 1936, the first awarded by Dalhousie University. Two years later he obtained his Doctor of Medicine degree.

Doctor Stewart's medical career began with a research appointment as First Secretary with the National Research Council (NRC) where he worked with Sir Frederick Banting, the co-discoverer of insulin. One of the projects Stewart undertook while with NRC was a cross-country tour that produced a report entitled *Survey of Facilities for Medical Research in Canada*, which was published in January 1939. He then participated in numerous national committees that followed including the Farquharson Committee, which ultimately led to the formation of the Medical Research Council in 1960.

Dr. Chester B. Stewart

He enlisted in the Royal Canadian Army Medical Corps in April 1940 as a Lieutenant (Lt) Medical Officer. While serving in the Army, Lt Stewart was assigned to the first School of Aviation Medicine in Ottawa, Ontario. In May 1940, he was sent to work with Major Sir Frederick Banting at his Medical Research Unit at the University of Toronto. While in this post, he was promoted to Captain, then transferred to the RCAF Medical Branch when it was formed in November 1940 and re-ranked to Flight Lieutenant (F/L).

No. 1 Clinical Investigation Unit at No. 1 Initial Training School located in Toronto, Ontario needed his talents, so F/L Stewart was promoted to Squadron Leader (S/L) and appointed Medical Officer-in-Charge for eight months. Other Clinical Investigation Units were being set up and S/L Stewart was assigned to No.2 CIU at Regina, Saskatchewan for seven months and then, in April 1942, to a similar unit, No1 Flying Personnel Medical Section of the Y Depot at Halifax, Nova Scotia. This unit was subsequently moved to Lachine, Québec with S/L Stewart in command.

Coming full circle, Wing Commander Stewart returned to Toronto in 1944 as Medical Officer in Charge of No. 1 Clinical Investigation Unit. These units assessed recruits' medical suitability for aircrew training, and trained airmen in the use of oxygen and safety equipment for high altitude flying. During this hectic period, W/C Stewart had short duty tours at Air Force Headquarters in Ottawa and at the Headquarters in London, England in 1942 .

Many of Wing Commander Stewart's research projects focused on the hazards of flying at high altitude where temperatures and oxygen levels could cause loss of function and acute or long term physical harm to aircrew. Decompression sickness was of particular interest. This condition, resulting in muscle spasms, difficulty in breathing and partial paralysis, is caused by too rapid a decrease in atmospheric pressure, such as might occur in an aircraft rapidly ascending to high altitude. His research included such topics as:

- decompression sickness from repeated ascents to 35,000 feet,
- a study of decompressions sickness observed on 17,000 exposures to simulated altitude of 35,000,
- relationship of certain factors to the incidence of decompression sickness,
- altitude selection and training of aircrew candidates,

- efficiency and practicability of the Schroder oxygen unions,
- acute otitic barotrauma resulting from low-pressure chamber tests,
- incidence and cause of dental pain at high altitude.

Wing Commander Stewart was exploring new fields in aviation medicine. He was truly a pioneer in aviation medical research.

After the war in 1945, Dr. Stewart undertook postgraduate work at Johns Hopkins University, obtaining his Masters degree in Public Health. He joined the Faculty of Medicine of Dalhousie University in Halifax, Nova Scotia in 1946 as professor of epidemiology and in 1951 returned to Johns Hopkins as a research associate earning the degree of Doctor of Public Health.

Dr. Stewart returned to Dalhousie University where he remained for the remainder of his career. His research projects, too numerous to list, included reports on histoplasmin and tuberculin sensitivity and BCG vaccination. BCG or bacilli Calmette Guérin vaccine is a tuberculosis vaccine containing living, avirulent, tubercle bacilli. This was followed by pioneer studies on the adaptation of epidemiological methods to the estimation of medical and hospital requirements in preparation for the introduction of the Canadian Hospital and Medicare Insurance Plans.

In 1954 Dr. Stewart was appointed Dean of Medicine of Dalhousie University. During his seventeen years in that position, planning and construction of the Sir Charles Tupper Medical Building was completed. There was also a complete modernization of the medical curriculum and a tremendous growth in medical research. In addition, Dalhousie developed one of the most extensive programs of continuing medical education in Canada. He was awarded a Fellowship of the American Public Health Association in 1952 and Fellowship of the Royal College of Physicians & Surgeons of Canada in 1961.

In 1971 Dr. Stewart was appointed Vice-President (Health Sciences) at Dalhousie. His term ended in 1976 on reaching retirement age. He was for a time thereafter a special consultant, holding the title Dean Emeritus.

In 1971, Governor General Roland Michener made Dr. Stewart an Officer of the Order of Canada for his contributions to medical education, research in aviation medicine and the planning of national and provincial health and hospital services. The citation read:

"For his pioneer service to aviation medicine, epidemiology and health services."

101

Dr. Stewart had four honorary degrees from universities in Atlantic Canada. He was past-president of the Association of Canadian Medical Colleges and of the Canadian Public Health Association. He was awarded senior membership in the Canadian Medical Association and was awarded the Canadian Medical Association Medal of Service. He was an honorary member of the College of Family Medicine, and was awarded the Duncan Graham award by the Royal College of Physicians and Surgeons in 1996 for outstanding contributions to medical education.

Dr. Stewart was a member of Rotary, Saraguay Club, Halifax Medical Society, former member of boards of governors of Dalhousie University, Victoria General Hospital, Izaak Walton Killam Hospital for Children and Northwood Centre. He had a passion for gardening, and reading from his extensive library. Since 1970, Dr. Stewart and his family have enjoyed their summer retreat at "Kintyre" Stanley Bridge, Prince Edward Island, a garden paradise, until his death on 12 January 1999.

Dr. Stewart was married to the former Kathleen French of Regina Saskatchewan and they have two daughters Joan and Moira. Joan is married to Dr. Lionel Teed and they live in Fredericton New Brunswick. Moira is a PhD and professor in family medicine at University of Western Ontario in London and married to Dr. Thomas Freeman, clinician in family medicine at University of Western Ontario.

Summary of Achievements

Officer of the Order of Canada (OC)
Canadian Forces Decoration (CD)
War Medal, 1939 - 1945
Canadian Volunteer Service Medal
Queen Elizabeth II Coronation Medal - 1952
Canadian Centennial Medal - 1967
Queen Elizabeth II Jubilee Medal - 1977
Doctor of Medicine - Dalhousie University - 1938 (MD)
Fellow American Public Health Association (FAPHA)
Diploma Public Health (DPH)
Master Public Health (Johns Hopkins) (MPH)
Fellow Royal College of Physicians (Canada) (FRCP C)
Doctor of Philosophy (PhD)

ROYSTON ALLEN STUBBS
CD, BSc
WING COMMANDER

Royston **Allen Stubbs,** known to many as "Roy" was born in 1922 in Toronto, Ontario. His primary and secondary schooling was also in the Toronto area. He joined the RCAF in 1941, was trained as a pilot, and served in Coastal Command. Flying Officer Stubbs flew Consolidated B-24 Liberators on anti-submarine patrols in Southeast Asia and in the western approaches to the United Kingdom.

After the war, he attended the University of Western Ontario in London, Ontario, graduating in 1950 with a Bachelor of Science, majoring in physics and mathematics.

Stubbs rejoined the RCAF as a Bioscience Officer and served at the RCAF Institute of Aviation Medicine (IAM) in Toronto, beginning in 1950. During 1951, Stubbs was conducting research on motion sickness under the direction of Dr. W.H. Johnson and Dr. Wilbur Franks, defining the physical characteristics of complex motions and the design of instruments to measure the motion of vehicles and the relative motions of the head and body.

W/C Royston A. Stubbs

This was followed by research on ejection seats. Stubbs computed basic escape system equations for ejection seats, defining ejection seat critical areas in terms of acceleration. He also designed man/seat coupling systems and introduced into the RCAF man/seat separation and parachute deployment devices to make ejection seats automatic. He also carried out ejections to confirm his data. These findings were reported in IAM Report 51/333: *The Characteristics of the IAM Emergency Seat Packs and Seat Pans Under Initial Seat Ejection Conditions.* Stubbs conceived and designed a new approach to a survival signaling device (radio) for minimum size and maximum range in the Canadian north. This was reported in IAM Report #53/2.

Roy Stubbs spent two years at the RAF Institute of Aviation Medicine in Farnborough England from 1954 to 1956 where he designed a simplified full-pressure breathing suit for the RAF, utilizing a new method of pressure control and fluid dynamic principles for which connection patents have been granted. He carried out tests of pressure suits and ventilation systems for the RAF for extreme climatic conditions of flight and ground use in the tropics.

Wing Commander (W/C) Stubbs assumed command of the Flying Personnel Medical Establishment at the RCAF IAM in September 1956 and, in September 1961, was named project co-ordinator at that unit.

It was during this time that Stubbs directed the research and development program for the IAM in cockpit layout, instrument presentation, escape systems, air conditioning systems, respiration and "G" re-protective systems and personal protective safety and survival equipment. In addition, he:

- conceived a new project of protective helmet design and introduced the design into service use,
- directed a program of design and development in new aircrew clothing in conjunction with Defence Research Medical Laboratories (DRML) staff. Designed a program to determine correlation between laboratory and field trials,
- was advisor to aircraft companies in the program of putting men efficiently into aircraft, interpreting man's limitations and requirements for escape from satellite vehicles,
- designed new Anti-G Valve providing features to permit the valve to operate under acceleration and pressure breathing,
- designed a new respiratory valve system to remove the critical nature of existing valves and to assist respiration in pressure breathing application,

- designed a compact oxygen system for high performance aircraft having compatibility with NATO requirements and adopted in various configurations by numerous European countries and Japan,
- defined the requirements and limitations of aircraft escape systems.

While project coordinator and Officer Commanding the IAM Detachment at the Defence Research Medical Laboratories (DRML) from 1961 to 1965, W/C Stubbs supervised research and development in the following areas:

- measurement of contamination in liquid oxygen,
- electromagnetic spatial orientation device,
- new design concept of an ear oximeter,
- measurement of oxygen partial pressure and development of aircrew hypoxia warning device. IAM Reports #61-RD04 and #64-RD-3,
- study into the mechanism of oxygen transportation in blood,
- measurement and control device for oxygen/helium measurement. RCAF IAM report #61-RD-6 (W/C R.A. Stubbs and R.S. Weaver, Ph.D.),
- closed and open-circuit diving breathing systems,
- diving decompression computer developed; Patent Application #L18-319507.

W/C Stubbs retired from RCAF on 30 December 1965. He joined the Defence Research Board, DRML, as head of the physics group.

Roy Stubbs continued his research work with the Defence Research Board and during 1965 to 1973 he designed and constructed electronic analogue decompression computers for operation in real time and faster than real time, to assist civilian and military divers in decompression difficulties at sea. The diving history of the person in distress could be fed into the device and the safe decompression requiremnts would be calculated immediately and relayed to the rescue team. There were many successful rescues of divers in trouble on the Atlantic and Pacific Oceans—all coordinated from the Defence and Civil Institute of Environmental Medicine (DCIEM) at Downsview. Stubbs designed and constructed methods of measuring and controlling oxygen-helium mixtures for deep diving.

105

Roy Stubbs was appointed chief scientist of the Defence and Civil Institure of Environmental Medicine (DCIEM), the organization created at the DRML site to join the IAM and DRML into a civil and defence research facility. He designed the deepest research diving facility in the world at the time and perhaps still - 6,000 feet capability for man and equipment testing. The facility was constructed and housed in a wing of DCIEM in 1973. When the wing was completed it was named after R.A. Stubbs.

Roy retired once more in January 1973. He lives in Spain and Waterloo, Ontario. In 1998, he was living in Ajijic, Jalisco, Mexico, researching the design of ultra-light aircraft among other interests.

Summary of Achievements

Canadian Forces Decoration (CD)
1939 - 1945 Star
Atlantic Star
Burma Star
Canadian Volunteer Service Medal
War Medal 1939 - 1945
Bachelor of Science - University of Western Ontario (BSc)

VINCENT J. TREMAINE
CD
FLIGHT-LIEUTENANT

Vincent J. Tremaine, known to friends and colleagues as "Vin," was born in Kenagimi, Québec, in 1915. After working in his father's hardware business for a short time, he enrolled in the RCAF in 1942. His original plan was to learn to fly, but he was selected for training as an Aeromedical Training Technician.

Tremaine's introduction to aviation medicine was when he was sent to the RCAF Institute of Aviation Medicine in Toronto as a test subject for some high-level decompression chamber trials. These trials were designed to select decompression chamber operators to man the chambers set up in Halifax, Nova Scotia in the Flying Personnel Medical Section to screen aircrew applicants for susceptability to decompression sickness. The decompression chamber, a large, two-chambered tank was capable of reproducing the rarified atmospheric conditions of very high

F/L Vince Tremaine

altitudes when oxygen was pumped out of the tank. The screening of the candidates consisted of a training run to 10,000 feet, during which the subject would become anoxic from a lack of oxygen. This familiarized the individual with behavioural changes brought about by oxygen lack. Each aircrew member then had three training runs to 35,000 feet. These results were documented into his logbook and those who had an acceptable tolelerance to high altitude could be employed on high altitude flying operations. Those who could not tolerate

107

conditions at high altitude went on to Coastal Command for low altitude flying duties such as mine laying or submarine patrols.

Vin, who had a high tolerance to high altitude atmospheric conditions, was kept on at the Institute of Aviation Medicine as a chamber operator. He also participated in cold weather trials of survival equipment in the winter of 1943. When he was assigned to work with Dr. Wilbur Franks *(see Franks elsewhere*

Corporal Tremaine in the observer's seat of the Human Accelerator.

in this chapter) in the development of Franks' anti- G suit, he became the principal observer on the accelerator, also known as the human centrifuge. This device consists of a gondola attached to an arm extending from a central pivot, was rotated at various speeds to create centrifugal forces on the candidate sitting in the gondola. In this early model of the accelerator, the observer sat with his back to the central pivot, visually monitoring the candidate for any signs of distress. Tremaine became Dr. Franks' right-hand man in his Anti-G suit research and made over 3,000 runs as an observer on the human accelator, a feat unsurpassed by any other individual.

The first workable Anti-G suit was a rubberized garment with water-filled bladders suitably position around the lower limbs and trunk. These suits were manufactured in twelve sizes. Tremaine wore one of them for trials in the accelerator, the cold room and the tropical room to evaluate its comfort or discomfort levels and its efficiency in preventing blackouts at high "G." It took over an hour to get into this cumbersome outfit for each of the trials and nearly as much time to get it off again.

In the early 1950s he went overseas and helped Wing Commander Romney Lowry fit RCAF pilots with a new American model G-suit as the

RCAF had gotten out of the G-suit business. W/C Lowry, a physician and a pilot, became the head of Defence and Civil Institute of Environmental Medicine from 1971-1978.

Tremaine then became head of the oxygen laboratory and instituted an inspection program for 0^2 regulators that maintained the reliability of the oxygen equipment in the field. He carried on this work until he retired in the early 1970s.

This talented individual was first an aeromedical technician until he was commissioned as a bioscience officer. He spent all of his career at the Institute except for a year at RAF Farnborough in 1944. This outstanding dedicated officer is proud of his contribution to aviation medical research.

Tremaine is quite ill in hospital. His friends have prepared this material.

Summary of Achievements

Canadian Forces Decoration (CD)
Defence Medal 1939 – 1945
Canadian Volunteer Service Medal
War Medal 1939 – 1945

O. Harold Warwick
CM, MD
Squadron Leader

Harold Warwick was born in 1915 just as WWI was getting underway. He got his early education in his home town of Saint John, New Brunswick and went on to Mount Allison University in Sackville where he earned a Bachelor of Arts (BA) degree in 1935. He was a bright student and was elected a Rhodes Scholar in 1936, leading to an honors BA from Oxford University in England in 1938.

Warwick returned to Canada to take his medical degree at MGill University in Montreal, Québec in 1940 with an internship at Royal Victoria Hospital in that city in 1941. WWII was in progress and Warwick enlisted in the Royal Canadian Air Force as a Flight Lieutenant Medical Officer.

Squadron Leader (S/L) Warwick earned rapid promotion and was assigned to the Flying Personnel Medical Section at Halifax, Nova Scotia. This unit assessed flying personnel from #1 Y Depot RCAF Halifax, providing decompression chamber training and assessing aircrew's ability to

S/L O. Harold Warwick

function at high altitudes. The high altitude indoctrination taught the effects of anoxia, the proper use of oxygen equipment and assessed the crewmen's susceptibility to decompression sickness. Their flying log books were annotated accordingly and this would determine their future flying duties, that is high altitude or low altitude flying.

S/L Warwick conducted numerous research projects while in this post on such varied subjects as:

- decompression sickness and its causes
- compression fractures of the spine as a complication of severe anoxia
- experimental felt oxygen masks
- aircrew preferences for various types of oxygen masks
- distortion of RCAF oxygen masks
- nasion-mention measurements of aircrew
- comparative comfort and efficiency of RCAF oxygen mask assemblies
- altitude selection and training
- efficiency of the Schroder Oxygen unions
- acute otitic barotrauma from low presssure chamber tests

S/L Warwick finally got an overseas posting and served in England until 1945 when he was returned to Canada and left the RCAF to take postgraduate training at the Royal Victoria Hospital in Montreal, Québec. In 1946, he was named a Nuffield Scholar and took postgraduate training at Hammersmith in London, England and the Royal Cancer Hospital in that city.

Following these studies, Dr. Warwick was appointed Assistant and Associate Professor of Medicine at the University of Toronto, then Executive Director of the National Cancer Institute of Canada. He was appointed Senior Physician at the Toronto General Hospital (1948-1958) and Senior Physician at the Princess Margaret Hospital in Toronto (1958-1961).

Dr. Warwick went on to become the Dean of the Faculty of Medicine at the University of Western Ontario at London from 1961 to 1965, Vice-President (Health Sciences) University of Western Ontario from 1965 to 1972. He continued to teach at the University following a sabbatical leave in 1973 and held a professorship in their Faculty of Medicine until 1980 during which he was also the Senior Physician of the Victoria Hospital and the Ontario Cancer Foundation Clinic in London Ontario. In 1980 Dr. Warwick was named Emeritus Professor of Medicine of the University of Western Ontario.

Summary of Achievements

Member - Order of Canada (CM)
War Medal, 1939 - 1945
Canadian Volunteer Service Medal
Doctor of Medicine, McGill University 1940 (MD)
Fellow Royal College of Physicians (Canada) (FRCPC)
Fellow Royal College of Physicians (London, England) (FRCP)
Fellow American College of Physicians (FACP)
LL.D. (honorary) Mount Allison University
LL.D. (honorary) University of Western Ontario

Publications

Dr. Warwick prepared and published forty papers on medical scientific subjects including aviation medicine, and various aspects of malignant disease.

Offices in Voluntary Organizations

Executive Director - National Cancer Institute of Canada, 1948-1955
Director - National Cancer Institute of Canada and Canadian Cancer Society, 1955-1966
Vice President - International Union Against Cancer (representing British Commonwealth), 1954-1958
President - National Cancer Institute of Canada, 1964-1966
Medical Advisory Board - Ontario Cancer Treatment and Research Foundation, 1955-
Governor for Ontario - The American College of Physicians, 1963-1970
Director - Physician Services Incorporated Foundation, 1971-1973

Note

Dr. Warwick was named a Member of the Order of Canada with the following citation:

> *Professor Emeritus at the University of Western Ontario, physician and administrator, he is a pioneer in cancer chemotherapy in Canada and was among the first to establish the importance of calcium metabolism in managing cancer patients. He played a vital role in the development of both the Ontario and the National Cancer Institutes and has dedicated his career to the advancement of health care and medical education in Canada.*

John C. Wickett
AFC, CD, MD
Group Captain

John C. **Wickett,** known as Jack, was born on 30 September 1915 in Lethbridge, Alberta. He died on 22 May 1976 in Ottawa, Ontario, after an illustrious career involving active service overseas as Squadron Commander, 418 Mosquito Fighter Squadron, incarceration as a prisoner of war in Germany, earning a degree as a medical doctor and thereafter being involved particularly in aviation medicine and its bioscience components. He was totally devoted to aviation medicine and pursued his work in this branch of the RCAF with integrity, enthusiasm and wisdom.

Wickett's interests in aviation began at age five, when intrigued by reports of machines that could fly, he made himself a pair of wings and jumped from a garage roof. This resulted in a broken arm and the necessity of carrying around a bucket of sand for several months in order to straighten out the arm. But it did not damage his interest, curiosity and enthusiasm for machines that can fly and most particularly, a deep concern for those who fly them.

G/C Jack Wickett

After graduating from high school in Medicine Hat, Alberta, he went on to earn a BSc at the University of Alberta. He started pilot training in 1938 at RCAF Station Trenton, Ontario, and in 1940, became an instructor. In 1942, he was posted to the Flying Instructor's School in Arnprior, Ontario as the Officer Commanding flying. At some point during this time, he wrote a flying instructors manual, which some 40 years later his nephew William Wickett Jr.

used as part of his training.

In January 1943, Wickett embarked for the first time for London, England, returning to Canada some six months later. While there, he was much involved with test flying and research. On his return to Canada, he was posted to #3 Training Command in Montreal as a staff officer. He was concerned, however, that he was not contributing to active duty overseas and welcomed the opportunity in May 1944 to attend the operational training unit at RCAF Station Greenwood, Nova Scotia. By September 1944, he was in England with 613 Squadron, first as pilot, then as squadron commander. In November, he was transferred to 418 Mosquito Fighter Squadron as its Commanding Officer.

In February 1945, at a time when there was a surge of low-level bombing, Wickett went missing. He was reportedly seen going down in flames. On crash landing, his navigator Jessop, who had a foot caught in the controls, and could not get out of the burning plane. With the strength born of desperation, Wickett pulled him right out of his boots and out of the plane and they both got safely away before the explosion. Jessop grabbed Wickett's hand in a wild handshake and exulted: "That's the best goddamned landing you ever made!"

Of course, they were taken prisoners, but Wickett, as Commanding Officer, was taken away by himself for interrogation and was badly treated. Life as a prisoner ended in April 1945 when a number of Canadians, and others, were sent on a long forced march and managed to capture their guards. Soon the war with Germany was over. Wickett spent several weeks in hospital in England before returning to Canada in May.

Then it was back to Trenton to become Commanding Officer of the Central Flying School. He already knew what he wanted to do in the Air Force and that was to work in the field of aviation medicine. First he had to get a degree in medicine, which he did at the University of Western Ontario in 1949. At the same time he got his Master's degree in biochemistry. He was now prepared to start a new career.

This took him to the RCAF Institute of Aviation Medicine in Toronto in 1950. First, he was Officer-in-Charge of Flying Personnel Section, then Officer-in-Charge of Flying Personnel Medical Establishment. He was much involved in research, and was always a champion of aviation medicine, promoting the need, and recruiting workers with great zeal. Workers in the same field in other countries began to call him even at home to discuss a situation, or ask him for input on a project. He was never too busy to listen or to help when he could.

It was not surprising that he was posted to the Canadian Joint Staff in Washington in 1956 as Senior Medical Officer and Flight Surgeon. Already he had colleagues in the United States who welcomed him. He worked there for three busy years travelling about the country from time to time for meetings, conferences, courses and consultations. In the community in which he lived, he was sought out by neighbours, most of them military, in cases of an accident or some other medical situation. Visiting colleagues from other states and from Canada were always welcomed at his home. Admiral Ruthven Libby called him one of Canada's most highly respected representatives. Admiral Smart maintained that Wickett had saved his life.

Wickett eventually married and had a family. His marriage to Beatrice (Bea) Enid Hall took place in 1939. Subsequently he had three children - Barbara Jean in 1940, Margaret Dell in 1947 and John Cameron Hall in 1949. An additional family member was acquired when Bea's father, Henry Hammel Hall came to visit them immediately after his retirement in 1947 and remained with them until his death in 1964.

The whole family cherished his presence and he travelled with them wherever they went, participating actively in the events of family life - both geographical and social. Wickett had a loving respect for his father-in-law and they had many interests in common - boating, fishing, camping, reading and current affairs. The children loved him dearly and to this day feel a family is not complete without a grandfather! It was during his time as part of the family that Barbara Jean died and Henry Hall was an important part of the healing that had to take place after such a loss.

On Wickett's return from Washington in 1959, he was posted to Air Force Headquarters in Ottawa as Director of Aviation Medicine. In 1960, he became Director of Bioscience on the staff of the Director General Medical Services (Air). Due to ill health, he retired from this position in 1969.

Ever since he was a prisoner of war, he suffered from ill-health, but in spite of this, carried on heroically in the forces, promoting his faith in the need for support for aviation medicine; not only for the military, but also for all those involved in Canadian aviation. During this time, he continued to be consulted frequently by colleagues from the United States who would phone him or come

115

in person to meet with him. His activity with NATO and the Advisory Group on Aerospace Research and Development (AGARD) continued, so that consultation often took place with other countries.

Wickett was always sensitive and helpful to out-of-the-country visitors by inviting them to his home, since he himself enjoyed the opportunities he was given, when travelling, to spend some time in the homes of his colleagues.

After retirement from the forces, he worked for Veterans Affairs and did some work with the Drug Directorate. His health continued to fail, but he was still working part time and promoting aviation medicine at the time of his death on 22 May 1976.

While Wickett did several articles on aviation medicine, his best known one was published in *Roundel* in 1955, entitled *Aviation Medicine*. In spite of his accomplishments, he was a gentleman who never sought fame or honour, and was very modest. It is noted that in group pictures, he invariably stood at the back!

Summary of Achievements

Air Force Cross (AFC)
Canadian Forces Decoration (CD)
1939 - 1945 Star
France and Germany Star
Canadian Volunteer Service Medal
War Medal 1939 - 1945
Coronation Medal - Queen Elizabeth II
Doctor of Medicine - University of Western Ontario - 1949 (MD)
Masters Degree in Biochemistry
Honorary Member of the Association of Military Surgeons of the United States - 1956

COLIN A. YELLAND
SBStJ, CD, MD
COLONEL

Colin Yelland is a native of Kilmarnock, Scotland and a 1950 graduate of the University of Glasgow's Faculty of Medicine. Dr. Yelland was recruited, following his internship, for service in the Royal Canadian Air Force. The RCAF was building up its forces at that time, so Colin, his brother and several of his classmates enrolled and came to Canada in 1951. The recruitment incentive was fairly attractive. Newly graduated physicians, working in hospitals in Glasgow, received a salary equivalent to seventy-five dollars a month. The RCAF was paying Flight Lieutenant Medical Officers seven hundred and fifty dollars per month. The job offer was very attractive and it is a move Yelland has never regretted.

Flight Lieutenant Yelland served as a General Duty Medical Officer at various RCAF stations in Ontario and in Alberta between 1951 and 1955. In 1955 Yelland was selected to enter postgraduate training in anaesthesia at the Victoria General Hospital in Halifax Nova, Scotia. He graduated from this program in 1958 and became a Fellow of the Royal College of Physicians of Canada (F.R.C.P.Anaesthesia). The following year he became a Fellow of the American College of Anesthesiologists (F.A.C.A.)

Col Colin A. Yelland

A promotion and a four-year European posting followed as Squadron Leader (S/L) Yelland joined the medical staff of the RCAF Hospital at 3 (Fighter) Wing Zweibruken, Germany as Chief of Anaesthesiology. This hospital provided major surgical care to Air Force members and their families from all the 1 Air Division bases in Germany and France.

117

At the end of his tour in 1962, Wing Commander (W/C)Yelland returned to Canada to the staff of the Canadian Navy hospital, HMCS Stadacona, in Halifax, Nova Scotia as Chief of Anaesthesiology. The Canadian Forces Medical Services were in the process of integration and doctors were cross-posted to units of any of the other services. Two years later, W/C Yelland was called to Ottawa join the staff of the Surgeon General at National Defence Headquarters. During his five years in Ottawa, he was given appointments of greater responsibility and a promotion to Group Captain, a rank that was changed to Colonel in 1968 when integration of the Forces came into effect. Colonel Yelland held appointments as Director of Treatment Services and later as Director of Staffing and Training.

In 1970, Colonel Yelland assumed command of the Canadian Forces Environmental Medicine Establishment and Deputy Chief of the Defence and Civil Institute of Environmental Medicine in Toronto. During this appointment, which he held for seven years, he made major contributions to research in aviation medicine and was an active member of two International Aviation Medicine Committees.

Colonel Yelland ended a thirty-year Royal Canadian Air Force and Canadian Forces Medical Services career with his appointment as Regional Surgeon Pacific on the staff of the Maritime Pacific Headquarters (MARPACHQ) at Esquimalt. His office was responsible for the provision of medical care and services throughout British Columbia, covering territory as far north as Masset in the Queen Charlotte Islands. This four-year posting (1977-1981) came to a close with Colonel Yelland's retirement on 19 June 1981.

On retirement he took a position with Health and Welfare Canada in Victoria until his second retirement. Colin Yelland's interest in aviation continues in his retirement and is reflected in his hobby of flying radio-controlled airplanes.

Summary of Achievements
Serving Brother of the Most Venerable Order of the Hospital of St. John of Jerusalem (SBStJ)
Canadian Forces Decoration (CD)
Special Services Medal - NATO
Glasgow, Scotland, 1950 (MB.ChB)
Licentiate, Royal College of Physicians (LRCP)
Licentiate, Royal College of Surgeons (LRCS)
Fellow, American College of Anaesthesia (FACA)
Fellow of Royal College of Physicians Canada (Anaesthesia) (FRCPC)

CHAPTER 3

THE FLIGHT SURGEONS

- **Lieutenant-Colonel S.E. "Sue" Aitken**

    A post-war female Medical Officer and Flight Surgeon who made parachute jumps and flew in a CF104 to experience flight conditions.

- **Group Captain A. Mansfield Beach**

    A war-time navigator with a Distinguished Flying Cross and Bar with 13 trips to Berlin who later became a doctor and psychiatrist.

- **Colonel R.J. "Jack" Hicks**

    A navigator and one of the first members of the Aircrew Medical Training Plan. He maintained a keen interest in aviation medicine.

- **Lieutenant-Colonel James R. Popplow**

    A post-war navigator and later a doctor, who earned a Master of Science degree and private pilot's licence since 1968.

- **Lieutenant-Colonel R.C. "Bud" Rud**

    Royal Military College graduate, pilot, chemical engineer then a doctor who specialized in occupational medicine.

- **Colonel David A. Salisbury**

    A doctor who later become a pilot and Flight Surgeon to the Snowbirds; maintains a keen interest in aviation medicine.

- **Lieutenant-Colonel W.J.C. "Joly" Stevenson**

    A war-time RAF pilot and civil airline pilot, who later joined the RCAF as a Medical Officer, became the Base Surgeon at Portage where he flew T-33 jet training aircraft, usually before starting morning sick parade.

- **Colonel Robert F. Thatcher**

    A navigator who later become a doctor, one of the first members of the Military Medical Training Plan, maintained an interest in aviation medicine and still employed in that field in civilian life.

Susan E. Aitken née Ball
OMM, CD, MD
Lieutenant-Colonel

Susan E. Ball, known to friends and colleagues as Sue, was born in London, Ontario. She proudly admits to being an Army Brat, the daughter of an officer in the Royal Canadian Electrical and Mechanical Engineers. Therefore, her early education was punctuated by many moves and different schools ending up in London, Ontario. Hence she attended and graduated from the University of Western Ontario in that city. Sue joined the Royal Canadin Air Force in 1967 in the Medical Officer Training Plan and completed her degree in medicine, graduating in 1969. A general internship in Toronto prepared her for her first posting as a General Duty Medical Officer at Canadian Forces Base (CFB) Winnipeg, Manitoba in July 1970.

It was at Winnipeg that Sue discovered the excitement of flying and working with the flying personnel of squadrons, attending to patients on aeromed evacuation flights, monitoring aircrew during high altitude chamber runs, and observing the search and rescue (SAR) teams at work. When time permitted the helmet and flight suit, hanging on the back of her office door, were in action racking up flying time as a passenger in a Lockheed T-33 jet trainer and other aircraft.

LCol Sue Aitken receives the Order of Military Merit from Her Excellency Governor General Jeanne Sauvé

While working with SAR crews, it became evident that the medical kits they were using were woefully inadequate for the changing profiles of the victims of aircraft crashes. Technological advances permitted earlier location of downed aircraft and

121

therefore the people aboard had a better chance of survival. Together the SAR technicians and their interested physician developed a new medical kit, but one thing leads to another. To complement the medical supplies and equipment in the new kit, the SAR Techs needed improved skills in first aid and medical techniques. To that end Captain Aitken "liberated" the US Army teaching manual used for training medics for service in Vietnam. Aitken adapted, plagiarized and re-wrote it to meet the needs of search and rescue in Canada. The SAR Squadron included medical exercises in their training that permitted real-time use of the kits and newly acquired medical training to refine both the supplies and the skills needed to use them.

The enthusiasm showed by the Winnipeg SAR techs spread to other squadrons and the approach of improving the medical kits and training became widespread. To this day the Canadian Air Force SAR Techs "take it to the US SAR Techs" during their yearly competitions, which include specific medical exercises built into the overall competition.

A posting to CFB Trenton followed. Susan was now a Flight Surgeon, the second female to so qualify, and continued her interest in flight medicine with the squadrons of Air

Major Aitken briefs SAR team, Master Corporal R. Clement and Master Corporal Jarbeau, on medical equipment before a search mission on a de Havilland DHC-4 Caribou

Transport Command and also continued her commitment to search and rescue with 426 Squadron.

In 1975, a posting to National Defence Medical Centre in Ottawa commenced the five-year quest to become a medical oncologist. Major Aiken acquired this specialty through a four-year program of studies at the University of Toronto in Internal Medicine and Medical Oncology in1976. Now a Fellow of the Royal College of Physicians and Surgeons of Canada, Lieutenant-Colonel (LCol) Aitken was posted back to Ottawa as a general internist and medical oncologist for the Canadian Forces at the National Defence Medical Centre in 1980. Thus the first Canadian Forces medical oncology clinic and referral service was established. She was appointed assistant professor at the University of Ottawa.

On 1 June 1988, Her Excellency Governor-General Jeanne Sauvé bestowed the Order of Military Merit on LCol. Aitken in the grade of Officer.

Dr. Aitken enjoyed her work as a flight surgeon. She has flown in many of the Air Force's aircraft, including the Lockheed T-33, the Canadair CF-5, the Canadair CL-41 Tutor and the Lockheed CF-104 Starfighter. One of her most memorable experiences was flying in a dual CF-104 over the Alberta Primrose Lake Alberta Gunnery Range. She also made two parachute jumps.

Susan retired in 1987 and became a civilian medical oncologist at the Ottawa Civic and General hospitals. From 1992-1999 she worked with the Ontario Breast Screening Program as both its Director and Senior Medical Advisor to improve the services for breast screening and breast assessment throughout the province. Retirement from this role occurred in September 1999.

She remains on the Board of Governors for the Corps of Commissionaires and expects new challenges on a regular basis.

Summary of Achievements

Officer of the Order of Military Merit (OMM)
Canadian Forces Decoration (CD)
Doctor of Medicine - University of Western Ontario, 1969 (MD)
Fellow Royal College of Physicians Canada - Internal Medicine (FRCPC)

ALBERT MANSFIELD BEACH
DFC, CD, MD
GROUP CAPTAIN

Albert M. Beach, known to everyone as "Mike" was born in Vancouver, British Columbia in April 1916. He was educated at the University of British Columbia, graduating with a Bachelor of Arts degree. Mike joined the Royal Canadian Air Force in April 1940 and served throughout World War II as a navigator, completing two tours of operations and winning the Distinguished Flying Cross and Bar for his actions. As a navigator and bomb aimer, he participated in numerous sorties against enemy targets. He took part in the first daylight attack on battle cruisers at Brest and made fifteen aerial attacks on Berlin.

On 30 August 1942 he was awarded the DFC with the following citation:

G/C A.M. "Mike" Beach

"As navigator and bomb aimer this officer participated in numerous sorties against targets in Germany, France, Belgium, Italy, Tripoli and Cyrenaica. While based in this country he took part in the first daylight attack on the battle cruisers at Brest. During engagements his gunners shot down an enemy fighter. During his operations in the Middle East P/O Beach has maintained his very high standards of navigation and bomb aiming. His coolness in attack is exceptional."

On 14 November 1944 he was awarded a Bar to his DFC with the following citation:

> *"This officer has a long record of successful sorties against a variety of targets, including 15 on Berlin. He has now completed a second tour of operational duty. On numerous occasions he has participated in attacks on heavily defended targets and secured valuable photographs. At all times an outstanding navigator, F/L Beach has continued to show admirable bravery."*

Upon repatriation to Canada in 1944, Mike Beach enrolled at McGill University in Montreal, Québec and graduated in 1949 with a medical degree. During his final year in university, he re-enlisted in the RCAF and upon graduation was transferred to RCAF Station Sea Island, British Columbia as a Flight Lieutenant Medical Officer. He was one of twenty-four medical students, all RCAF veterans initially in the RCAF Reserves, who were employed during the summer months on research and survey work for the RCAF Institute of Aviation Medicine. He was one of two officers working on personnel selection research.

In July 1950, he was attached to 426 Squadron at Lachine, Québec as a medical officer, and served with that Squadron until May 1952 when it operated out of Tacoma, Washington, the Hawaiian Islands and Tokyo, Japan on the Korean airlift of supplies and casualties during the Korean War. In May 1952, he was transferred to 14 Training Group in Winnipeg, Manitoba for four months and then assigned duties with 2 (Fighter) Wing at Grostenquin in France.

Squadron Leader Beach returned to Canada in August 1954 and spent three years in postgraduate training in psychiatry at the Essondale Hospital near Vancouver, British Columbia and at the Montreal General Hospital.

In September 1957, he was transferred to the Medical Selection Unit in London as a psychiatrist, and in August 1958, Wing Commander Beach moved with the Medical Selection Unit to RCAF Station Centralia, just north of London. While serving at Centralia he became Officer Commanding the Medical Selection Unit.

In July 1963, Wing Commander Beach joined the staff of the National

Defence Medical Centre in Ottawa as Chief of Psychiatry, a position he held until August 1965. In August of that year, Beach was again promoted to Group Captain and given command of the RCAF Institute of Aviation Medicine in Toronto, from which he retired in 1966.

He married the former Margaret Catherine Porter and had two children: Susan Margaret and Michael Robert.

Summary of Achievements

Distinguished Flying Cross and Bar (DFC)
Canadian Forces Decoration (CD)
1939 - 1945 Star
Aircrew Europe Star
France and Germany Star
Defence Medal
Canadian Volunteer Service Medal
War Medal, 1939 - 1945
UN Medal - Korea
Operations Wing and Bar
Doctor of Medicine - McGill University, 1949 (MD)
Diploma in Psychiatry (D Psy)

RAYMOND JACK HICKS
CD, MD
COLONEL

Raymond Jack Hicks was born near Bloomfield, Ontario in 1935. He graduated from Prince Edward Collegiate Institute in 1953 and joined the Royal Canadian Air Force as an Officer Cadet for enrolment at Royal Roads Military College in Victoria, British Columbia. He graduated from the Royal Military College at Kingston, Ontario in 1957 with a Bachelor of Arts degree, majoring in English and History.

Summers were spent at the Air Navigation School in Winnipeg, Manitoba and Hicks qualified for his AI (Air Interceptor) Observer Wings in August 1956. In May 1958, upon completing training at 3 AW(F)OTU, an all-weather fighter operational training unit, he and his pilot F/O Roy Dunbar were posted to 419 AW(F) Squadron, based at 4 (Fighter) Wing in Baden-Soellingen, West Germany.

Flight Lieutenant Hicks completed some 800 operational flying hours over Europe on the Avro CF-100 Canuck, a twin-engine, all-weather jet interceptor.

Col R. Jack Hicks

There was a change of pace as Hicks returned to Canada in December 1962 and started long range navigation training at the Air Navigation School Winnipeg. From high altitude jet interceptors, F/L Hicks went to the Canadair CP-107 Argus, a long-range, low level, maritime patrol aircraft. These were located at Greenwood, Nova Scotia as part of VP405 a maritime patrol squadron. After nearly 1,200 hours of maritime patrol operations, with the principal aim of detecting Soviet submarines, but often in search and rescue and in aid to other government departments such as fisheries and police, Hicks decided to change careers. He was accepted into the RCAF Military Medical Training Plan in September 1965. Doctor Hicks graduated from Dalhousie University Medical School in Halifax, Nova Scotia in 1970. His first posting as a medical officer was to Canadian Forces Base Trenton, Ontario.

The flight surgeon's course was completed that autumn and Major Hicks subsequently became Flight Surgeon and Base Surgeon at CFB Trenton. Medical support to global air operations with the Air Transport Command squadrons at Trenton was a satisfying challenge at this time. The Tropical Medicine Course at Walter Reed Army Institute of Research in Washington, DC was completed in 1973. He also served six months with the United Nations Emergency Force at Ismailia, Egypt during his Trenton posting.

Promotion to Lieutenant-Colonel (LCol) and a posting to the Directorate of Medical Treatment Services at NDHQ followed in 1977. LCol Hicks was appointed Commanding Officer of the Canadian Field Hospital during this time, to assume those responsibilities at any time that the Hospital was activated for an operational role.

With a promotion to full Colonel, Hicks assumed his new duties as Commanding Officer of the Canadian Forces Environmental Medicine Establishment and Deputy Chief of the Defence and Civil Institute of Environmental Medicine (DCIEM) at Downsview in 1980. A personal association with Dr. Wilbur Franks, remembered for his original anti-G suit and human centrifuge research, remains a cherished memory. Through participation in the on-going research at DCIEM and as a member of the Aerospace Medical Panel of the NATO Advisory Group for Aerospace Research and Development (AGARD) Colonel Hicks strongly promoted aviation medicine research and its relevance in support of the Air operation in the overall mandate of DCIEM.

A voluntary release from the Canadian Forces was taken in 1986 and Hicks continued part-time occupational medicine employment first with Petro-

Canada, then to Central Medical Board at DCIEM, and more recently with the Civil Aviation Medicine Branch of Health Canada.

Dr. Hicks, after a varied and rewarding 33-year career in the RCAF and Canadian Forces, is now completely retired from the medical field. He and his wife Elinor presently reside in Prince Edward County near Picton, Ontario, where they enjoy visits from their three children and five grandchildren. A winter residence on the island of Montserrat in the West Indies allows year-round enjoyment of gardening and hiking which are favourite activities.

Summary of Achievements

Canadian Forces Decoration (CD)
Special Service Medal - NATO
United Nations Force Middle East
Doctor of Medicine Dalhousie University, 1970 (MD)
Bachelor of Arts RMC – Royal Roads and Kingston (BA)

James R. Popplow
SBStJ, CD, MD
Lieutenant-Colonel

J**ames Popplow** joined the Royal Canadian Air Force in March 1961. Selected for aircrew training, he was trained as a navigator at the Air Navigation School located at RCAF Station Winnipeg, Manitoba. On completion of his training, Flying Officer Popplow was assigned to 415 (Maritime Patrol) Squadron at RCAF Station Summerside, Prince Edward Island. The Squadron was flying Canadair CP-107 Argus, a long-range maritime patrol aircraft. After three-and-one-half years flying with 415 (MP) Squadron, Flight Lieutenant Popplow was assigned to a radar site at RCAF Station Moosonee, Ontario as Operations Officer. This was one of the radar stations in the Pinetree Line that formed part of the North American defences against aerial attacks. While at this Station in 1966, Popplow decided to leave the RCAF, temporarily, to return to university.

At Queen's University Kingston, Ontario, Jim completed degree programs, graduating Bachelor of Science (Physiology) in 1970 and a Bachelor of Education (Biology). In 1971 he rejoined the Canadian Forces to complete his degree in medicine, graduating in 1975. This was followed by a medical intern year at Kingston General Hospital, one year at Canadian Forces Base Kingston at the Base Hospital and three years as Base Surgeon/Flight Surgeon at CFB Portage la Prairie, Manitoba.

LCol James R. Popplow

Major Popplow's post-M.D. residency training was taken at Ohio State University and Wright-Patterson Air

Force Base, Dayton, Ohio, where he completed a Master of Science degree in Aerospace Medicine in 1980 and was elected a Fellow of the American College of Preventive Medicine.

The subsequent two years (1982-1984) were spent in the Aerospace Medicine Section on the Surgeon General's staff at National Defence Headquarters in Ottawa. This led to a promotion in July 1984 and Lieutenant-Colonel Popplow was appointed Director of the Medical Life Support Division of the Defence and Civil Institute of Environmental Medicine in Toronto.

From July of 1988 to June 1995 he served as the Staff Officer Aeromedical Operations and Clinical Services at Air Command Headquarters, Winnipeg, Manitoba, and was elected a Fellow of the Aerospace Medical Association in 1989. After retiring from the Canadian Forces in 1995, he joined Manitoba Health as the Provincial Medical Officer of Health for the Environment.

He has been a private pilot since 1968 and completed 150 hours of dual flying on the Kiowa helicopter (Bell 206 Jetranger) during his three years at CFB Portage la Prairie.

Dr. Popplow is married to the former Jeanette Clark of Brandon, Manitoba. They have two daughters, Katherine and Carolyn.

Summary of Achievements

Serving Brother of the Most Venerable Order of the Hospital of St. John of Jerusalem (SBStJ)

Canadian Forces Decoration (CD)

Doctor of Medicine – Queen's University, 1975 (MD)

Bachelor of Science (Psychology) 1970 (BSc)

Bachelor of Education (Biology) 1971 (B.Ed)

Master of Science in Aerospace Medicine 1980 (MSc)

Fellow of the American College Preventative Medicine (FACPM)

Publications
LCol Popplow authored or co-authored a number of papers on aviation medicine and its related matters with such varied titles as:
- A Review of Canadian Forces Search and Rescue Technician Medical Training and Operations. *Aviation Space and Environmental*

Medicine. 1996; 67(5):486-490.

- Survival. Flight Comment, *CAF Flight Safety Digest. 1992; 5*
- *The Psychological, Physiological and Performance Impact of Sustained NBC Operations on CF-18 Fighter Pilots.* DCIEM Report No. 90-RR-08, DCIEM, P.O. Box 2000, 1133 Sheppard Avenue West, Downsview, Ont., M3M 3B9
- Coping with Critical Incident Stress. *Flight Comment, CAF Flight Safety Digest. 1990; 6*
- Scott Emergency Escape Breathing Device Evaluation for Use by Aircraft Cabin Crew Passengers. *Aviation Space and Environmental Medicine. 1987; 58(8): 747-753*
- Fooling Yourself - The Deadly Game. *Canadian Flight. 1986; May/June:6-7*
- The Field Treatment of Hypothermia. *Canadian Aeronautics and Space Journal. 1984; 30(2): 114-119*
- After the Fire-Ball. Flight Comment, *CAF Flight Safety Digest. 1983; 4: 2-5 and reprinted in Aviation Space and Environmental Medicine. 1984; 55(4): 337-338*
- Cardiopulmonary Responses to Combined Lateral and Vertical Acceleration. *Aviation Space and Environmental Medicine. 1983; 54: 632-636*
- Some Physiological Changes in Lateral (Gy) Acceleration. *Proceedings of the Workshop on Flight Testing to Identify Pilot Workload and Pilot Dynamics.* AFFTC Technical Report, Air Force Flight Test Center, Edwards AFB, California. 1982
- *Human Performance and Cardiopulmonary Effects of Combined Lateral and Vertical Acceleration.* M.Sc. Thesis, Wright State University, Dayton, Ohio, 45435. 1982
- Performance Effects Resulting from a Complex G Experiment. *Preprints of the Annual Meeting of the Aerospace Medical Association*, 320 South Henry St., Alexandria, VA 22314. 1982
- The influence of Gy and Gz Forces on Biodynamic Measurements. *Preprints of the Annual Meeting of the Aerospace Medical Association*, 320 South Henry St., Alexandria, VA 22314. 1982
- Why Am I G2O2 if He's G1O1? *Flight Comment, CAF Flight Safety Digest. 1979;*
- Salmonallae Isolation From Surface Waters. *Proc. 11th Conference Great Lakes Research, International Association for Great Lakes Research. 1968; 537-561*

R. C. "Bud" Rud
CD, MD
Lieutenant-Colonel

R.C. **"Bud" Rud** was born in Camrose, Alberta on 25 April 1935. He entered Royal Roads Military College September 1952 and, in September 1954, enrolled at Royal Military College at Kingston, Ontario. Bud graduated in Chemical Engineering, University of Alberta in 1957.

Following successful completion of pilot training in the RCAF, Bud was retained as a flight instructor at RCAF Station Penhold, Alberta during the period 1957-1960, flying North American Harvard aircraft.

In 1961, Flight Lieutenant Rud was given an operational posting to 445 AW(F) Squadron, an all-weather interceptor, fighter squadron stationed at Marville, France. The Squadron flew the Avro CF-100 Canuck, jet all-weather interceptor in aerial patrols over Europe as part of Canada's NATO forces in Europe.

Rud switched from flying duties to an engineering role while in Europe and transferred to Base Construction and Engineering at 3 (F) Wing at Zweibrucken, Germany to complete his tour during 1962 to 1965. On his return to Canada, he continued in the engineering role and was posted to Canadian Forces Station Chibougamau, Québec, one of the Pine Tree Line radar stations. While at this last post, he applied for and was selected for training as a physician in the Military Medical Training Plan in 1967.

LCol R.C. "Bud" Rud

Captain Rud completed his medical degree at the University of Alberta and interned at the Edmonton

General Hospital, returning to military duty in 1972. Major Rud assumed his duties as Base Surgeon at Canadian Forces Base Portage la Prairie, Manitoba later that year and served there for four years. This station was conducting flying training, and Major Rud's experience served him well in working with student pilots on the base.

Rud was selected for further training in aviation medicine and sent to Brooks Air Force Base in San Antonio, Texas for a residency in Aerospace Medicine for the year 1976-1977.

This prepared Lieutenant-Colonel (LCol) Rud for his next post, during 1977-1978 as Staff Officer Medical Air Operations at Air Command Headquarters in Winnipeg, Manitoba.

His expertise was next required at the Defence and Civil Institute of Environmental Medicine (DCIEM) in Toronto where Rud became the Director Medical Life Support Division for the years 1978-1981. This was followed by another directorship at the DCIEM, that of Director of the School of Operational and Aerospace Medicine and Central Aircrew Medical Board. LCol Rud held this appointment until his retirement from the Canadian Forces in 1982.

Dr. Rud had a private practice in family medicine in Edmonton for eight years until he accepted an appointment with Alcan Aluminum at Kitimat, British Columbia as its Medical Director.

When Dr. Rud left Alcan Aluminum in 1993, he continued in aviation medicine with a consulting practice in Edmonton, an active occupation as of this writing.

Summary of Achievements

Canadian Forces Decoration (CD)
Special Services Medal NATO
Doctor of Medicine, University of Alberta, 1967 (MD)
Bachelor of Science, Chemical Engineering, University of Alberta (BSc)
Certificate, Canadian Board of Occupational Medicine (CcBOM)

DAVID A. SALISBURY
CD, MD
COLONEL

David Salisbury was born and raised in Ottawa, Ontario. He enrolled in the Canadian Forces in 1975 under the auspices of the Medical Officer Training Plan (MOTP) program. Captain Salisbury graduated from Queen's University Medical School at Kingston, Ontario in 1978. After internship at McMaster University he was posted as a General Duty Medical Officer to Canadian Forces Base Portage la Prairie, Manitoba. In 1982 he was selected for the flight surgeon/pilot program and commenced pilot training. He received his pilot wings in 1983 and stayed on at CFB Moose Jaw, Saskatchewan as the Base Surgeon. He was the pilot/physician in charge of the CF Motion Sickness treatment program and he was the Flight Surgeon to the Snowbirds, the Air Force flying demonstration squadron.

In 1986 he was selected for postgraduate training in aerospace medicine. He obtained his Master's degree in Occupational Health from the University of British Columbia in 1987. In 1988 he attended the United States Air Force Residency in Aerospace Medicine at USAF School of Aviation Medicine at Brooks AFB, San Antonio, Texas and earned his USAF Senior Flight Surgeon Wings. He is Board certified in Aerospace Medicine by the American Board of Preventive Medicine and has his Royal College Fellowship in Community Medicine.

Col David A. Salisbury

In 1990 he was posted as the Head of Central Medical Board at the Defence and Civil Institute of Environmental Medicine (DCIEM) in Toronto. In 1993

135

he became the Special Projects Officer at DCIEM where he worked on revision of the Flight Surgeon's Course, the aircrew medical database, and the use of Modafanil in improving human performance during sustained operations.

In 1994 he was promoted to Lieutenant-Colonel (LCol) and was posted as the Chief of Ambulatory Care at the National Defence Medical Centre in Ottawa. In January 1995 he began working on Operation Phoenix, the re-engineering of the Canadian Forces Medical Service.

In June 1996 he was sent to Zagreb, Croatia as part of the NATO led peacekeeping effort in the former Yugoslavia. He returned to Ottawa after his six-month tour and served as the head of Public Health for the Canadian Forces on the staff of the Chief of Health Services, the organization formerly known as the Surgeon General.

In July 1997, with the reorganization of the Navy, Army and Air Force as separate operational entities, LCol Salisbury assumed the newly created position of Medical Advisor to the Chief of the Air Staff at National Defence Headquarters in Ottawa.

In 1998, with a promotion to Colonel, David Salisbury assumed command of the Canadian Forces Environmental Medicine Establishment and Deputy Chief of the Defence and Civil Institute of Environmental Medicine in Toronto. He has published numerous papers in occupational, aerospace and community medicine. His research interests concern aircrew selection and the use of computerized databases in the study of occupational epidemiology. He recently completed a four-year term as the Executive Secretary of the Clinical Reasoning Skills Test Committee of the Medical Council of Canada. He is the co-president of the Canadian Aerospace Medicine and Aeromedical Transport Association (CAMATA), a past-president of the International Association of Military Flight Surgeon Pilots, and he has been honoured as a Fellow of the Aerospace Medicine Association.

Colonel Salisbury is the only serving Medical Officer included in this work. He, his wife Els, and their two children (Jenny and Shelagh) live in Toronto.

Summary of Achievements

Canadian Forces Decoration (CD)
NATO - Implementation Force, Bosnia
Queen's 1978 (MD)
Master Health Science (Occupational Health) - UBC 1987 (MHSc)
Fellow American College Physical Medicine (Aero Space Medicine) (FACPM)
Fellow Royal College of Physicians Canada (FRCPC)

W. Joly Stevenson
CD, MD
Lieutenant-Colonel

Born and educated in Dublin, Ireland, Joly Stevenson enlisted in the Royal Air Force in 1941 during his pre-medical year at Trinity College Dublin. Stevenson's initial pilot flying training was completed in England, but he was sent to Canada for service flying training under the British Commonwealth Air Training Plan. Pilot Officer Stevenson arrived in Halifax, Nova Scotia on 1 January 1942 and proceeded to RCAF Station Penhold, Alberta where he trained on the Airspeed Oxford, a twin engine aircraft. There was a surplus of pilots in Britain at that time, so Stevenson was kept on in Canada as a staff pilot at 37 Service Flying Training School at Calgary, Alberta.

He returned to Britain in September 1942, sailing on the Queen Mary from New York City and without a convoy. The "Queen" was faster than most subs and having to slow down to stay in a convoy would have put her in greater jeopardy, hence she sailed alone at top speed.

On arrival, Flying Officer Stevenson was first assigned duties as a flying instructor at an advanced flying unit in England. He eventually was assigned to operational training on the Martin Baltimore aircraft at Shallufa, Egypt in the "night armed reconnaissance role" (low level flying at night). By this time, the war in Europe had come to an end, so he transferred back to Britain with his crew to convert to Douglas

LCol W. Joly Stevenson

Dakota DC-3 transport aircraft and was then sent to Burma to serve with 194 Transport Squadron and subsequently 267 Transport Squadron.

Released from the RAF in 1946, Stevenson joined Aer Lingus, the Irish airlines, as a pilot. He was selected for training on the Lockheed Super Constellation, a four-engine, long-range, passenger aircraft just coming into commercial airline service, but he had to decide whether to take this training or accept an offer of a grant from the British government to complete his medical studies.

After a great deal of soul searching, he resigned from Aer Lingus and enrolled in Trinity College's medical program in Dublin. Succesfully completing his medical degree, he undertook a one-year rotating internship at St. Albans Hospital in Hartfordshire, England. This was followed by an appointment as senior house officer at the Chest Surgical Unit of St. Charles Hospital at Ladbrook Grove in London, England.

The Royal Canadian Air Force was recruiting physicians in Ireland and England so he enlisted in the RCAF in 1954. Because of his aviation background he was selected for training as a Flight Surgeon at the RCAF Institute Aviation Medicine at Toronto, Ontario. In 1956, Flight Lieutenant Stevenson was sent on a conversion course on the Lockheed T-33 jet aircraft at Portage La Prairie, Manitoba where he was Senior Medical Officer. Squadron Leader Stevenson (S/L) maintained a medical office on the flight line and a T-33 was parked nearby on the tarmac. This afforded him the luxury of flying an hour of aerobatics prior to starting his morning sick parade.

Stevenson attended Harvard University's School of Public Health in 1958 under the tutelage of the renowned Professor Ross McFarland who was probably best known for his research and books on human factors in aviation. Following completion of his studies at Harvard in 1959, S/L Stevenson was transferred to Europe to the RCAF No. 1 Air Division as Flight Surgeon. During this four-year posting Stevenson continued to fly the T-33 whenever his duties permitted.

On his return from Europe in 1963, Wing Commander Stevenson was transferred to Winnipeg, Manitoba as the Training Command Flight Surgeon. He continued in this assignment until 1967 when he was transferred to the RCAF Institute Aviation Medicine in Toronto as Director of the Central Medical Board where he remained until retirement from RCAF in 1975. By this time he had logged a total of 2,500 flying hours as a pilot.

While in the RCAF, Lieutenant-Colonel (LCol) Stevenson prepared various scientific papers, some of which were presented at international meetings. These covered such varied subjects as;

•studies of morbidity in aircrew in the RCAF,
•diabetes mellitus in flying personnel,
•human factors in fatal aircraft accident,
•unusual injury on ejection from aircraft, and
•antihistamine and aircrew.

LCol Stevenson was a medical member of numerous boards of inquiry investigating aircraft accidents and incidents. Prior to retirement from the RCAF LCol Stevenson completed a four-month sabbatical as a special intern at Toronto Western Hospital and Hospital for Sick Children. Subsequently he joined Imperial Life Assurance Company as a medical underwriter of life insurance and disability claims. He also worked for IMPCO Health (now Laurentian Health Services) as a consultant in occupational and aviation medicine. Dr. Stevenson retired from these companies in 1989 and now works part-time in the same field as an aviation medical examiner.

Dr. Stevenson was certified by the Canadian Board of Occupational Medicine in 1982. He is a founding member and was later president of the Canadian Society of Aerospace Medicine. He is also a Fellow of the American Aerospace Association and Canadian Aeronautics and Space Institute. In November 1995 he was honoured by the Royal College of Physicians in Ireland with their Fellowship in Occupational Medicine. The ceremony took place in Ireland.

Since 1991, he continues to practice Aviation and Occupational Medicine. Currently he is a Civil Aviation Medicine Examiner for the Ministry of Transport. As well, he is a Medical Adviser to three small companies and makes a weekly visit to the Evans Occupational Clinic in Toronto.

Joly Stevenson married Ann Mary Kiernan, an Irish girl he met while a medical student in Dublin. He was married in Los Angeles in 1956; the best man at the wedding was Peter Allenshaw an old RAF buddy who subsequently won an academy award for his art work in the Walt Disney movie "Mary

Poppins."

Joly and Ann had four children, twin girls, a boy and another girl. One of the twins is a Ph. D. candidate at the University of Western Ontario. The youngest daughter is married and is living in Moncton, N.B. Their son is a private pilot.

Summary of Achievements

Canadian Forces Decoration (CD)
General Service Medal and Clasp, South East Asia
Defence Medal
War Medal, 1939 - 1945
Special Service Medal, NATO
Doctor of Medicine Trinity College, Dublin, Ireland, 1953 (MD)
Bachelor of Medicine (MB)
Bachelor of Chirurgie (BChirg)
Master of Obstetrics (MAO)
Master of Public Health, Harvard, 1958 (MPH)
Fellow of The Faculty of Occupational Medicine, Royal College of Physicians of Ireland (FFOM)
Certificant, Canadian Board of Occupational Medicine - 1982 (CCBOM)

ROBERT F. THATCHER
SBStJ, CD, MD
COLONEL

Robert Thatcher, known to everyone as "Bob," was born on a farm in Chatham, Ontario on 26 November 1936. His early schooling was received in Chatham and Ridgetown, Ontario before attending the University of Western Ontario in London, Ontario. Bob joined the Royal Canadian Air Force while at university in September 1955 and, during the summers, trained as a navigator. Pilot Officer Thatcher was awarded Navigator's wings in August 1958.

After graduation in 1959, Pilot Officer Thatcher flew with 409 (F) AW Squadron at Comox, British Columbia, flying the Avro CF-100 Canuck all-weather interceptor and then on the McDonnell CF-101 Voodoo interceptor aircraft. These aircraft flew patrols over the northwest, intercepting Russian bombers flying too close to Canadian territory. Flight Lieutenant Thatcher left the military in August 1962 to enter medical school at the University of Western Ontario. Bob rejoined the RCAF in August 1963 as one of the

Col Robert F. Thatcher

first members of aircrew to train as a doctor under the Military Medical Training Plan.

After graduation in 1966 and completing his internship at St. Paul's Hospital in Vancouver, British Columbia, Squadron Leader Thatcher was assigned to his old flying base at RCAF Staion Comox as Senior Medical Officer and Flight Surgeon. This was a very busy flying base with a fifteen-bed hospital and eighteen hundred personnel. Base operations included air defence patrols, search and rescue flights and medical evacuation of sick and injured from many remote areas of northern British Columbia, numbering as many as one hundred per year. In his role as Flight Surgeon, Thatcher was responsible for the support of three flying squadrons, which included accident investigation, crash response and disaster planning. He found time in his busy schedule to complete the Flight Surgeon's course in 1967 at the Defence and Civil Institute of Environmental Medicine in Toronto and the Canadian Forces Advanced Management Course in 1969.

In 1971, Major Thatcher's education in aviation medicine began in earnest, first with a diploma program in public health from the University of Toronto, graduating in 1972. This was followed by Arctic, Sea and Land Survival Courses in 1972 and with a program in aerospace medicine at Brooks Air Force Base in San Antonio, Texas in 1973.

Putting all this education to good use, Lieutenant-Colonel Thatcher was appointed Director of the Medical Life Support Division, Defence and Civil Institute of Environmental Medicine. As director, he was responsible for research and development of life support equipment, physiological research in the high altitude environment, human factor analysis of aircraft accidents, the medical selection of aircrew candidates and consulting and advising on the disposition of experienced aircrew with medical problems.

Positions of ever greater responsibility were in store as Colonel Thatcher was sent on the Canadian Forces' Senior Staff Course, at the National Defence College in 1977 to prepare him to for his next appointment in 1978 at National Defence Headquarters in Ottawa Ontario. Col Thatcher was appointed Director of Medical Staffing and Training on the Surgeon General's staff. This directorate was responsible for career planning and programming of training for all Canadian Forces Medical Service personnel.

Colonel Thatcher took time out to attend the Canadian Forces French Language Course in 1983 before assuming a new responsibility, that of Director of Preventive Medicine in the Office of the Surgeon General. As Director, he was responsible to the Surgeon General for advising on measures to prevent disease and to provide and maintain health in the Canadian Forces. These measures included policy development, establishing and monitoring research and development and promoting health through education. The areas of responsibility included communicable disease control, hygiene and sanitation, occupational health, environmental medicine, addiction and rehabilitation, life quality improvement, prevention of drug and alcohol misuse and community health nursing.

In 1983, Colonel Thatcher made another move, this one as Command Surgeon of Air Command at its headquarters in Winnipeg, Manitoba. The Command Surgeon was responsible to the Commander Air Command, for the provision and maintenance of proper standards of preventive medicine and treatment services within his jurisdiction. As well, he was the advisor on the human factors and medical implications as applied to all air operations and training.

As administrator of the preventive medicine program, he had the responsibility for the traditional aspects of disease control through hygiene and sanitation, immunization, occupational health monitoring, inspection and investigation and as well, the more recent programs of drug and alcohol education, anti-smoking, obesity and hypertension.

As administrator of treatment services, his responsibilities included ensuring quality medical care administration of medical finances, and alcohol treatment clinic and social work services.

Colonel Thatcher retired from the Canadian Forces in December 1984 after approximately 30 years of service and started a second career with Petro Canada. This second career was most rewarding and satisfying and was most helpful in providing the means to educate his five children.

Currently, Dr. Thatcher is doing contract work with DND at the Defence and Civil Institute of Environmental Medicine primarily in the medical selection of aircrew. He works with Dr. Gary Gray *(see Aviation Medicine Pioneers)* who has probably provided the most continuous expertise in aviation and space medicine since World War II.

Summary of Achievements

Decorations
Serving Brother of the Most Venerable Order of the Hospital of St. John of Jerusalem (SBStJ)
Canadian Forces Decoration (CD)

Education - Academic
Bachelor of Science, Honours Chemistry, UWO, 1959
Medical Doctor, UWO, 1962 - 1966
Internship, St. Paul's Hospital, Vancouver, B.C., 1966 - 1967
Diploma in Public Health - University of Toronto, 1971 - 1972
Certified American College of Preventive Medicine (Aerospace Medicine), San Antonio, Texas, 1973
Military Flight Surgeon Course, Defence and Civil Institute of Environmental Medicine, 1967
Canadian Forces Advanced Management Course, 1969
Arctic, Sea and Land Survival Courses, 1972
National Defence College, 1967 - 1977
French Language Training, 1982 - 1983

Publications
Transport of Sick and Injured by Air: R.F. Thatcher
Pilot Workload and Work Capacity in Tactical Support Aircraft: R.F. Thatcher and P.J. Dean
Burns in Aircrew - Case Report: R.F. Thatcher and R.E. Noble
An Approach to the Study of Pilot Workload and Low-Level High-Speed Roles: R.F. Thatcher and P.J. Dean
A Conceptual Model for the Effects of Operational Stress: W.A. LePage, P.J. Dean and R.F. Thatcher
The Canadian Forces Immunization Program: G.R. Humphries, R.F. Thatcher

Memberships and Associations
Licence to Practice - College of Physicians and Surgeons of Ontario
Aerospace Medical Association - Associate Fellow
Canadian Society of Aviation Medicine - Member
Ontario Medical Association - Member
American Occupational Medical Association - Member
Defence Medical Association - Member

CHAPTER 4

THE PARA-RESCUE MEDICS

PARA-RESCUE MEDICAL OFFICERS,
NURSING OFFICERS
& MEDICAL ASSISTANTS

- **Wing Commander D.O. "Nig" Coons**
  One of the first post-war Medical Officers to earn para-rescue wings in 1951. Later worked for NASA as a medical advisor; monitored the astronauts of Apollo 1 as they died on the launch pad in a capsule fire during rehearsal.

- **Lieutenant Commander Herbert Duncan "Dutch" Fader**
  As a corporal medical assistant, was one of the eight para-rescue graduated in 1952.

- **Chief Warrant Officer George Westwood**
  A Sergeant Medical Assistant, he was one of the ten para-rescue graduates in 1951; a "D" Day veteran, he landed in Normandy on D+5.

- **Flying Officer Grace MacEachern née Woodman**

  One of seven nursing officers to graduate in para-rescue and made the first operational jump for a para-rescue by a nurse in the western world.

- **Colonel J.R. "Dick" Wynne**

  One of four Medical Officer awarded the para-rescue badge. Jumped on several para-rescue missions.

Dwight Owen "Nig" Coons
SBStJ, MD
Wing Commander

Dwight Owen Coons, usually called "Nig" or fondly as "Doc" was born in Hamilton, Ontario on 26 September 1925. He died 24 December 1997 in Dallas, Texas after an epic battle with cancer, a battle that extended his active life years beyond any medical reasoning or prognosis. Doc brought new definition to the term "one-of-a-kind" in his personal and professional life.

A graduate of the University of Toronto Medical School, he served as a Flight Surgeon in the Royal Canadian Air Force for 16 years, attaining the rank of Wing Commander.

His RCAF service included qualification as a para-rescue physician and he was on a number of para-rescue exercises and operations into extremely difficult conditions. Flight Lieutenant Coons was on the first para-rescue course in 1951 and was one of only four medical officers trained in this specialty. This course is no longer given to medical personnel, and he was proud of this achievement.

W/C D.O. "Nig" Coons

Squadron Leader Coons served in Europe as Flight Surgeon with Canadair F-86 Sabre fighter squadrons, and Avro CF-100 All-Weather Interceptor Squadrons. Following his overseas duties, he studied for a year at Harvard University where he received a Master's degree in Public Health.

He was then assigned to high level staff positions in Canada and the United States and served for a year on an aircraft carrier. He was the first RCAF Medical Officer to serve on HMCS Bonaventure.

In 1963, Doc retired from the RCAF to join the NASA Spacecraft Center in Houston, Texas where he served as Deputy Medical Director. During six years with the space program he was instrumental in the development of medical programs for the astronauts, with whom he established many close friendships. While employed at the NASA Spacecraft Centre in Houston at 6:30 a.m. on 27 January 1967 he was conducting medical monitoring on three astronauts, Virgil "Gus" Grissom, Edward White and Roger Chaffee as they were enveloped in flames in the cabin of Apollo 1 as it sat on the pad, conducting a launch rehearsal at the Kennedy Space Centre in Florida.

In 1969, Doc left NASA to establish a private practice in Dallas, Texas devoted to Aerospace Medicine. He specialized in working with professional pilots and their families, achieving an international reputation in the field and building a loyal following amongst "his pilots."

A pioneer in preventive medicine, Doc cared deeply about his patients and their well-being, to the point of making house-calls when needed. There is no question that many lives were enhanced and careers extended by his firm and steady devotion to the health of his patients.

On 26 September 1997 nearly 400 patients, friends and admirers joined together at the Monarch Air Hangar in Dallas to honour his 72nd birthday in a celebration of respect, affection and appreciation.

Summary of Achievements

Serving Brother of the Most Venerable Order of the Hospital of St. John of Jerusalem (SBStJ)
Canadian Forces Decoration (CD)
Special Service Medal - NATO
Doctor of Medicine, University of Toronto (MD)
Master of Public Health - Harvard (MPH)

Professional memberships included:

American Medical Association

Texas Medical Association

Dallas County Medical Society

Aerospace Medical Association

Civil Aviation Medical Association

Texas Air Medics

Fellow of the Royal Society of Medicine

Fellow of the American College of Preventive Medicine

Fellow of Canadian Aeronautics and Space Institute

Fellow of the Aerospace Medical Association

Canadian Society of Aviation and Human Factors Society

Doc was a member of the Southwest Medical Student Relations Committee and an adult leader of the Boy Scouts of America for 16 years.

Herbert Duncan "Dutch" Fader
CD
Lieutenant Commander

Herbert **Duncan Fader** was born in Halifax, Nova Scotia and received his early schooling and initial military training as a Sea Cadet at RCSCC Nelson from 1943-1947. He enrolled in the Royal Canadian Air Force in October 1947 at Eastern Air Command Headquarters in Halifax, and was subsequently drafted to the newly formed Manning Depot at RCAF Station Trenton, Ontario in March 1948. Manning Depot turned young civilians into airmen with uniforms, inoculations, drill and other basic training. He reluctantly acquired "Dutch" as his sobriquet during basic training as a result of ``Wet Canteen'' conversations with German-speaking Kitchener-Waterloo area recruits often referred to as "those Pennsylvania Dutchmen."

LCdr H.D. "Dutch" Fader

Fader's trades training as an airman was in the medical field. He qualified as a Medical Assistant and Laboratory Assistant and worked in the medical facilities of a number of RCAF stations. The work involved the management of the out-patient clinics, known in the Air Force as Medical Inspection Rooms (MIRs), assisting with mercy flights and aeromed evacuation flights, and supporting squadron personnel when they were deployed away from their main base.

Dutch received specialized training in para-rescue, air search and rescue, and survival training. He also worked as an instructor in para-rescue and survival training. The working conditions in para-rescue for medical personnel was rather different than that for non-medical search and rescue (SAR)

150

specialists. Those in other than medical trades were attached to a squadron for their SAR duties and training, to which they could devote most if not all of their day. The medical SAR specialists' primary duties were to the medical facility and they were responsible to the Senior Medical Officer. Medical commitments frequently prevented them from joining their non-med colleagues for operations and exercises. A great deal depended on cooperation between the Senior Medical Officer and the Senior Air Operations Officer if the medical SAR specialists were to be given sufficient training to stay current. This dichotomy was recognized and eventually alleviated with the formation of the Search and Rescue Technician (SAR Tech) Trade in the early 1980's.

The aforementioned notwithstanding, "Dutch" managed to accumulate 65 jumps including one operational jump to a downed USAF pilot in the Yukon in November 1956 during his active para-rescue period.

Fader was commissioned from the ranks (CFR) in early 1965 from the rank of Flight Sergeant and promoted to the rank of Flying Officer (F/O) in the Medical Secretarial Officer Branch. After unification of the Forces, this branch became known as Medical Associate Officer (Administration). At the time of commissioning,

Dutch prepares for a jump from a Norseman aircraft.

Dutch was serving at 4 (Fighter) Wing in Baden-Soellingen, West Germany. On his return from his commissioning course in Canada, F/O Fader was posted to 1 (Fighter) Wing at Marville in France. Later, when Canadian Forces Europe relocated its headquarters to Lahr Germany in the spring of 1967, F/O Fader was named a member of the advance party to go to Lahr and assist in the preparations for the Canadian take-over of the air base then occupied by the French Air Force.

He and his family returned to Canada, on the second last Yukon flight from Marville, on their way to the Canadian Forces Medical Training Centre at Camp Borden, Ontario in 1967. With unification of the Canadian Forces in 1968, "Dutch" was re-ranked to Captain and the School was renamed the Canadian Forces Medical Service School (CFMSS). He successfully completed studies in instructional techniques and training standards, both useful for his duties at the School.

During the summer of 1970, Dutch joined the staff of the Surgeon General at National Defence Headquarters in Ottawa, Ontario. He was assigned to the Directorate of Staffing and Training. As a logical progression from these duties, Major Fader moved on to the staff of the Director General Postings and Careers as Posting and Careers Officer/Medical (PCO/Med) in 1972 and remained in that post until 1978.

During this latter period, Major Fader took French language training and attended the advanced management course. He was selected for and completed training in hospital administration through the Canadian Hospital Association and the University of Manitoba. One of the highlights of his tour of duty as PCO/Med was his work as a member of the team that recruited twenty-five physicians from Great Britain during the years 1974 to 1977.

Major Fader's final posting was to the staff of the Regional Surgeon Pacific in Victoria, British Columbia on 1 August 1978. His duties in this post were the administration of medical support for all military units in the Pacific Region and to all the ships of the Pacific Fleet. Consequently, he acquired Sea Environmental Qualification and went to sea whenever possible to better appreciate fleet support medical requirements. His rank was officially changed to Lieutenant Commander by NDHQ during this period and he held this rank on transfer to the Canadian Forces Supplementary Reserve on retirement in 1985.

Summary of Achievements

Canadian Forces Decoration (CD)
Special Service Medal, NATO
Queen Elizabeth II Silver Jubilee Medal

GEORGE WESTWOOD, CD
CHIEF WARRANT OFFICER

George Westwood, a native of Windsor, Ontario, was born there on 26 March, 1924. He was barely 18 years old when he enlisted in the Royal Canadian Air Force on 7 July 1942. George's first military training was given at the Manning Depot at RCAF Staton Lachine, Québec. Properly kitted, inoculated and made into an airman, George volunteered to become a Medical Assistant. He was immediately sent to RCAF Station Trenton, Ontario to take this training. On graduation, George completed the circle and went to his first duty post at #7 Elementary Flying Training School in Windsor, Ontario. This was one of the many flying training schools of the British Commonwealth Air Training Plan.

Leading Aircraftman
George Westwood

There was a great build-up of troops in England in preparation for the invasion of Europe, so Leading Aircraftman Westwood was posted to England in the spring of 1943. He recalls the impression he had that Canadians in England were proud of their country and their service. An interesting note to Westwood's departure for overseas service is that he had a chance to visit with his father, who was a member of the Veteran's Guard guarding the troop ship in Halifax on which George sailed overseas.

George joined 416 Squadron medical staff at Rigby Links. There were four squadrons integrated into a wing called 126 Fighter Wing located at Biggin Hill. Eventually the Wing was sent to Tangmere and waited for the invasion of Europe. The advanced medical section of the Fighter Wing landed in Normandy on D-Day + 5, that is five days after the main invasion assault on the beaches. No. 126 Wing proceeded through France, Belgium and Holland where Canadians were respected and revered. The Wing was located at Utersen

Germany when the war came to an end.

With Germany's surrender, things moved rather quickly and Westwood was shipped back to Canada in March 1946 and demobilized from the RCAF. Six months later in September 1946, George re-enlisted in the RCAF as a

Para-Rescue Course #5-1951. Left to right: LAC Sandy Deschenes, LAC Campbell, F/O Marion Neely, Sgt George Westwood

Medical Assistant and was posted to RCAF StationTrenton.

Several postings followed, including RCAF Station Fort Nelson and Detachment at Smith River on the Alaskan Highway. Sergeant (Sgt) Westwood eventually ended up at RCAF Station Rockcliffe, Ontario where he volunteered for para-rescue duties in 1952. All para-rescue personnel were required to take regular training, involving parachute jumps and George continued in these duties until late in that year.

In the fall of 1952, Sgt Westwood was posted to RCAF Langar, England. Langar was the staging and supply base in England for the RCAF Air Division in Europe. A part of this base was a large medical supply depot that provided all of the medical equipment and pharmaceuticals for the Air Division.

Flight Sergeant Westwood returned to Canada in 1954 and spent the next ten years in instructional duties at RCAF Station Aylmer, Ontario, in the station hospital at RCAF Station Calgary, Alberta, at RCAF Hospital Rockcliffe, Ontario and finally at the National Defence Medical Centre in Ottawa, Ontario.

On Warrant Officer Westwood's third overseas posting in 1964, he was sent to 3 (Fighter) Wing at Zweibrucken, Germany. This base had the definitive care hospital to support the other two Wings and Air Division staff. It was a busy five years and one with its share of stress in the midst of the Cold War and the frequent exercises to prepare the Wings to meet a possible military threat.

When Master Warrant Officer Westwood returned to Canada in 1969, it was to join the Surgeon General's staff at National Defence Headquarters in Ottawa, Ontario. This three-year posting brought with it another promotion to Chief Warrant Officer (CWO), the highest non-commissioned rank in the Canadian Forces. He was then posted to Canadian Forces Hospital Kingston, Ontario as the Hospital CWO.

George Westwood retired from this last post with 35 years of dedicated and exemplary service. After retirement George took an appointment with the Federal Regional Psychiatric Centre of the Correctional Service of Canada in Kingston, Ontario.

There is a saying in correctional institutions that all inmates are either mad, sad or bad. George's military experiences served him well in his work and he says that the "cons" thought him a little crazy as well, so they got along well. Westwood must have enjoyed his time with Correctional Services, he continued in this work for eleven years.

George and Mrs. Westwood have two children, one who was a nurse at the National Defence Medical Centre, Ottawa and has since retired. Now in his second retirement, George enjoys golf in the summer and curling in the winter.

Summary of Achievements

Canadian Forces Decoration and Clasps (CD)
1939-1945 Star
France and Germany Star
Defence Medal
Canadian Volunteer Service Medal
War Medal 1939 - 1945
Special Service Medal - NATO

155

GRACE M. MACEACHERN
NÉE WOODMAN
R.N.
FLYING OFFICER

Grace Woodman is a native of Pembroke, Ontario, where she grew up and received her early schooling and nursing training. She is a graduate of the General Hospital in Pembroke, but received further nursing training at Ste-Agathe Des Mont, Québec in the Tuberculosis Sanitarium, at McGill University for Public Health Nursing, and at Queen's University Kingston, Ontario for a Bachelor of Science degree in Psychology.

In 1951 the RCAF commenced training doctors, nurses and medical assistants for para-rescue work. There were two courses, running July to September 1951 and January to June 1952. Each course consisted of two Medical Officers, five Nursing Officers and six Medical Assistants. Grace was on the second and last course in 1952. She was one of seven nurses to finish the programme.

When asked why she had chosen such a perilous course, she said, "I have always loved sports and the outdoors and the training in

F/O Grace Woodman

para-rescue was learning to survive and help others in accidents in isolated areas, mountains, bush etc." In July 1952, just one month after completing the five and a half month course of which most was outdoors, she made her first operational jump and reputedly a world first for para-rescue jump by a Nursing Officer.

A team of three rescuers was sent into the rocky slopes of Mount Coquitlam about thirty miles north east of Vancouver to rescue an injured surveyor from a geology party. The casualty was reported to have a fractured pelvis and punctured lung.

Grace was accompanied on this jump by Squadron Leader Dick Wynne, a para-rescue trained doctor, and Sergeant Red Jamieson, a full time para-rescue safety equipment supervisor. This was the first operational jump by a doctor and nurse and jumpmaster team. On the drop, the three became separated because of high winds. The team landed into high trees and Grace became entangled in branches about 125 feet from the ground. She carried "let-down" ropes for just such an eventuality, but the rope was only one hundred feet long, leaving a drop of twenty-five feet to the ground. Wynne and Jamieson managed to make it to the ground and were able to contact each other by shouting; however Woodman was too far away from the team to hear or to be heard.

Woodman describes the descent and subsequent activities as follows: "I managed to get myself untangled from the tree and to secure my let-down rope. However, in attempting to get untangled, I lost my gloves. The descent on the 100-foot rope, which should have been slow and easy, tended to be a bit faster than I would have liked. The speedy descent, holding the rope in my bare hands, was so painful that I had to let go and risk the chance of injury. All my fingers had deep burns and I had a deep, large gash across my left palm. The wind was knocked out of me and it took me a while to breathe at somewhere near a normal rate.

Although my right leg was painful, there was no sign of bleeding on my jump suit. My lower back and thoracic area were uncomfortable. I stood up, collected my belongings and started up the mountainside. By this time I had lost the little bit of daylight that was left and it was getting dark. I retraced my steps back to my parachute to avoid getting lost in the dark. Meanwhile, the pilot of the jump airplane kept circling until well after midnight giving me the direction that I had to take since I was separated from the other two. The country was very rough and was known to be inhabited by cougar and grizzly bear. However, the sound of the airplane motors probably scared everything away. I was so tired at this point I crawled under a bush and fell asleep. Around 5 a.m. the following morning, I was awakened by the sound of the search airplane and by Wynne and Jamieson calling out to me. I found my gloves at the foot of the tree and put them on to protect my burned and injured hands."

157

Guided by a circling DC-3 Dakota, Wynne and Jamieson located Woodman. The team continued to care for the injured geologist until the U.S. Coast Guard sent in a helicopter to evacuate the patient and the team to Sea Island. Para-rescue jumps and evacuation were very tough and hazardous for all concerned. In this case it was a successful combination of effort by the RCMP, the ground personnel, the US Coast Guard, helicopter and crew and last but not least the aircrew and para-rescue team. The hard work and danger was well rewarded when the para-rescue team saw the look of the patient's mother, to see her son alive and safe.

Grace Woodman married Major Charles MacEachern, RCAF Engineering Officer and left the service in 1955. She now lives in Trenton, Ontario. The MacEacherns have two children, a daughter married and living in Trenton and a son, a Royal Military College graduate in electrical engineering stationed at National Defence Headquarters in Ottawa.

Summary of Achievements

RN - General Hospital, Pembroke, 1940 - 1943
Post Graduate Training, Ste. Agathe Des Mont, 1945 - 1949
Nursing Sister Development Course, London
Para-Rescue Wings Graduate Course 6, 1952
McGill University Public Health Nursing
Queen's University, B Sc in Psychology

J.R. "Dick" Wynne
OStJ, CD, MD
Colonel

Richard Wynne, known to everyone as "Dick" was born 20 January 1921 in Vermilion, Alberta. He grew up in Anyox in northern British Columbia, a copper mine and smelter town, reportedly the largest in the British Empire. It was an isolated, one-industry town, accessible only by coastal vessels from Vancouver that made regular scheduled calls. In 1935, the mine closed and everyone had to move. Dick's father, who was with Canada Customs, was moved south to Ocean Falls, which was then a pulp and paper mill town.

Col J.R. "Dick" Wynne

Dick Wynne attended Granby Bay Public School at Anyox and St. George's School in Vancouver, graduating from high school in 1935. In 1936 he went to Epsom College in Surrey, England where he completed his education for entrance to university and his pre-medical sciences in 1939, the first Bachelor of Medicine (MB) for the University of London. He was awarded a scholarship for free medical education at University College Hospital Medical School in London, England.

After Wynne completed his pre-clinical training, or second MB as it was called, he left and enrolled in the RCAF for aircrew training. He had applied to join the RAF as aircrew, but was rejected medically because of a cartilage injury to one knee, a result of playing rugby. He had about six weeks to wait before reporting for induction in the RCAF, so he bought a book on aerial navigation to study. This, as it turned out, was a good idea. Wynne had also worked to make himself physically fit, riding a bicycle about twenty miles a day rather than use public transport.

In September 1942, he went to the Aircrew Reception Centre (ACRC) in London. Here, he and his colleagues were given uniforms and equipment, and received their inoculations before going to 13 Initial Training Wing (ITW) in Torquay, Devon. He joined a number of Canadians who had transferred from the Canadian Army to the RCAF and a very pleasant group it was. Airman Wynne had been in an Officers' Training Corps (OTC) at College and so had no difficulty with drill. This group of trainees, known as a Flight, were half RCAF and half RAF. Amongst the latter were five Americans who had joined the RAF.

In the group were people who had been in the Signals Corps in the army. They were able to help others with Morse code. Others, who knew more about armament and engines, were able to help the group with this knowledge. Wynne, who had prepared himself in navigation and mathematics, made his contribution in these areas. The RAF had taken over a number of hotels to be used to house or billet troops. The ITW trainees were billeted in the Grand Hotel, but it was anything but grand. It had been stripped of everything, the elevators were not in use and, of course, the trainees were on the top floor.

Training was completed in December, but there was the usual delay waiting for the next move. The trainees were put to work building an assault course, but they were already learning how to exist in a military system. They made sure that it took long enough to complete the project that they never had to go over it themselves.

Almost three months later, in February, they were sent to 21 Elementary Flying Training School (EFTS) at Booker for Grading School to determine their suitability for training. Here they were given about twelve hours of instruction in a de Havilland Tiger Moth. Their performance on this airplane and their ground school results determined whether they would be trained as pilots, navigators, or bomb aimers. They were not required to fly the airplane solo, but Wynne managed to do so.

Then they were billeted in private homes next to an RAF Station called a Disposal Centre located near Manchester. There was little to do but wait for a draft, but they were required to appear on parade each morning. Invariably, many would be late arriving, and this upset the NCO i/c (non-commissioned officer in charge) because he could never identify who was coming on parade late in order to get their names. They would just crawl along, bent over and hiding, to reach their Flight unobserved. This was at Heaton Park at a large depressed area surrounded by higher ground and an RAF Station. It was here that the parades were held. If there was nothing for the trainees to do, they were free for the day. There was little to do, so several of the group saw *Casablanca* three times in one week and they just about knew the dialogue by heart.

They were sent to Canada on the Queen Elizabeth, sailing from the Clyde to New York, but not in convoy. There were about 3,000 on board, but all were put in the upper decks and crammed thirty-six to a stateroom in bunks four tiers high.

In a typical SNAFU (situation normal, all fouled up) they went from NewYork to Moncton, New Brunswick to 31 Personnel Depot an RAF holding unit. They should not have gone there, so they were on a train again and on their way to Rockcliffe, Ontario where they were given a furlough before reporting to various Elementary Flying Training Schools (EFTSs) located across the country.

Wynne journeyed to Vancouver by train, and then up the coast by ship to Ocean Falls. The long slow journey gave him just 24 hours at home before having to leave to get back on time. Enroute to Ottawa to report to RCAF Station Rockcliffe, Wynne was advised, on arriving at Fort William, to turn around and head back west to report to No. 3 EFTS at High River Alberta. Eight weeks there, training on single engine Cornell aircraft and off again to No. 5 Service Flying Training School at Calgary, Alberta. This was for training on the twin-engine Cessna T-50 Crane bringing pilots to wing standard. He was commissioned in December 1943 when he was awarded his wings. After furlough, he went to No. 34 Operational Training Unit (OTU) at Pennfield Ridge, New Brunswick, an RAF Station in the British Commonwealth Air Training Plan, near the Bay of Fundy.

After OTU, members of the group who were trained as crews, got priority in posting overseas and they sailed back to England on the Isle de France, a 73,000 ton, pre-war luxury liner. Wynne and his crew did not get assigned to Douglas Bostons or North American B-25 Mitchells (twin-engine medium bombers) as they had expected. Pilot Officer Wynne, his Navigator and Wireless Airgunner (WAG) were posted to another OTU at Leicester East, where the crew was rounded out with a co-pilot. This OTU was preparing crews for 46 Group of Transport Command. A special group formed in February 1944 for the invasion of Normandy and equipped with Douglas DC-3 Dakotas, a twin-engine transport aircraft. Their role would be to supply the armies, evacuate casualties, and also take part in airborne operations by towing gliders. These large gliders, Airspeed Horsas, carried troops and even jeeps for landings in the battle zone. DC-3s were also used to drop paratroops, containers and panniers of arms and supplies. All the other course members were sent out to India, but Wynne's group was kept at the OTU as instructors, which they hated. Wynne managed to persuade a very pleasant RAF Squadron Leader that the group was not suited for instructional duties and, after a week, they were posted to 437 Transport Squadron RCAF, which was being formed at Blakehill Farm in Wiltshire.

For a time in September, Wynne and his crew were employed out of Netheravon towing salvaged Horsa gliders back from Normandy in France. They got back to their squadron just as re-supply flights to the airborne troops at Arnhem, Holland came to an end. The crew learned of this as they arrived at Blakehill Farm with a Horsa glider in tow. Wynne went to the Squadron Commanding Officer and pleaded to be allowed to return to the Squadron, The CO readily agreed and the crew was returned to Squadron duties.

The crew stayed with the squadron right through to the end of the war in Europe and was able to take part in the largest airborne operation in the history of warfare. Operation Varsity dropped paratroops to take part in the Rhine River crossing. This four-hour flight was in the midst of the largest mass of airplanes Wynne had ever seen. It was, he says, a sight to remember.

Transport flight crews did not get a credit for each operational flight as did bomber crews. Transport crews' credits were tallied in terms of operational hours. Wynne's crew put in about 660 hours on the Squadron and at #1Horsa Glider Support Unit, plus one trip at the OTU.

After VE Day, the Squadron moved to Nivelles in Belgium where they lived in tents. Then they were flying out of both airports in Brussels. From there, Wynne and his crew were sent to Norway, based at Oslo. This location they found much to their liking both for accommodation and duties. Dick Wynne was in Oslo when he was notified to return to London, England to be processed for demobilization. He immediately went to see the Dean of his Medical School to see if he could get back to finish his three clinical years. He was not only welcomed back, the Dean said he would get him back, even if he had to kick somebody out to make a place for him.

Dick Wynne had been on a full scholarship for all of his medical education when he left to join the RCAF. The Dean, at that time, would give no assurances, and in fact doubted that the scholarship would still be available at a later time. However, the new Dean was much more amenable and held a board meeting at which the scholarship was re-instated. Wynne's fees would have been paid by the Department of Veterans Affairs as part of veterans gratuities, but as a matter of principle he wanted this scholarship reinstated. All DVA paid was his $60-a-month subsistence allowance. This went up to $80 when Wynne was married.

The University of London, as well as all other universities in the United Kingdom, does not grant a degree of MD to those who graduate in medicine. The degree from London is Bachelor of Medicine, Bachelor of Surgery [MB, BS (London)]. This is the equivalent of the degree of MD awarded by Canadian and US universities. There are other bodies, such as the Royal Colleges, through which students can be licensed to practice medicine. The first "final exams" Dr. Wynne wrote were for these, granting him the degrees Member Royal College Surgery (England) [MRCS (Eng)] and Licentiate Royal College of Physicians (London) [LRCP (London)]. He wrote and passed these exams in 1948. A lot of people did it this way as an insurance and some did not bother about getting their degree or may not have been registered as a student of London University. Wynne wrote his degree exams after this, completing them in 1955 while in the UK.

The MD (London) is a specialist degree taken by only a very small percentage of doctors, usually those in academic medicine. It is not a degree one needs to practice medicine. It covers just a small field of particular interest to the individual, such as a PhD and is taken by less than five per cent of doctors. It is quite different from the MD handed out in Canada and it has no Canadian equivalent. Incidentally, all UK graduates and those who wrote and passed only the Royal College exams, are titled doctor. In England surgeons, when they pass their FRCS of any of the Royal Colleges revert to being called Mister.

Wynne interned at St. Paul's Hospital in Vancouver, British Columbia in 1949-50, after writing his Medical Council of Canada examinations in April 1949. These were required to register in BC, which then had no reciprocity with the UK where he first registered.

An interesting fact was the difference in training at medical school in London and that received in Canada. Before final exams were written, Dr. Wynne already had responsibility for patients as part of his medical and surgical training. Duties included writing their histories and examining them when admitted to beds in the ward, taking all blood for any tests and doing lumbar punctures. These initially were under instruction and they also assisted during operations on their patients. They had to do a minimum of twenty deliveries when on obstetrics and a minimum of twenty anaesthetics, an experience that Dr. Wynne enjoyed.

He found that Alberta graduates had not even pushed a needle into a patient, University of Western Ontario graduates were somewhat better. It seemed the University of Alberta graduated students not doctors.

As his Canadian certifications were nearing completion, Dr. Wynne decided to rejoin the RCAF as a doctor in May 1950. Early duty posts were RCAF Station Edmonton, Alberta for a few months, then to Sea Island, British Columbia in 1950-52 as Senior Medical Officer (SMO). Squadron Leader (S/L) Wynne took the para-rescue course in 1951, Course No. 5, while at Sea Island. He volunteered because there was a need for a doctor on the para-rescue team in Western Canada, and a non-commissioned officer (NCO) whom he knew well asked him if he would join. The NCO told of a recent para-rescue jump to rescue passengers from a Canadian Pacific Airline crash near Penticton, British

F/L Wynne, kneeling, practices with the Aldis signalling lamp under an instructor's watchful eye.

Columbia. He said they could have done with the help of a physician.

When Wynne dropped paratroops in England during war-time parachute training he thought they were crazy and said that he would never jump out of a serviceable aircraft, and only if it were on fire, or in a situation where he could not find a field on which to land, such as over mountains. But as training progressed, he got to enjoy it!

While SMO at RCAF Station Comox, British Columbia during the period 1952 to 1954, S/L Wynne took part in two "operational jumps." The first was in the coast range of the Rockies to rescue an injured geologist in July 1952 and the second in June 1953 to tend a seriously ill officer of the Royal Canadian Mounted Police at Coppermine in the Northwest Territories. This latter jump was necessary because no aircraft could land on the thin ice of the lake as it was just about to break up.

The patient had a large pleural effusion, which Wynne suspected was tuberculosis and this was later confirmed. With the help of a para-rescue

Medical Assistant named Sergeant Jack Strachan, S/L Wynne aspirated the lung to make breathing easier and then stayed with the patient until the lake was sufficiently open to allow an RCMP Noorduyn Norseman float plane to come in and evacuate the patient and team to Yellowknife in the Northwest Territories. Wynne recalls that the situation called for basic medicine with no X-rays. There was a quick turn-around at Yellowknife to a Beech 18 "Expeditor" aircraft for the last leg of the trip to Edmonton, Alberta, where the patient could receive definitive care.

S/L Wynne was sent to England in 1954 for postgraduate studies. He completed his MB,BS degree work in 1955 and was posted to the RCAF No. 1 Air Division for duties as Senior Medical Officer at 3 (Fighter) Wing Zweibrucken, Germany. This was one of four RCAF fighter wings in France and Germany with the Air Division Headquarters at Metz, France. The medical facilities were required to provide full care to the Air Force members as well as to their families.

On his return to Canada in 1958, S/L Wynne's rotated between the Navy hospital, HMCS Stadacona, Camp Hill Hospital and Victoria General Hospital at Halifax, Nova Scotia for duty and postgraduate studies until 1964.

The next three years, 1964 to 1967, were busy but satisfying as S/L Wynne took on the duties of SMO RCAF Hospital Cold Lake, Alberta. RCAF Station Cold Lake was the largest operational training base in Canada and the medical facility provided full care for the Air Force as well as their dependents. This facility was later reorganized as a Canadian Forces Hospital and Wing Commander Wynne became its Commanding Officer.

Lieutenant-Colonel (LCol) Wynne came to Ottawa, Ontario in 1967 for duties at the National Defence Medical Centre and for a short time on the staff of the Surgeon General in the Directorate of Medical Treatment Services. Neither of these appointments was particularly satisfying, so, in 1970 Wynne was very pleased to move on to Air Transport Command with the rank of Colonel and the appointment of Command Surgeon. The Command Headquarters (ATCHQ) was located at Trenton, Ontario. When the Canadian Forces reorganized and the Canadian Forces Training Systems Headquarters was located at Trenton, replacing ATCHQ, Colonel Wynne stayed in Trenton as its Command Surgeon. However, he was involved in the planning for staffing the new headquarters in Winnipeg, Manitoba.

In December 1976, Colonel Wynne retired and eventually moved back to British Columbia. He remained in the Canadian Forces Supplementary Reserve until 24 March 1982. There were no planned activities for the Supplementary

Reserve and Col Wynne felt that he might not be physically fit, so he asked that his name be removed from the Reserve list.

During the summer of 1997, Dr.Wynne was asked to man a display at the Canadian War Museum on Search and Rescue. This was one of the Canadian Forces displays put on for the summer months. Regular Force personnel could not be spared due to commitments, postings, etc so they asked the Public Relations Association for volunteers. Wynne offered to do two weeks in July. His para-rescue experiences were valuable in informing the public of the work of Search and Rescue Technicians and of their medical training.

Next to the display was a Canadair Tutor jet aircraft currently used in flying training. Dick Wynne's flying experience allowed him to fill for the Tutor demonstration team when they were on a break. He took great delight in explaining the functions of the various instruments and equipment to the young people visiting the aircraft and sat in its cockpit. The Tutor is essentially the same as the aircraft on which Wynne had learned to fly.

Dick Wynne was married in Llanwrda, Wales in 1947 to Celia Jones, a nurse at the hospital where he was a student. Dick and Celia have three children - Elaine, born in Vancouver 1949 when Wynne was interning. She graduated from UBC MD, 1977. She is in Vancouver, British Columbia. Michael, born in Vancouver in 1951, is manager of the Holiday Inn Express in Kelowna, British Columbia. John, born in Zweibrucken, Germany in 1957, lives in London, England where he works at the Prince of Wales School of Architecture and does computer music.

Wynne's retirement activities include family history and genealogy. He is also involved in military history. As a hobby, Dick makes wooden toys with moving parts, all just wood and glue, for grandchildren and some other little people. It is great fun.

Summary of Achievements
Officer of the Most Venerable Order of St. John of Jerusalem (OStJ)
Canadian Forces Decoration (CD)
1939-45 Star
France Germany Star
Defence of Britain Medal
Canadian Volunteer Service Medal and Maple Leaf Clasp
War Medal
Special Services Medal - NATO
Bachelor of Medicine, Bachelor of Surgery (MB BS)
Member of the Royal College of Surgeons (England) (MRCS)
Licentiate Royal College of Physicians (London) (LRCP)

CHAPTER 5
THE PHYSICIANS

WWII and POST-WAR MEDICAL OFFICERS

- **Colonel Ada M. Arthur née Steele**
  First female Medical Officer to command the Canadian Forces Medical Service School.

- **Colonel J. Keith Besley**
  A war-time Hurricane and Spitfire pilot who flew in Tehran, later a doctor who served in Korea, Europe and Canada.

- **Commander F. John Blatherwick**
  Served in the Reserves of all three services and later named to the Order of Canada.

- **Group Captain Hugh Bright**
  An early RCAF war-time doctor; the first Commandant of the National Defence Medical Centre in 1961.

- **Wing Commander Roy Brown**
  Trained as a Royal Navy Pilot at Kingston, served as an RCAF psychiatrist; carried the Olympic Flame in Kingston in 1976.

- **Capt. Wilhelmina de Groot**
  Survived the C-130 Hercules crash at Alert with injuries, but continued to treat casualties.

- **Wing Commander Gerald M. FitzGibbon**
  Interest in aircrew cardiology research led to specialty in this field. Transferred to the public service as the consultant cardiologist at the National Defence Medical Centre. An Officer of the Order of Military Merit and a Member of the Order of Canada.

- **Colonel Robert E. Forgie**
  Served in Libya as a Medical Officer, joined the RCAF and later became a specialist in ophthalmology.

- **Surgeon-Captain Ross B. Irwin**
  A war-time flight engineer awarded the Distinguished Flying Medal, became a physician and served in Korea, Europe and Canada.

- **Lieutenant-Colonel R.B. "Bud" Pritchard**
  The only Medical Officer with a Master of Science in Nuclear Medicine.

- **Wing Commander A.G. "Sandy" Watson**
  Last RCAF doctor to leave England at the end of WWII. Became manager of the RCAF Olympic hockey team, The RCAF Flyers; member of the Order of Canada.

ADA M. ARTHUR NÉE STEELE
SSStJ, CD, MD
COLONEL

Ada Steele was born in Sarnia, Ontario. She completed her medical studies at McMaster University in Hamilton, Ontario in 1978 under the Medical Officer Training Plan and completed her internship at Dalhousie University in Halifax, Nova Scotia in 1979.

She served at Canadian Forces Base (CFB) Summerside, Prince Edward Island as a Captain General Duty Medical Officer and Flight Surgeon until 1980 and then completed one year of residency in general surgery at Canadian Forces Hospital Halifax and Dalhousie University at Halifax.

In 1981, Captain Arthur was posted to CFB Comox, British Columbia as a Flight Surgeon. While at this base in 1982, Ada was promoted to Major and was appointed Senior Medical Officer at Canadian Forces Station Masset, British Columbia. Masset is located on the northern point of the Queen Charlotte Islands and is a radio listening post for the Canadian Forces. The hospital, however, was required to care for all the military and dependent personnel as well as some members of the local community, of which a large number were first nations Haida.

Col Ada M. Arthur

In 1983, Major Arthur returned to CFB Comox as the Base Surgeon. Comox was a busy flying base that conducted all-weather flying operations as part of the North American air defences and search and rescue operations for the west coast.

A series of brief postings followed Major Arthur's stay in Comox. In 1985, she took on duties at Maritime Forces Pacific Headquarters at Esquimalt, British Columbia as the Deputy Regional Surgeon. In 1986, Ada was called to join the staff of the Surgeon General in Ottawa, Ontario where she was assigned to staff duties in the Directorate of Preventive Medicine. In 1987 she became the Medical Officer Career Manager in National Defence Headquarters, a position she retained until 1989.

With a promotion to Lieutenant-Colonel (LCol), Ada moved to the Surgeon General's office to serve in the Directorate of Health Care Personnel Training and Development. This last assignment was good preparation for her next task, which was to assume command of the Canadian Forces Medical Service School (CFMSS) at CFB Borden in 1992. LCol Arthur was the first female to hold the appointment of Commandant of the CFMSS.

In 1994, LCol Arthur was appointed Deputy Chief of Staff Medicine at Maritime Forces Pacific Headquarters at Esquimalt, British Columbia, an appointment she only held for a year when she was promoted to full Colonel and moved to Air Command Headquarters in Winnipeg, Manitoba as Command Surgeon.

Colonel Arthur retired from the Canadian Forces in October 1997 and returned to live in Victoria, British Columbia with her husband, Rad, who is a retired Canadian Forces air navigator.

Summary of Achievements

Serving Sister of the Most Venerable Order of the Hospital of St. John of Jerusalem (SSStJ)
Canadian Forces Decoration (CD)
125th Anniversary of the Confederation of Canada Medal
Doctor of Medicine, McMaster University - 1978 (MD)
Flight Surgeon - 1980

JOHN KEITH BESLEY
KStJ, CD, MD
COLONEL

John Keith Besley was born on 4 September 1919 in Shelburne, Ontario, a small farming town north of Toronto. He was the third child in a family of eight. His paternal grandparents came to Canada in 1850 from Devonshire, England. His maternal relatives were United Empire Loyalists. Besley completed his schooling at Shelburne Public and High School and, in 1938, left home to become an apprentice in pharmacy in Toronto.

On 10 September 1940, barely 21 years old, he joined the RCAF, served a few months on guard duty and then began pilot training. Keith attended the Initial Flying Training School at the Eglinton Hunt Club on Avenue Road in Toronto. This location eventually housed the famous RCAF Institute of Aviation Medicine. He successfully qualified as a pilot-trainee and did his elementary flying training on the Fleet Finch aircraft at London, Ontario in January and February 1941. Service flying training was completed on the North American Harvard at No. 8 Service Flying

Flying Officer J. Keith Besley

Training School at Moncton, New Brunswick, qualifying Keith to wings standard and he received his pilot's wings and a commission in June 1941.

Now a Pilot Officer, Keith was posted to RCAF Station Trenton, Ontario as a flight instructor pending his posting overseas in February 1942. In England, Besley went to an operational training unit for conversion training on the

171

Hawker Hurricane, the pre-eminent fighter aircraft of the Royal Air Force (RAF). Training completed, Flying Officer (F/O) Besley was posted to the Middle East as part of the formation of the British 8th Army in Egypt.

Keith's sea journey to Africa was twice interrupted by the threat of German submarines and the ship took refuge in Ireland. When it finally got underway, the ship made for the west coast of Africa and made port on the African Gold Coast, now the country of Ghana, after a 32-day crossing. F/O Besley had to continue his journey, backtracking to Cairo on an RAF Shorts Sunderland flying boat for a flight across Africa. When Keith finally arrived in Cairo he was immediately admitted to hospital with severe jaundice and malaria. Three weeks later, F/O Besley was well enough to join the famous 74th Squadron RAF in Alexandria and took part in the battle that was just beginning between General Montgomery and General Rommel at El Alamein. Although air combat was rare as the allies had air superiority, there was a great deal of ground strafing amidst tremendous dust and sandy conditions. Fine sand rose as high as 10,000 feet due to military activity and the movement of thousands of tanks and vehicles. The Squadron continued forward until early December 1942, when 74th Squadron was ordered up to Iran (Tehran) to join the 10th British Army. The reason for the move was the possibility of a Russian defeat at Stalingrad. The Allied troops were to prevent further advancement by German troops across the country.

Conditions in Iran were near unbearable. The pilots were billeted in an old unheated horse stable at temperatures near zero degrees and musty army canvas stretchers for beds. Stretchers were supported on empty petrol cans to keep them off the ground and to keep rats out of the bed. The mattress consisted of folded army blankets and more were piled on top to try to keep from freezing. The rations were entirely British, actually consisting of a daily allotment of bully beef and hard tack. The squadron expected to have a very lean Christmas, but a supply aircraft arrived the day before Christmas with thirty geese and the squadron enjoyed a wonderful goose dinner on December 25th.

The 74th Squadron along with the 274th South African Squadron remained in this position for three months. The Russians wanted these Squadrons to give them their Hurricanes, but the squadron commanders refused. The Russians declared they could pay for aircraft, but it was more difficult to repay lost lives.

For their refusal, the Russians would not allow the Squadrons to go into combat for them on the Stalingrad front.

In March 1943, orders came through for the Squadrons to fly to Abadan on the Persian Gulf to do sea patrol over the Gulf where Japanese submarines had been sighted. Abadan, at that time, had the second largest oil refinery in the world and was vital to the Allied war effort. Abadan was also the marshalling point for lend-lease shipments to the Russians. Convoys of vehicles and aircraft passed onward to Russia around the clock. It was a magnificent effort by the Allies.

An advance party was sent from Tehran to set up a base at Abadan from which to operate two flights of three Hurricanes, for a total of six airplanes. For navigation purposes, the two flights of fighters were led on this cross-country journey by a Bristol Blenheim bomber. There were a number of problems with this operation. The route crossed 14,000-foot-high mountains and the fighters, normally used for low level operations, were not equipped with oxygen. Oxygen is required at altitudes over 10,000 feet to prevent hypoxia. The crossing, therefore would require precise daily meteorological reports to allow flying at a lower altitude and through mountain passes to stay below 10,000 feet. But weather reports were non-existent. The radio systems between the bomber and the fighters were not compatible. Fighter pilots could talk to each other, but had to use hand signals to communicate with the bomber. On 24 March 1943, conditions were bright and clear in Tehran and the aircraft were ordered airborne. The fine weather lasted for about half an hour and then a bank of dense, thick cloud enveloped the airplanes. The aircraft continued to climb, passing 19,000 feet before breaking clear. Two Hurricanes were lost in the climb alone. Nothing but disaster lay ahead. The remaining Hurricane pilots were suffering severe hypoxia and all its dangers. The Blenheim crew continued flying on the planned route, unaware of these problem and landed safely at Abadan but without any Hurricanes. Those that remained had come down at various places throughout the lower part of Iran. Besley did a wheels-up crash landing in the mountains at a village called Shushtar and spent eight days with the natives. He was able to send a message of his whereabouts by a native runner down the Anglo-Iranian pipeline to Basra and he was rescued by an RAF maintenance crew who drove into the mountains and took him and his aircraft back to Basra. A full account of this escapade was published in a book called *We Few* by the Canadian Fighter Pilots Association in Ottawa.

The Squadron was regrouped and flew patrols over the Persian Gulf from an RAF station in Iraq. From one extreme to another, the temperatures here were among the hottest in the world. The squadron endured heat in the range of 120 to 130 degrees Fahrenheit for the entire period of deployment. The aircraft became so hot that they could only be flown prior to 6 a.m. The rest of the day was spent in underground barracks to escape the tremendous heat.

The squadron was posted back to the western desert in June 1943 to an airdrome at kilo 10 on the Mediterranean Sea. Convoy patrol was the order of the day but extensive flying training was carried out to convince Air Force Headquarters in Alexandria, Egypt of the Squadron's capabilities. As a result, they were rewarded with brand new Spitfire Mk IXs and bade farewell to their trusty Hurricanes.

In late September 1943, Churchill, at the urging of Stalin to appease the Russian people, decided to strike a blow to the underbelly of Europe. Many wonderful men died and hundreds were taken prisoner in this operation, but it was not until thirty years later that those involved in this assault would realize that it was just a feint with no real military value. The 74th Squadron RAF and the 274th Squadron South Africa were ordered to fly to Cyprus and on to Cos Island - a tiny island in the Dodecanese chain in the Aegean Sea. The ground crew, along with the British Durham Light Infantry, landed on the neighbouring Island of Leros.

The plan was to advance through Greece and create a second front. The two squadrons with their new Spitfires landed on the evening of 12 September 1943 at the salt flats of Cos Island. Petrol and supplies were to be dropped in early the next morning by a transport squadron commanded by Group Captain Max Aitken, son of Lord Beaverbrook. Squadron pilots waited on a hilltop throughout the night waiting for their supplies to arrive. Fog settled in and shore visibility was nil. At 5 a.m. the sound of droning motors awakened the sleeping pilots. They were horrified to find not the expected airdrop but a large host of gray uniformed German assault troops breaking through the fog. The motor noise was their landing craft.

The pilots were completely cut off from their aircraft and fled rapidly on foot across the island. A few others fled into the hills on Cos. The pilots succeeded in running the three miles to the opposite shore where a British yacht, converted to look like an old Greek freighter, was waiting. It took off at once for the shore of Turkey, unloaded the pilots to a British destroyer and the squadron was back at home base in the desert thirty-six hours after leaving, but minus one flight commander and their new Spitfires. All members of the ground crew, including the Medical Officer, who won the Military Cross on Leros Island, were either killed or taken prisoner.

The Germans knew the value of Cos and Leros. They had been forewarned of the attack and they knew these two islands were suitable bases for the Royal Air Force and also that there was a harbour for the Navy. If the operation had been successful it would have meant freedom for the Greek people. Consequently the Germans threw everything into the effort to stop it, and succeeded. It appears that the Allied attack was never meant to succeed.

After a short time back in the desert, the squadron was returned to England, given new Spitfires, and trained to knock out V-1 Buzz-Bombs in flight as they approached England from the continent.

F/O Besley, following an accident, was sent home in March 1944. He married Shirley Bell a month later in Toronto. The injury to his left shoulder required surgery, which was done at the old Christie Street Hospital in Toronto. Following recovery, Flight Lieutenant Besley was posted to RCAF Station Uplands near Ottawa as a flight instructor once again. He applied to go to the Pacific, but that war was coming to an end following the bombing of Hiroshima and Nagasaki, so he was discharged to the Air Force Reserve.

Keith Besley applied for admission to the Faculty of Medicine at Toronto University in 1945 and was accepted. The Department of Veterans Affairs provided tuition and a subsistence allowance of $80 a month for a married veteran, which didn't leave much spending money to support a family. In 1949, the Royal Canadian Army Medical Corps (RCAMC) approached these veteran students and offered them a commission as 2nd Lieutenants with full pay and promotion to Captain on graduation. The RCAF had no such plan. A number of students accepted this plan and, after graduation in 1950, they continued their service in the RCAMC.

Captain Besley began his internship at St. Michael's Hospital in Toronto,

175

but after three months interning, the Korean conflict broke out and he was again in a war zone, this time as a Battalion Medical Officer. There were a number of his classmates called upon at the same time and these veterans of WW II were the mainstay of the Medical Service during the Korean conflict. Besley was "mentioned in dispatches" for his outstanding services in Korea.

On his return from Korea he completed his internship at St. Michael's Hospital in Toronto. Then, drawing on his Korean experiences, Major Besley was sent to Québec City where he spent two years organizing and training Field Ambulances units for service in Europe and in Korea. At the end of his time in Québec City, Major Besley returned to Toronto and began surgical training, primarily at the famous Sunnybrook Hospital, which had been built at the end of WW II to care for war veterans.

After three years of extensive training in surgery, he was posted to Europe to be the surgeon for the Canadian Army in Northerwest Germany. He was situated at Iserlohn in a British Army Hospital serving the Canadian Army and the British Army on the Rhine. This was an exciting experience; there was much major surgery and the British, in the early 1950s, did not have enough money to buy and supply up-to-date surgical equipment. It was a tremendous time to learn to do things the hard way and it was also a time to travel Europe with his family and see the beauty of the different European countries.

Major Besley and his family returned to Toronto and he completed his fellowship examinations in general surgery and was immediately posted to the one remaining isolated post for a full time surgeon - Whitehorse General Hospital in the Yukon Territory. He was the Chief Surgeon and Senior Medical Officer (SMO) for the Northwest Highway System (NWHS). This turned out to be one of the most exciting postings of his career.

Major Besley looked after all the military personnel and their families, provided surgical services to the native people and for all other Yukon inhabitants. Providing surgical services to the native Indians proved to be a real problem on occasions and the living conditions in the territory brought with it many interesting surgical problems. Every morning brought a new and often different cases to deal with, ranging from open skull surgery, open chest surgery and cardiac arrests, to hysterectomies and cesarean sections. Keith considered himself the last of the truly general surgeons known in the Royal Canadian

Army Medical Corps.

The Yukon stretched from mile zero in Alberta for more than 1,200 miles to the Alaska border. It was a dusty gravel road in summer and snow covered and dangerous in the winter. There was never-ending road repair to rebuild damage from washouts and landslides. It was a challenging posting and the land was exciting and beautiful with unexcelled fishing, camping and hunting.

While in the Yukon, he was also instrumental in teaching first aid to the workers at maintenance camps, the Armed Forces and the Boy Scouts. For this tremendous task he was given a formal Vote of Thanks from the Most Venerable Order of the Hospital of St. John of Jerusalem and admitted to the Order in the grade of the Serving Brother. He remained active in the Order from then until the completion of his career. He was promoted to Lieutenant-Colonel while in the Yukon.

In 1963 he was posted to the new National Defence Medical Centre (NCMC) in Ottawa, Ontario where he became Assistant Chief of Surgery under Colonel A.B. Powell.

Keith wanted to specialize his surgical training, so he returned to surgical training in Urology in 1965 at the Ottawa Civic Hospital and received his specialty in this field in 1967. During his specialty training in Urology, he was part of the newly formed Urology Transplantation Unit and participated for a number of years in this unit at the Ottawa Civic Hospital. He was also a member of the team that carried out the first kidney transplant in Ottawa and the first father-to-daughter kidney transplant in Ottawa.

Colonel J. Keith Besley

Besley was promoted to Colonel in 1966 and became Chief of Urology at NDMC in 1967, a position he held until his retirement in December 1985. His was the only urology service in the

177

Canadian Forces, so Colonel Besley's practice was large and diverse.

He continued his first aid work and in 1981 became Chief Medical Officer for St. John Ambulance in Canada and was elevated in the Order to the grade Knight of Grace in 1985. He was serving on Chapter of the Order of St. John in Ottawa at the time of his death.

Early in his surgical practice of urology, he realized the need for control of bleeding in the post operative phase of transurethral prostatectomy, so he designed and had manufactured a hypothermia machine, which proved extremely efficient in the control of bleeding in the post-op period. The hypothermia machine was so good that the Head of Urology at the University of Ottawa borrowed it when he carried out a prostatectomy on one of his more famous patients, a gentleman who was then Governor General of Canada.

Keith Besley lived with a number of serious disabilities. He had bilateral total hip replacements and back fusions, resulting from wartime injuries and this led to his retirement from medical practice at age 65. He was happily married for forty-five years and had two sons. He was a clinical teacher in surgery at Ottawa University for twenty years. He died on 6 October 1998.

Summary of Achievements
Knight of the Most Venerable Order of the Hospital of St. John of Jerusalem (KStJ)
Canadian Forces Decoration (CD)
1939 - 45 Star
Africa Star
Italy Star
Defence Medal
Canadian Volunteer Services Medal
Korea Medal (with Mention in Despatches)
United Nations Service Medical (Korea)
Special Services Medal - NATO
Queen Elizabeth II Coronation Medal (1953)
Doctor of Medicine, University of Toronto, 1950 (MD)
Fellow Royal College of Surgeons Canada (FRCSC)
Note
Although this work is primarily to recognize RCAF Medical Branch members, Keith Besley's wartime RCAF service and his continuing interest in that service warrants his inclusion.

JOHN BLATHERWICK
CM, CSTJ, CD, MD
COMMANDER

John Blatherwick started his military career in 1961 with the Governor General's Foot Guards in the rank of guardsman. However, his association with the military predates this. John proudly admits to being an Air Force brat who lived for some time in Permanent Married Quarters (PMQs) at RCAF Station Rockcliffe. In 1963, he joined the RCAF University Reserve Training Plan at 107 University of Alberta Squadron. In 1967, while attending medical school in Edmonton, he joined 418 Squadron serving as medical officer. During his internship in Calgary in 1970 he joined the Royal Canadian Army Medical Corps and served as the Officer Commanding the medical company in their reserve medical unit. On graduation, he joined the naval reserve in 1971 at HMCS Discovery. He served in the reserves for twenty-six years before retiring in 1997.

Flying Officer John Blatherwick with his brother Brian as an Aircraftman 1ˢᵗ Class and father Earl Blatherwick a Warrant Officer 1ˢᵗ Class and the longest serving warrant officer in the RCAF.

Commander Blatherwick served as the Assistant Secretary General

179

(Canada) and Vice-President (Canada) of the Confederation of Interallied Reserve Medical Officers (CIOMR) in each appointment for three years. His outstanding contribution to the CIOMR earned him the CIOMR Gold Medal.

Dr. Blatherwick was admitted to the Order of Canada in 1994 in the grade of Member for his work as the Medical Officer of Health for the City of Vancouver. The citation read:

"As Vancouver's Medical Health Officer, he has been the moving force behind a number of important programs, including the move to abolish smoking in the workplace, and especially those involving youth, people with disabilities, and people living with AIDS. He is also involved in educating health professionals, as well as being active in his community."

Commander Blatherwick served a term as President of the Defence Medical Association of Canada from 1988 to 1989. This Association, an affiliate of the Conference of Defence Associations, supports serving members of the Canadian Forces Medical Service both Regular Force and Reserves. It has Branches located throughout Canada.

From 1989 to 1990, Dr. Blatherwick was the Provincial Commissioner of St. John Ambulance in British Columbia. St. John Ambulance is the uniformed arm of The Most Venerable Order of the Hospital of St. John of Jerusalem. The familiar black uniformed members are highly visible at public functions to provide first aid to the general public. The Provincial Commissioner directs these operations for the province. In recognition of his work in this field, John Blatherwick was admitted to the Order of St. John and promoted through the grades to Commander.

John Blatherwick authored several books, including *Canadian Orders, Decorations and Medals, Honors and Awards to the RCAF (also RCN and Canadian Army), 1000 Brave Canadians* and *A History of the Airlines of Canada.*

Summary of Achievements
Member of the Order of Canada (CM)
Commander of the Most Venerable Order of the Hospital of St. John of Jerusalem (CStJ)
Canadian Forces Decoration (CD)
Doctor University of Alberta - 1969 (MD)
Diploma of Public Health (DPH)
Fellow Royal College of Physicians Canada (FRCPC)
Clinical Professor University of British Columbia
Medical Health Officer - Vancouver/Richmond Health Board
Note
This work was intended to recognize RCAF Medical Branch members, however Commander Blatherwick's RCAF service and his outstanding achievements seem to warrant his inclusion.

Hugh Bright
SBStJ, CD, MD
Group Captain

Hugh **Bright** was born 9 May 1911 and got his primary and secondary education in Toronto, Ontario, graduating from the University of Toronto with a degree in medicine in 1936. Dr. Bright was in private practice, but he felt the need to get involved in the war effort, so he joined the Royal Canadian Air Force in 1942. Flight Lieutenant Bright's interests in aviation medicine were soon recognized, so, in 1944, he was brought to the RCAF Institute of Aviation Medicine in Toronto to conduct medical research.

Following the end of WWII, the RCAF reorganized into a peace-time regional command structure. Squadron Leader Bright became the Principal Medical Officer of Northwestern Air Command at Edmonton, Alberta in 1947. This was followed by another Command appointment in 1955 as the Staff Officer Medical Services (SOMS) at 1 Air Division in Metz, France, responsible for medical services for the four RCAF fighter wings in France and Germany. Wing Commander (W/C) Bright held this appointment until 1958 when he returned to Canada to take postgraduate studies.

G/C Hugh Bright

During the period 1958 to 1960, W/C Bright attended the University of Toronto's public health program, earning a Diploma in Public Health. He was promoted to Group Captain (G/C) on his graduation and given command of the newly built National Defence Medical Centre in Ottawa, Ontario. G/C Bright became the hospital's first Commandant in 1961, an appointment he held until his retirement in 1967.

Dr. Bright was the medical superintendent of Victoria Hospital in London Ontario until his retirement from medical practice. Circulatory problems led to a lower limb amputation in 1976 and periods of hospitalization at the National Defence Medical Centre, where he died on 28 December 1988.

Dr. Bright's son, Hugh, graduated in medicine from the University of Toronto in 1968 and, after a short time in the Canadian Forces Medical Service, went into private practice in Kingston, Ontario.

Summary of Achievements
Serving Brother of the Most Venerable Order of the Hospital of St. John of Jerusalem (SBStJ)
Canadian Forces Decoration (CD)
1939 - 1945 Star
Atlantic Star
Canadian Volunteer Service Medal with Maple Leaf
War Medal, 1939 - 1945
Special Service Medal - NATO
Diploma Public Health (DPH)
Diploma Hospital Administration (DHA)
Fellow of American Board of Preventive Medicine (FABPM)
Diploma American Board of Physical Medicine (DABPM)

Note
This biographical sketch has been compiled with assistance of Mrs. Bright, G/C Bright's widow, and is incomplete.

ROY BROWN
CD, MD
WING COMMANDER

Roy Brown was born in Kilmarnock, Scotland in 1925, where he received his early education at Kilmarnock Academy and Aberdeen Grammar School. He graduated from high school in 1943 and, at age 17, joined the Fleet Air Arm of the Royal Navy as a trainee pilot. In 1944, he came to Canada to complete his flying training under the British Commonwealth Air Training Plan (BCATP)'s No. 31 Service Flying Training School at Kingston, Ontario. He graduated in June of that year with his naval pilot's wings and a commission.

On his return to England, Brown underwent operational training on Vought F-4U Corsair aircraft. These aircraft were in service on the Royal Navy carrier, HMS Victorious, stationed in the area of Ceylon, now Sri Lanka. Therefore, Brown was flown out to Ceylon to join his squadron and complete his operational training before joining his ship. Lieutenant Brown served with the British Pacific Fleet until September 1945, a month after V-J Day, which marked the end of the war with Japan.

W/C Roy Brown

Roy was demobilized from the Royal Navy in 1946. He took the opportunity to study medicine, using his veterans' benefits to attend Medical School at Aberdeen University. Dr. Brown graduated MB, ChB in 1951.

In June 1952, the Royal Canadian Air Force was recruiting doctors from the UK for its expanding force. Roy was one those enrolled as a medical officer in the RCAF. Flight Lieutenant (F/L) Brown returned to Canada, bringing with him his wife, Meg, and daughter, Lesley, to his new post at RCAF Station Uplands near Ottawa. The Cold War was at a fever pitch and Uplands, as one of the stations of Air Defence Command, had a high level of flying activity, flying air defence patrols north of the capital in all-weather interceptors. F/L Brown's pilot experience, combined with his medical skills were invaluable in working with young aircrew members and in flying accident investigation.

In 1953, F/L Brown was asked to bring these skills to a new appointment on the staff of the Director General Medical Services (Air) at Air Force Headquarters in Ottawa. Here, F/L Brown served with Air Commodore Corbet and Group Captains Nelson, Caldbick and Brown. His work earned him a promotion in 1954 to Squadron Leader (S/L).

A year later, in 1955, S/L Brown was one of the first to be offered postgraduate training in a specialty of his choice. He trained in psychiatry at various hospitals in Toronto and was awarded the Diploma in Psychiatry in 1958. This resulted in another promotion to Wing Commander (W/C) and a posting to Halifax, Nova Scotia as the Staff Officer Medical Services at Maritime Air Command Headquarters. W/C Brown combined the duties of providing medical services to air force stations in the maritime region with clinical services in psychiatry.

W/C Brown and his family, now of three children, were transferred to Metz, France in 1959 where he served as the Senior Medical Officer at the 1 Air Division Headquarters for four years. When the Brown family returned to Canada in 1963, it was to take up a clinical post at the National Defence Medical Centre in Ottawa. During this tour of duty, W/C Brown completed another program in psychiatry earning him the Certificate of the Royal College of Psychiatry (Canada) and later a fellowship from the College.

In 1968, W/C Brown was transferred to Canadian Forces Hospital Kingston at Kingston, Ontario. He was appointed Chief of Psychiatry, Base Surgeon and Deputy Commanding Officer until the hospital was closed in 1975. At that time, he was moved to Training Command Headquarters in Trenton, Ontario as Senior Staff Officer (Medical). Dr. Brown retired in February 1976 to accept the position of Medical Director, Regional Psychiatric Centre (Ontario), with the Federal Correctional Service of Canada in Kingston.

He retired again in 1980, but soon began work again as a contract consultant at Canadian Forces Base Kingston and at Kingston Penitentiary, Warkwork Institution, Bath Institution and the Prison for Women. Roy finally retired from clinical practice in 1996.

Roy's interests in Air Force and athletics have involved him in a number of projects such as:

•Rowing Blue and Founder Member of Aberdeen University Boat Club 1949 - 1951

• MO i/c Medical Rescue Force at the Sailing Olympics in Kingston in 1976

•Carrying the Olympic Flame in Kingston in 1976

•Supervising the building of the Harvard Memorial at RCAF Association's 416 Wing Kingston to honor all those who served at No. 31 Service Flying Training School as part of the British Commonwealth Air Training Plan).

He remains active in several associations and is an avid golfer and curler. Since 1990, he has organized and participated in seven golf-tours of Scotland and has played nearly fifty of the top courses, including several rounds at the famed Old Course in St. Andrews.

Summary of Achievements

Canadian Forces Decoration (CD)
War Medal, 1939 - 1945
1939 - 1945 Star
Pacific Star
Burma Star
Defence Medal
Special Services Medal - NATO
Bachelor of Medicine, Aberdeen, Scotland, 1951 MB -
Bachelor of Chirugie, Aberdeen, Scotland, 1951 Ch B -
1965 - Certificate Royal College of Psychiatry (Canada) [CRCP(C)]
1967 - Fellow, Royal College of Physicians (Canada) [FRCP(C)]
Diploma, Psychiatry (D Psych)

WILHELMINA HELENE DE GROOT
MD
CAPTAIN

Wilhelmina Helene de Groot was born and raised in Collingwood, Ontario. She graduated from high school with honors and entered the University of Toronto with an academic scholarship. She maintained the scholarship through two years at the University of Toronto and was accepted in 1986 into the Faculty of Medicine at Queen's University in Kingston, Ontario. She joined the Medical Officer Training Plan of the Canadian Forces during her second year and completed Basic Officer Training in the summer of 1988.

In the spring of 1990, Dr. de Groot completed her M.D. and started her internship. This included two-month rotations in various specialties, including six months spent in Thunder Bay studying surgery, pediatrics and family medicine, and in Oshawa, where she delivered sixty babies.

On completion of internship in June 1991, she was posted to Canadian Forces Base Trenton, now known as 8 Wing, as a General Duty Medical Officer. The first summer she was the Medical Officer for the Air Cadet Training Camps at CFB

Capt Wilhelmina DeGroot

Trenton. On 14 September 1991 she married George Iwanchyshyn, a classmate from medical school.

Six weeks later, on 30 October 1991, Captain DeGroot was on a special assignment to Canadian Forces Station Alert in the North West Territories to review the work of the Medical Assistants who work there on six-month rotations. She was to be there for one week but the Lockheed C-130 Hercules transport aircraft in which she and twelve other passengers and five aircrew were travelling crashed on the approach to the base. Ten passengers and four crew survived but the pilot died of hypothermia before rescue crews arrived thirty-two hours later. Rescue efforts, which included aircraft from the United States and Canada, were hampered by blizzard conditions and rough terrain in total seasonal darkness. Captain DeGroot suffered a fracture of her right ankle that was subsequently reduced at the National Defence Medical Centre in Ottawa on her return. Despite her injuries in the crash, Captain DeGroot gave whatever medical aid she could to the other survivors.

After four weeks she was back to full duty in Trenton. In recognition of her actions at the crash site she was awarded the Air Command Commander's Commendation in May 1992. In the summer of 1993 she returned to Canadian Forces Base Alert with her husband and a group of crash survivors and family for a ceremony unveiling a monument to those killed in the accident.

In the spring of 1992 she completed the Flight Surgeon's course at Defence and Civil Institute on Environmental Medicine in Toronto. This included training in the altitude chambers and centrifuge and one week flying with 424 Squadron, Search and Rescue at CFB Trenton.

In April 1993 she completed a tropical medicine course and in early 1994 was assigned to Nairobi, Kenya for six months as a Medical Officer supporting the airlift of humanitarian aid into Somalia.

In May 1993, Captain Degroot addressed the Advisory Group for Aerospace Research and Development (AGARD) conference in Victoria, British Columbia. She presented the paper *Survival from a C-130 Accident in the Canadian High Arctic*. The advisory group had researchers from NATO presenting papers on *The Support of Air Operations under Extreme Hot and Cold Weather Conditions*. Captain DeGroot was asked to present her paper again at the International Aerospace Medical Association (ASMA) meeting in Toronto.

In April 1994, when her first child, Mark, was born, she left the Canadian Forces and established, together with her husband, a private practice, in Etobicoke, Ontario. Her second child, Tamara, was born in April 1996. She is currently working part-time as a general practitioner which includes assisting at surgery at Etobicoke General Hospital.

Summary of Achievements
MD - Queen's University 1990

GERALD M. FITZGIBBON
CM, OMM, OSTJ, CD, MD
WING COMMANDER

Dr. Gerald FitzGibbon, clinician, cardiologist, clinical researcher, was closely associated with the Canadian Forces and its veterans for the forty-three years of his active professional life, eighteen of them in uniform, the remainder as a full-time DND civilian employee in a military hospital. Always with a military focus, he pursued excellence in diagnosing and treating cardiovascular disorders, providing optimal patient care, doing research into early detection and prompt treatment of heart disease and the long-term effectiveness of surgical and other interventional therapy.

Gerald FitzGibbon was born on 24 November, 1926 in La Paz, Bolivia, married Maud Eileen (Molly) Rouse on 21 February, 1949 and had daughters, Hilary Jane (1956) and Gillian Ruth (1959), and a grandson, Nicholas Michael Pacella (1984). He went to school in South America, England, Malaysia and South Africa. His undergraduate medical education was undertaken at the Royal College of Surgeons in Ireland, Dublin, Eire, and his postgraduate studies in Dublin, Toronto, London and Kingston, Ontario. He gained the following professional qualifications: Licentiate in Medicine, Surgery, and Midwifery,

W/C Gerald FitzGibbon receives the Order of Military Merit from His Excellency Governor General Jules Léger

Royal College of Surgeons in Ireland; Licentiate, Medical Council of Canada; Specialty Certification, Royal College of Physicians of Canada; Fellowships, Royal College of Physicians of Canada, American College of Cardiology,

American College of Physicians; Membership, Canadian Cardiovascular Society.

Dr. FitzGibbon joined the Royal Canadian Air Force in the UK, on 3 November, 1952, as a Flight Lieutenant Medical Officer, and entered Canada on 6 December, 1952. A temporary posting to Air Defence Command Headquarters at St-Hubert, Québec, introduced him to the Canadian winter on the bush survival course in Alberta and to aviation medicine on a course at the RCAF Institute of Aviation Medicine (IAM) in Toronto Ontario. This was succeeded by a posting to clinical duties at the Central Medical Establishment of the IAM, where he served from June 1953 until July 1956. There followed postgraduate training in internal medicine, with special emphasis on cardiology, in Toronto, London and Queen's University at Kingston, Ontario, the last associated with duties as a specialist internist at the Canadian Forces Hospital Kingston.

This was followed in August 1961 by his most important posting, to the National Defence Medical Centre (NDMC) in Ottawa. He was tasked to head

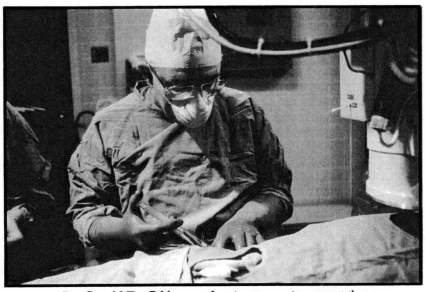

Dr. Gerald FitzGibbon performing an angiogram at the
National Defence Medical Centre

a department to investigate and treat cardiovascular disorders in this new hospital, an innovation for a Canadian military establishment. He directed the Cardio-Pulmonary Unit (CPU) as a regular force officer until August 1970 when he was released from the service to take up the same position immediately as a public servant (Medical Specialist 3).

On retirement from the public service in April 1989, Dr. FitzGibbon continued to work in the Cardio-Pulmonary Unit as a full-time consultant in cardiology until July 1994. Thereafter he was engaged in documenting a number of research studies, funded by a research grant from the Department of National Defence's Chief of Research and Development (CRAD), until he retired from active medical practice in 1996.

Other positions held during his career included Chief of Medical Staff, NDMC, member and chairman of many medical staff committees, associate professor of medicine (cardiology), University of Ottawa, and member, advisory board, University of Ottawa Heart Institute. He was also a Member of the Committee on Research Using Human Subjects, a Member of the Ad Hoc Committee Evaluating Biomedical Research, and Chairman, Committee on Biomedical Engineering Research, at the National Research Council of Canada.

On retirement he became Scientific Advisor to the University of Ottawa Heart Institute, Adjunct Professor of Cardiology at the University of Ottawa, Consultant, Canadian Forces Support Unit (Ottawa) Health Care Centre, Custodian of Administrative and Patient Records, and of 18,000 selective coronary angiograms, on some eight million feet of 35 mm cine film, legacies of the CPU at NDMC. He also continued to write and engage in research.

Contributions to Medical Care and Research
1. Set up a central RCAF electrocardiogram reading and filing system at the Institute of Aviation Medicine.
2. Introduced multi-channel ECG recording and Master's two-step exercise testing for cardiac ischaemia at the IAM.
3. Studied and publicly described a large series of aircrew members having ECG exercise testing at the IAM.
4. Made contacts with US and UK Military and civilian cardiac departments and was invited for valuable visits.
5. Organized the first International Conference on Aviation Cardiology at the

IAM on October 1955.

6. Organized the third Conference on Aviation Cardiology at NDMC, in June 1962.

7. Planned, organized and brought into full operation at NDMC, the first unit for the investigation and treatment of cardiovascular disease in a Canadian military hospital, and the first such department in any hospital in the Ottawa area (the University of Ottawa Cardiac Unit at the Ottawa Civic Hospital opened in 1969).

8. Offered a full range of investigation, including ambulatory ECG recording, echocardiography, stress-testing, cardiovascular catheterisation and selective coronary angiography, at the Cardio-Pulmonary Unit of NDMC, which became the cardiovascular referral facility for the Canadian Forces.

9. Set-up a sophisticated pulmonary function testing laboratory, which for years was unequalled in the Ottawa area.

10. Offered comprehensive medical treatment, including pacemaking, with an emphasis on lifestyle modification.

11. Established in 1963, in collaboration with Dr. G. David Hooper, a cardiac surgical consultant, a cardiac surgical program, which led to performance of a large number and a wide spectrum of cardiovascular operations at NDMC, from treatment of congenital and valvular lesions to myocardial revascularization.

12. Was responsible, with Dr. G. D. Hooper, for initiating at the NDMC in 1965, and accumulating the largest (with the exception of Dr. Vineberg's personal series), most complex, thoroughly studied and followed-up Canadian experience with the Vineberg myocardial revascularization procedure, which was the first effective surgical treatment for obstructive coronary artery disease and prefigured the coronary bypass operation.

13. When Dr. G. D. Hooper introduced the Ottawa cardiopulmonary bypass ('open-heart") surgical program in 1967, he began a continuing fruitful association with the Ottawa Civic Hospital and, later, with the University of Ottawa Cardiac Unit and its successor, Dr. W. J. Keon's University of Ottawa Heart Institute.

14. One year after its momentous introduction at the Cleveland Clinic, Dr. Hooper did a coronary bypass procedure, in 1969 at the Civic Hospital on a military patient investigated at NDMC, the first of a total of nine such NDMC patients with coronary disease, on whom he performed this

operation without a death.

15. In 1975, established the Clinical "Link Nurse" position at CPU/NDMC, the first in the Canadian Forces.

16. From 1982, referred patients with suitable coronary narrowing for percutaneous-trans-luminal coronary angioplasty (PTCA), initially to the Institute of Cardiology in Montreal, later to the University of Ottawa Heart Institute, this new procedure being contraindicated at NDMC due to absence of immediate access to "open heart" surgery.

17. Followed CPU patients with great care and maintained a long-term surveillance of those having coronary operations or other interventions at or through NDMC. In particular, the unique follow-up study of coronary bypass grafts, was unequaled in the entire medical literature for its comprehensive nature and detail, culminating in the 1996 publication: *Coronary Bypass Graft Fate and Patient Outcome: Angiographic Follow-Up of 5,065 Grafts Related to Survival and Reoperation of 1,388 Patients Over 25 Years*, and the complementary *Interventions For Coronary Stenosis: A Canadian Experience of 30 Revolutionary Years*.

18. Made many 16mm movies for teaching and for illustrations of papers of professional meetings, with assistance of CF Graphic Arts and the National Film Board, which rendered B&W 35mm film to stunning 16mm colour; film editing was done at NDMC, with help from Sgt. K. Oberlin of the Canadian Forces Photo Section.

19. Made more than 100 formal presentations relating to cardiovascular disease, especially in military personnel, at professional meetings in Canada, the United States, the United Kingdom and Europe.

20. Published, almost all as principal author, more than 50 papers, dealing with heart disease detection, diagnosis, treatment and, especially, long-term consequences, in national and international professional journals.

Publications Included

1. The first in the literature on the use of coronary angiography in members of Aircrew;

2. The first paper on the frequency of failure to diagnose coronary artery disease in young military patients, presenting with typical and readily identifiable symptoms - a problem of youth rather than military service;

3. The first to correlate the results of Master Two-step exercise testing with coronary angiographic findings;

4. The first on the use of the Vineberg procedure in patients with coronary

disease, without angina pectoris;

5. The first Canadian Case Report (two cases) of emergency coronary bypass for impending cardiac infarction;

6. The first series of patients without angina pectoris, treated with the coronary bypass operation, compared with a control group having typical anginal pain, a later publication showing no difference in benefit after 15 years;

7. The first paper showing quantitatively the adverse effects of smoking on coronary bypass graft survival;

8. Description of a method of classifying disease and narrowing of bypass grafts which is now used internationally;

9. Description of a simple apparatus and technique for making large prints of single 35mm cine-film frames;

10. Demonstration of the mechanism of occurrence of myocardial infarction in a case occurring at reoperation;

11. Reporting the incidence and angiographic findings associated with peri-operative cardiac infarction;

12. Reporting in detail the largest group of coronary patients requiring surgical treatment below the age of 39;

13. Documenting, in a large series, the occurrence and incidence of graft spasm during selective angiography;

14. Documenting correlation between coronary bypass angiography and echocardiography, in a large series;

15. Clarifying and defining the influence of coronary disease diagnosis on occupational risk in the Canadian Forces;

16. Reporting the first Case, a Canadian Forces officer, in the world literature, of the diagnosis and successful surgical treatment of cardiac rupture after myocardial infarction, previous attempts by others having failed;

17. Collaborating with psychiatrists, previous CPU-residents, prepared two papers on psycho-social aspects of coronary artery disease diagnosis and interventional therapy in Canadian military versus civilian patients;

18. A series of detailed papers, published over 16 years, on angiographic studies of coronary bypass grafts, documenting, during a 25-year period, long-term follow-up changes, describing new methods of assessing disease and narrowing, and providing definitive information on the relationship between graft disease, graft blockage the requirement for re-operation, and finally, mortality in all patients and in various subgroups.

Publications

Publications appeared in the following journals: Aerospace Medicine * AGARD/NATO Conference Proceedings * Annals of Internal Medicine * Annals of Thoracic Surgery * Archives of Surgery * Aviation Space and Environmental Medicine * British Medical Journal * Canadian Journal of Cardiology * Canadian Journal of Psychiatry * Canadian Journal of Surgery * Canadian Medical Association Journal * Cardiology Board Review * Chest * Circulation * Current Medical Digest * Diagnosis * Dokumentation Offentlicher Sozialmedisin Gesundheitdienst Arbeitsmedizin * Irish Journal of Medical Science * Journal of the American Medical Association * Journal of the American College of Cardiology * Journal of Aviation Medicine * Journal of the Royal Army Medical Corps * Journal of Thoracic and Cardiovascular Surgery Lancet * Medical Services Journal of Canada * Medicus * Military Medicine * Modern Medicine * Modern Medicine of Canada * New England Journal of Medicine * Physical Fitness and its Laboratory Assessment (Book) * Silent Myocardial Ischaemia (Book) * Sportarzt Und Sportmedizin * Year Book of Cardiovascular Medicine and Surgery * Year Book of Medicine

Summary of Achievements

Member - Order of Canada, 1989 (CM)
Officer - Order of Military Merit, 1974 (OMM)
Officer of the Most Venerable Order of the Hospital St. John of Jerusalem, 1974 (OStJ)
Canadian Forces Decoration (CD)
Queen's Silver Jubilee Medal, 1977
Canada 125 Years of Confederation Medal, 1992
Licentiate in Medicine, Surgery and Midwifery, Royal College of Surgeons Ireland LRCP&S (Ireland) -
Licentiate Medical Council of Canada (LMCC)
Fellow Royal College of Physicians Canada (FRCPC)
Fellow American College of Physicians (FACP)
Fellow American College of Cardiology (FACC)
Note

Summation

Dr. FitzGibbon was very proud of his Canadian citizenship and believed himself fortunate to have served DND, in uniform and as a public servant, during his entire 43-year professional career. He never "moonlighted." He believed that the military environment permitted the best medical practice, needing only commitment, enthusiasm, concern for the health of service personnel, and understanding of the interaction between medical care and operational requirements, to elicit support from superiors.

He said that no one had ever prevented him from undertaking a project he could substantiate to be in the best interest of the organization he served, and he repaid this support by documenting his activities thoroughly, by presenting this work at professional meetings by publishing in respected journals, many papers of generally accepted values to military and civilian cardiology.

Dr. FitzGibbon was named a Member of the Order Of Canada with the following citation:

"An outstanding clinical cardiologist and medical scientist, he has devoted his life to the pursuit of excellence in his clinical practice, teaching and research and has contributed a great deal both locally and internationally to the general field of cardiac diseases. Despite carrying a heavy workload as Head of Cardiology at the National Defence Medical Centre in Ottawa, he has been unstinting in the time and personal concern he has devoted to his patients."

Robert E. Forgie
OStJ, CD, MB, BS
Colonel

Robert E. Forgie was born in Aberdeen, Scotland on 17 July 1932. He received medical training at Charing Cross Hospital Medical School, University of London, graduating with MB BS in 1954. Captain Forgie served in Libya with the British Army from 1956 to 1958 as a regimental medical officer for the Queen's Bays, 2nd Dragoon Guards.

In 1958, Dr. Forgie joined the Royal Canadian Air Force as a Flight Lieutenant (F/L) Medical Officer and immigrated to Canada. After basic officer training in Centralia, Ontario, F/L Forgie was posted to 4 Flying Training School in Penhold, Alberta where he served from 1959 to 1962.

F/L Forgie was selected for training in ophthalmology at the Walter Reed General Hospital in Washington, D.C., which he undertook from 1962 to 1965. He was promoted to Squadron Leader (S/L) during that time.

After completion of specialty training and obtaining certification by the Royal College of Physicians and Surgeons of Canada, S/L Forgie was posted to HMCS Stadacona, the Navy's hospital in Halifax, Nova Scotia, as consultant ophthalmologist for a four-year tour from 1965 to 1969. During part of that tour of

Col Robert E. Forgie

duty he was clinical instructor in ophthalmology at Dalhousie University in Halifax.

With a promotion to Lieutenant-Colonel (LCol) in 1969, Forgie was posted to Canadian Forces Base Lahr, West Germany for a four-year tour of duty. All Canadian forces in Europe , Army and Air Force, had now been concentrated in this part of Germany - at Lahr and at Baden-Soellingen.

On LCol Forgie's return to Canada in 1974, he was promoted to Colonel (Col) and appointed Chief of Ophthalmology at the National Defence Medical Centre in Ottawa, Ontario. Col Forgie was also consultant to the Surgeon General in ophthalmology and Assistant Professor of Ophthalmology at the University of Ottawa.

Col Forgie was involved in expansion and international accreditation of the ophthalmic technician training program in the Canadian Forces Medical Service and in a similar training program in Yellowknife, NWT. He served as Commissioner on the Joint Commission for Allied Health Personnel in Ophthalmology for nine years and received the Statesmanship Award from this organization. He found time, in his busy schedule, to qualify for a private pilot's licence, which he held for several years.

After his retirement in 1985, Dr. Forgie established a private practice, which he continues now on a part-time basis. He continues to serve as member of the Vision and Colour Perception Study Group for the International Civil Aviation Organization (ICAO) of the United Nations. He also acts as consultant in ophthalmology for the Department of Transport.

Summary of Achievements

Officer of the Most Venerable Order of the Hospital of St. John of Jerusalem (OStJ)
Canadian Forces Decoration (CD)
Special Service Medal - NATO
Fellow Royal College of Surgeons Canada (FRCSC)
Licentiate Medical Council of Canada (LMCC)
Bachelor of Medicine, Bachelor of Science (MB, BS)
Diploma Ophthalmology (DO)

ROSS B. IRWIN
DFM, CD, MD
SURGEON CAPTAIN

Ross B. Irwin was born in Sarnia, Ontario in 1921. He moved to South River, Ontario in 1928 where he attended public and high school. Ross graduated from grade 13 in North Bay, Ontario. During the fall and winter of 1938-1939 he worked as a clerk in a lumber camp in Algonquin Park before moving to Toronto, Ontario, where he took a course in airframe and aeroengine mechanics to prepare himself for employment by the de Havilland Aircraft Company. The Royal Canadian Air Force badly needed airframe and aeroengine mechanics so Ross joined up in August 1940.

Following his basic training at the Manning Pool at Brandon Manitoba, Aircraftman 1st (AC1) Irwin was sent to the RCAF's Technical Training School at St. Thomas, Ontario. This huge complex of buildings connected by underground tunnels had just been completed by the Ontario Government to be used as a hospital for the mentally ill. It was commandeered as a trades training school and did not see its intended use until well after the war was over. AC1 Irwin was re-trained as an airframe technician and put to work at a Service Flying Training School in Dunville, Ontario, one of

Warrant Officer Ross B. Irwin
Flight Engineer

the stations of the British Commonwealth Air Training Plan.

There was a call for aircrew volunteers and Leading Aircraftman Irwin was selected for training at No. 3 Wireless School in Winnipeg, Manitoba. On graduation, Ross was promoted to Corporal (Cpl) and posted to England in December 1941. Cpl Irwin served as a wireless operator with 418 Squadron

RCAF until he was again posted to the RAF Station at St. Athans in Wales. In Wales, he was trained as a flight engineer on the Handley Page Halifax bomber, was promoted to Sergeant and was awarded the Flight Engineer half wing.

Following this, he flew on bomber operations for a brief period with 102 Squadron RAF and then with 78 Squadron RAF until January 1944 when, during a raid on Magdeburg, his aircraft was badly shot up.

According to the citation for the decorations awarded as the result of this action, Flight Lieutenant Shard and Flight Sergeant Irwin were pilot and flight engineer respectively of an aircraft detailed to attack Magdeburg on the night of 21 January 1944. The aircraft was attacked by a night-fighter and sustained severe damage. The astrodome was shot away, the mid-upper and rear turrets were put out of action and the hydraulic gear was damaged. One of the port propeller blade was also damaged. The fighter made repeated attacks, but Flight Sergeant Irwin, standing with his head protruding through the fuselage, at the aperture that had previously been covered by the astrodome, gave the necessary instructions to his pilot, who was thus able to out-manoeuvre and eventually evade the attacker.

Later, one of the starboard engines had to be feathered (that is the engine was shut down and the propeller blades turned so that their thin edge was parallel to the line of flight to prevent windmilling and destruction of the damaged engine). Nevertheless, Shard flew the aircraft back to England where he landed safely in spite of badly damaged flaps and burst tires in two landing wheels. This officer and airman displayed great courage, determination and devotion to duty.

The rear gunner was killed and Irwin and the mid-upper gunner were wounded. For action on this raid the pilot was granted an immediate award of the Distinguished Flying Cross and Flight Sergeant Ross was awarded the Distinguished Flying Medal.

He returned to Canada in the fall of 1944 and was demobilized from the RCAF in February 1945. He had decided to take advantage of university training offered to veterans and he was accepted to study medicine at the University of Toronto. While awaiting the beginning of the university year, Ross returned to work at the de Havilland Aircraft Co. It was that summer that he met Elfrieda and they were married within six months. They recently celebrated their 52nd wedding anniversary.

He started his pre-med studies at the University of Toronto in September in an all-veterans class and graduated in 1950. In his final year, he joined the Royal Canadian Navy along with seven other classmates. The Korean War started that summer and several medical officers on both coasts sailed in destroyers for Korean waters. Surgeon Lieutenant Irwin and two other classmates volunteered to postpone their internship for a year to fill the gaps left by those MO's who had sailed. He was posted to Esquimalt British Columbia to serve at the Naval Hospital. The following year, he began his internship at the Vancouver General Hospital and when the year ended he sailed in HMCS Athabaska for Korea and was there for fourteen months. On return to Canada he was promoted to Surgeon Lieutenant Commander and was posted to Ottawa.

A year later he began training in anaesthesia. He spent two years in Halifax and passed the certification exams in anaesthesia in the fall of 1958. He was appointed Chief of Anaesthesia at HMCS Stadacona, the Navy hospital at Halifax, Nova Scotia. With another promotion to Surgeon Commander, Irwin was posted to 3 (Fighter) Wing Zweibrucken, Germany as Chief of Anaesthesia. He held the post for four years, during which time he was promoted to Surgeon Captain.

Surgeon Captain Irwin return to Halifax after his European tour and was appointed Commanding Officer and Chief of Anaesthesia of Canadian Forces Hospital Halifax. This facility was formerly known as HMCS Stadacona.

Three years later Colonel Irwin was posted back to Europe to command the Hospital at the Canadian Forces Base at Lahr, Germany and to act as Regional Surgeon for Canadian Forces Europe. This appointment lasted for two years and took

Surgeon Captain Ross Irwin

place at a time when there were drastic cuts in the forces in Germany and the army moved from the north to share space with the much reduced air force in Southern Germany. Colonel Irwin returned to Canada in 1971 to become Chief of Anaesthesia and later Commanding Officer of Canadian Forces Hospital Kingston, an appointment he held until retirement from the forces in 1975.

Summary of Achievements

Distinguished Flying Medal - (DFM)
Canadian Forces Decoration (CD)
1939 - 1945 Star
Aircrew Europe Star
Defence Medal
Canadian Volunteer Service Medal
War Medal 1939 - 1945
Korean War Medal 1950 - 1953
United Nations Service - Korea
Centennial Medal
Special Services Medal - NATO
University of Toronto, Veterans Class - 1950 (MD)
Fellow of the Royal College of Physicians Canada - 1958 (FRCPC)

Note
This work was intended to recognize RCAF Medical Branch personnel, but Ross Irwin's distinguished wartime RCAF service and his continued interest in this service warrants his inclusion.

R.B. "Bud" Pritchard
CD, MD
Lieutenant Colonel

R.B. **"Bud" Pritchard** was born in Calgary, Alberta on 3 March 1930 and got his early education in Vancouver. With financial support from the Royal Canadian Air Force and moral support from his wife Muriel, he completed his medical degree at the University of British Columbia, graduating in 1956. During medical school, he wrote his MD thesis on decompression sickness, using the decompression chamber at the University for his research under the supervision of Wing Commander Bill Gibson.

When he came to full time duty with the RCAF Medical Branch in 1957, he served in a wide range of stations and posts. These were interesting times with the constant threat of the Cold War and its nuclear implications, with North American Air Defence (NORAD) commitments for the air defence of the north, with the radar screens across the Canadian north, most manned by the RCAF, with missile sites at various points in Canada, armed with Bomarc missles capable of delivering a nuclear warhead, and with North Atlantic Treaty Organi-

LCol R.B. "Bud" Pritchard

zation (NATO) commitments in Europe, there were no end to the challenges facing a new medical officer in the RCAF.

Postings seemed to criss-cross the country as needs arose in remote and urban locations. First to Fort Nelson, British Columbia in 1957 where Flight Lieutenant (F/L) Pritchard cared for Air Force members as well as their families and the few first nations people in the area. Then to RCAF Station Borden, Ontario in 1958 to care for Air Force trainees in one of the service's largest training centres. A short two years later, F/L Pritchard was on his way to the Air Force's manning depot at St-Jean, Québec in 1960 where he was responsible for the health care of new recruits, many who were unilingual French. A year later, F/L Pritchard packed his bags again in 1962 to go a few miles further east to St-Hubert, Québec. This was the site of RCAF Station St-Hubert and the location of Air Defence Command Headquarters.

Finally in 1965, a respite and a chance to recharge his academic batteries with a one year program at the University of Toronto in Public Health. With a Diploma in Public Health in his hands, Squadron Leader (S/L) Pritchard was despatched to the University of Rochester in Rochester New York in 1966 for a master degree program in Nuclear Medicine. With his Master of Science in Nuclear Medicine attained in 1967, S/L Pritchard became the only specialist of this kind in the RCAF.

One of the problems of holding unique qualifications is that you are inevitably headed for Headquarters and so S/L Pritchard was assigned to the Surgeon General's staff in the office of the Director of Preventive Medicine where he served from 1967 until 1970. With a rank change from Squadron Leader to Major, Pritchard managed to get out of the clutches of headquarters and get back to clinical medicine in 1970 as Base Surgeon at Canadian Forces Base North Bay, Ontario. This is the Canadian headquarters of NORAD (North American Air Defence), it was an Air Defence Command flying base and the site of one of the Bomarc missile stations. When Bud announced to his family that they were going to North Bay, Ontario, his daughter Alison wondered why they couldn't go to South Bay, Florida instead.

Major Pritchard's next posting in 1974 was one the family did not object to. He was assigned as Base Surgeon at 4 (Fighter) Wing at Baden-Soellingen, Germany. Although the majority of the Canadian Forces in Europe were concentrated at Lahr, Baden-Soellingen was still a very active flying base and also accommodated units of the Army. There was a large dependent population as well as the military to keep the medical facilities extremely busy.

On Major Pritchard's return to Canada in 1977, he continued in clinical medicine at the National Defence Medical Centre and at National Defence

Headquarters. During this time, Bud was promoted to Lieutenant-Colonel, a rank he held on retirement in 1980.

After retirement, Dr. Pritchard worked for the Department of Veterans Affairs (D.V.A.) in Ottawa and in Charlottetown, Prince Edward Island for three years. He moved back to beautiful B.C. in 1984 and continued to work for D.V.A. there until his retirement from clinical medicine in April 1999.

He married Muriel Bryce in May, 1953. They have two daughters; Nancy married a serving Naval Officer and is living in Ottawa, Alison lives in Chilliwack, British Columbia. They have five grandchildren, four boys and one girl, ranging in age from two to 16. In 1999 and on, they plan to travel in their motor home, golf, swim, bike and just enjoy themselves.

Summary of Achievements

Canadian Forces Decoration (CD)
NATO - Special Services Medal
Doctor of Medicine, UBC in 1956 (MD)
Diploma in Public Health, Toronto (DPH)
Master of Science, (Nuclear Medicine), University of Rochester, NY, 1967. (MSc)
Fellow, Royal College of Physicians of Canada, Public Health, 1968 [FRCP(C)]

ALEXANDER G. "SANDY" WATSON
CM, MD
WING COMMANDER

Alexander G. "Sandy" Watson was in England when he joined the Royal Canadian Air Force in London in December 1944. Flight Lieutenant Watson was sent to Bournemouth to No. 3 Personnel Reception Center as a General Duty Medical Officer. He was recalled to London in February 1945 to work in a medical facility that was set up in Harrods Department Store. The RCAF occupied the entire second floor of this building, a part of which was set aside for out-patient care.

When the RCAF moved out of Harrods, Watson moved to Lincoln Inn's Fields across the street from RCAF headquarters in London, where he operated a Medical Inspection Room (MIR), the term then used to designate an outpatient facility.

Sandy finally got closer to the action in May 1945 with a posting to an Artillery Observation Post Squadron at Eastbourne. The Squadron flew Oster aircraft, a light single engine plane with STOL (short take-off and landing characteristics).

W/C Alexander G. "Sandy" Watson

These planes were used to spot artillery targets and to relay information to the artillery batteries as to where their rounds were falling, helping them to correct their aim. The operation was commanded by the Canadian Army but had RCAF administrative officers and RCAF medical officers attached.

With the end of the war and the declaration of V.E. Day on 5 June 1945,

Sandy was posted to RCAF Headquarters in London in its Medical Branch. As headquarters officers were returned to Canada, Sandy took over their duties. But the work was not pressing and he found time to attend to the RCAF's official hockey team in London. His late enrolment meant that he was one of the last to return to Canada in September 1946.

On his return to Canada, Flight Lieutenant Watson was assigned to the RCAF Institute of Aviation Medicine in Toronto, Ontario. He worked on various projects at the IAM until 1947 when he was moved to Ottawa, Ontario to Air Force Headquarters with a promotion to Squadron Leader and the appointment of Senior Medical Officer in the outpatient facility.

The first Winter Olympic Games were planned for St. Moritz, Switzerland for 1948 and Canada was unable to field an amateur hockey team to represent the country. It was 1947 and time was running out, but Sandy Watson persuaded the Chief of the Air Staff, Air Marshal W. Curtis, and the Minister of Defence, Brooke Claxton, that he could form an RCAF team that could be contenders for the Olympics. With their agreement and the support of the RCAF, Sandy got the RCAF Flyers together and they went into practice.

The press gave the Flyers poor reviews prior to their arrival in St. Moritz, but they were determined and went on to win the Olympic gold medal and the World Hockey Championship in St. Moritz in February 1948. This was followed by a month's exhibition tour throughout Europe, which Mike Pearson, a future Minister of External Affairs and Prime Minister, claimed was the finest diplomatic feat ever for Canada.

Following this great achievement, Sandy returned from the Olympic trip to resume his duties as Senior Medical Officer at Air Force Headquarters in Ottawa. Watson remained active as an executive of the Senior Eastern Hockey League.

In May 1951, the RCAF, due to expansion for the Korean War, suffered a severe shortage of medical officers and there were none available from Canadian sources. Sandy Watson suggested to the Director General Medical Services (Air) that he could persuade twenty recent graduates in Medicine from Scotland to immigrate to Canada to join the RCAF Medical Branch. Medical graduates in Great Britain were obliged to serve two years "national service" with Britain's armed forces, whose pay was extremely low. In four weeks, Sandy was able to persuade thirty Scots medical graduates to join the RCAF and come to Canada. They provided excellent medical services and eighty percent of them remained here and became Canadian citizens.

The Air Force was also short of specialists and relied on the civilian community for its specialty services. In September 1951, Watson was selected to take specialty training in Ophthalmology, a subject in which he had been keenly interested. He spent three years at the Institute of Ophthalmology of the Columbus Presbyterian Hospital in New York City. At that time, it was the premier eye centre in the world.

On completion of his studies, Wing Commander Watson returned to RCAF Station Rockcliffe Station Hospital where he became the Senior Staff Officer in Ophthalmology. He was also invited to join the Ophthalmology Department at the University of Ottawa Medical School and he was also given full surgical privileges at the Ottawa General Hospital where he carried out the intricate eye surgery for which he had been trained.

As time went on, it was obvious that he was too well trained for routine eye service for the shrinking military population and he asked to be released from the RCAF. He was promoted to Acting Group Captain in an attempt to persuade him to stay, but this only delayed the inevitable. In September 1959, Dr. Watson obtained his release, but only after paying back part of the cost of his specialty training and waiving all rights to a service pension.

After resigning from the RCAF, Dr. Watson became Professor and Head of the Department of Ophthalmology at the University of Ottawa where he served for seventeen years. He was instrumental in creating and building the Eye Institute, which is recognized as the finest eye hospital and research centre in Canada.

In 1987, he was made a Member of the Order of Canada with the following citation:

> *"He is one of Canada's foremost ophthalmologists, former Chairman and Professor and now Professor Emeritus of the Department of Ophthalmology at the University of Ottawa and the force behind the establishment of the Ottawa General Hospital Eye Institute. His interest in hockey led him to assemble and manage the RCAF Flyers who won the Olympic Gold Medal in hockey in 1948 and to serve as Manager of Canada's Olympic Hockey Team in 1984."*

Summary of Achievements

Member of the Order of Canada (CM)
Defence Medal
Canadian Volunteer Service Medal
St Andrews (Scotland) 1944 (M.B., Ch. B.)
Diploma, American Board of Opthalmology (DABOph)
Fellow, American College of Surgeons (FACS-Oph)
Fellow Royal College of Surgeons Canada, Opthalmology (FRCSC)
Emeritus Professor Opthalmology, University of Ottawa

CHAPTER 6
THE NIGHTINGALES

NURSING OFFICERS

- **Colonel Anne-Marie Bélanger**
  A graduate of the National Defence College and Officer of the Order of Military Merit.

- **Squadron Leader Mary Deneau (Cunningham)**
  Served on the Korean aeromedevac airlift with over 450 flying hours logged in three months.

- **Colonel Marielle A. Gagné**
  An operating room nurse and nursing administrator, now serving as the Director of Health Care Personnel Training and Development.

- **Colonel M. Joan Fitzgerald**
  Served in the Army in Italy and Europe in WWII and in the RCAF post-war as an instructor, flight nurse and nursing administrator. First female colonel and first selected to attend the National Defence College.

- **Colonel Jessie E. Lawson**

  A public health nurse, flight nurse and nursing administrator with twenty-eight years service ending her career as the senior nurse in the Canadian Forces Medical Service.

- **Wing Commander Muriel McArthur**

  Senior RCAF post-war nurse who served in the transition period of the RCAF Medical Branch to the Canadian Forces Medical Service.

- **Lieutenant-Colonel Dorothy McClelland**

  An operating room nurse, and Nursing Branch Career Manager with 32 years RCAF and Canadian Forces Medical Service experience.

- **Colonel V.A. "Roni" McKee (Lowe)**

  German nurse immigrant who rose to the senior nurse appointment, Director of Nursing Service, for the Canadian Forces Medical Service.

- **Squadron Leader F.M. "Fran" Oakes**

  One of 20 RCAF nurses out of 781 in WW II to win the Associate Red Cross Class 2 Award; an associate member of the Guinea Pig Club; was the Senior RCAF Nursing Officer on retirement.

- **Lieutenant-Colonel Shirley M. Robinson**

  A nurse with a 30-year career who was politically active in efforts to gain career equity for service women.

ANNE MARIE BÉLANGER
OMM, OSTJ, CD, RN
COLONEL

Anne-Marie Bélanger was born in Levis, Quebec in July 1931. At the age of 23, Anne-Marie enrolled in the Royal Canadian Air Force as a nursing officer in June 1954. Pilot Officer Bélanger spoke no English when she enrolled, but worked hard at acquiring English skills. Following initial training, she served as general duty nurse and head nurse at RCAF Station Rockcliffe Hospital in Ottawa, Ontario. This was followed by a tour of duty at 4 (Fighter) Wing at Baden-Soellingen, Germany. Anne-Marie improved her English skills so well in Germany that she was appointed the senior nursing officer at RCAF Station Centralia, Ontario and then clinical instructor at the Canadian Forces Hospital at RCAF Station Cold Lake, Alberta. Subsequently, Captain Bélanger was posted to the National Defence Medical Centre in Ottawa where she held senior nursing staff appointments.

Bélanger's leadership and management skills were so apparent that she was promoted to the rank of major in 1970, and selected for university training. Major Bélanger attended the University of Ottawa and graduated with a Bachelor of Science degree in Nursing in 1971.

Major Bélanger completed two tours of duty at the Canadian Forces Medical Service School at Canadian Forces Base Borden, Ontario. The first as Officer-in-Charge of Basic Nursing Officer course in which she prepared young nursing officers for military duty. During her second tour, Major Bélanger was Officer Commanding the Medical

Major Anne-Marie Bélanger admitted to the Order of Military Merit by Her Majesty Queen Elizabeth II

Assistants Training Company. In this appointment, she was responsible for all trades training for Medical Assistants from the basic entry level to that of physician's assistants.

Following graduation from Canadian Forces Staff College in 1974, she was appointed Director of Nursing of the Canadian Forces Hospital Valcartier at Canadian Forces Base Valcartier, Québec. This two-year appointed resulted in another promotion in May 1976 and Lieutenant-Colonel Bélanger moved on to National Defence Headquarters in Ottawa to be the Career Manager for the Nursing Officer Classification.

More military training was in store and in September 1978, newly promoted Colonel Bélanger was off to the National Defence College in Kingston, Ontario, the second nursing officer to be selected for this program. Following graduation from National Defence College in July 1979, she returned to NDHQ as Director of Women Personnel.

There were more promotions in store for Anne-Marie Bélanger, including one to the rank of Brigadier-General, but she elected to leave the service in 1983 to care for her mother, who was quite ill.

Anne-Marie Bélanger was given many honors during her service career. These included the Order of Military Merit in the grade of Officer of the Most Venerable Order of St. John of Jerusalem, the Silver Jubilee medal and the Canadian Forces Decoration. On 1 April 1980, she was appointed Honourary Aide-de-Camp to the Governor General.

After her retirement, Anne-Marie valiantly fought a losing battle against cancer and passed away in August 1992.

Summary of Achievements

Order of Military Merit (OMM)
Officer of the Most Venerable Order of the Hospital of St. John of Jerusalem (OStJ)
Canadian Forces Decoration (CD)
Special Services Medal - NATO
Silver Jubilee Medal
Bachelor of Science Nursing, University of Ottawa - 1971 (BSc)

MARY CUNNINGHAM NÉE DENEAU
CD, RN
SQUADRON LEADER

Mary Deneau grew up in Essex County in western Ontario. Her nursing training was taken at Victoria Hospital in London, Ontario and, in 1942, she completed a Bachelor of Science degree in Nursing at the University of Western Ontario in that city as well. Mary had been a nursing instructor at the Belleville General Hospital in Belleville, Ontario for two years when, in 1944, she decided to get into the war effort, so she joined the Royal Canadian Air Force.

Pilot Officer Deneau's first duty post was No. 2 Command Medical Board Hospital (2 CMBH) located in a temporary wing of Deer Lodge Hospital, a veterans hospital administered by the Department of Veterans Affairs (DVA) in Winnipeg, Manitoba. Mary served here until after VE Day and VJ Day that signaled the end of the war in Europe and with Japan. No. 2 CMBH was then closed and the space returned to the DVA.

Following the closure of No. 2 CMBH, Flying Officer Deneau was sent to No. 4 CMBH in Calgary,

S/L Mary Deneau

Alberta, then to No. 6 Repair Depot at Trenton, Ontario for a short period before moving, literally across the road, to RCAF Station Trenton Hospital. This was the period of RCAF expansion and Flying Officer Deneau was moved frequently and served at RCAF Station Aylmer, Ontario; RCAF Station Clinton, Ontario; RCAF Station Centralia, Ontario; RCAF Station Edmonton, Alberta; RCAF Station Fort Nelson, Yukon Territory; RCAF Station Rockcliffe, Ontario; RCAF Station Summerside, Prince Edward Island; RCAF Station St-Jean, Québec; RCAF Station Goose Bay, Labrador; 3 (Fighter) Wing Zweibrucken, Germany; and finally at the National Defence Medical Centre in Ottawa.

There was a great deal of personnel activity at Trenton in early 1946, and Deneau worked with a Flight Sergeant Medical Assistant setting up medical documents for those leaving the RCAF in the mornings, and those returning or enlisting in the afternoons.

Later at Trenton, with the help of a Flight Sergeant and Corporal Medical Assistant she helped set up a program, wrote the precis, and taught the first few Medical Assistant courses, until training was moved to RCAF Station Hospital Rockcliffe.

In her third posting to Trenton, she was assigned to Training Command Headquarters on the staff of the Staff Officer Medical Services (SOMS) in the capacity of Command Matron. Flight Lieutenant (F/L) Deneau was responsible for the quality of nursing services throughout the Command. This required her to visit RCAF stations from St-Jean, Québec to Claresholm, Alberta about twice a year during her three year tour of duty. Sometimes she travelled alone at other times with the SOMS, Wing Commander (later Group Captain) Ian Barclay. Junior nursing officers gained from her visits, discussing their problems and improving Medical Assistant training and nursing services.

During the Korean War, the RCAF sent several nurses to the United States, one or two at a time, to learn and practice aeromedical evacuation techniques. F/L Deneau and F/L Doris Thompson went to the Air Evac School at Montgomery, Alabama, then to Hickam Air Force Base in Hawaii for practical experience. From there they flew to Tokyo Japan and returned with a full load of patients who were being returned from the Korean War. Most of these were U.S. soldiers, but some were Canadians. These patients were taken to a hospital in Hawaii for a period of stabilization before continuing their air journey to the US and Canada. After a stop-over rest, the nurses then left with patients going to Travis Air Force Base, north of San Francisco California. After a further period of stabilization, the patients were again transported by air to the hospital nearest their home base for continued care. F/L Deneau had one trip with a USAF nurse out to the Philippines. In three months Deneau accumulated more than 450 flying hours.

When the RCAF began giving regular force nurses postgraduate training at various universities, F/L Deneau was given the opportunity to take a Master of Arts degree program in nursing service and administration at Teachers

College of Colombia University in New York City. The students on this course were mostly American military nurses, some from the army, navy and air force. In addition to the two Canadians nursing officers, there were military nurses from Trinidad, Puerto Rico, India, Pakistan and Norway. Needless to say, they all spoke "American" English. They worked hard but also found time to play, go to theatres and restaurants and see the sights. New York was a much safer city to explore in 1955 than it is today.

F/L Deneau was pleased to be posted to the hospital at 3(Fighter) Wing at Zweibrucken, Germany. This was the largest of the Canadian medical facilities and the definitive care hospital for the other three wings and for the Air Division Headquarters. Deneau worked with specialists in medicine, surgery, obstetrics and other specialties. These doctors visited the other units on a regular schedule and sent the patients who needed extra care to 3 (F) Wing. So the hospital was kept busy, but Deneau managed to find time to see some of Europe, including Holland in tulip time, Munich for Octoberfest, London on Christmas leave and places farther afield on annual leave.

Squadron Leader Deneau came home from 3 Wing in September 1961 to be the matron of the new National Defence Medical Centre (NDMC) on its opening. Military doctors, pharmacists, administraters and nurses, especially Wing Commander John Kettles and Matron (Squadron Leader) Frances Oakes, planned the hospital. When it opened, NDMC was considered the finest hospital in Ottawa. The staff was drawn from all three services, army, navy and air force. While there she was pleased to serve on the advisory committee at the School of Nursing of the University of Ottawa. She and her colleagues helped by providing field experience for the University's postgraduate nursing students.

Mary Deneau was married in February 1965 to Squadron Leader Cunningham and retired at her own request in November 1966. She and her husband later adopted a little girl. She didn't really leave the RCAF, since her husband continued to serve until 1973.

Summary of Achievements
Canadian Forces Decoration (CD)
Canadian Volunteer Service Medal
War Medal 1939 - 1945
UN Service Medal Korea
Special Service Medal - NATO
Registered Nurse, Victoria Hospital - London (RN)
Bachelor Science Nursing (B ScN)
Master of Arts - Columbia (MA)

215

MARY JOAN FITZGERALD
OMM, OSTJ, CD, RN
COLONEL

Joan Fitzgerald was born in 1920 in Halifax, Nova Scotia where she received her early education and nursing training, graduating from the Halifax Infirmary School of Nursing in 1941. Joan came from a military family. Her father, a Military Cross winner of World War I served in the militia after the war. A younger brother served in the Royal Canadian Air Force in Bomber Command and was lost over Europe, another served in the Royal Canadian Navy as a submariner. It was only natural, therefore that Joan should want to be involved in the war effort, so barely a year after graduation in 1942, she joined the Royal Canadian Army Medical Corps as a Lieutenant (Lt) Nursing Sister (N/S).

Squadron Leader Joan Fitzgerald

Lt Fitzgerald's first "overseas" posting was to Newfoundland - St. John's for six months and then for another six months to Botwood where a military hospital was situated. Newfoundland was then considered overseas because it had not yet joined Confederation and was "outside" Canada. The journey by ferry from North Sidney, Nova Scotia to Port-aux-Basque on the south-western tip of Newfoundland was not without its hazards. German submarines had been operating in the mouth of the St. Lawrence River and indeed had sunk one of the ferry boats on this route with great loss of life. The railroad journey north of the port and then east across the island was perhaps not as hazardous, but it certainly came near it in discomfort. The narrow-gauge railroad, irreverently called "The Newfie Bullet" because of its remarkable lack of speed, provided hard straight-back seats and not much heat. An army officer, a friend of the family, offered welcome support and made Lt Fitzgerald's journey bearable.

Nursing Sister Fitzgerald was soon on her way to England where she joined the staff of No. 18 General Hospital RCAMC. Lt Fitzgerald was one of the nurses sent as reinforcements to No. 5 General Hospital then in Italy to care for casualties of that campaign. Twelve-hour shifts were routine and accommodation for the nurses was in an old school building that still had its blackboards in place. The diet was sometimes unusual and a late supper might consist of a sandwich of raw onion slices on dark bread. The abundance of oranges, however, made up for the other dietary irregularities.

When the 1st Canadian Division left Italy, No 5 General Hospital was moved as a unit, first by sea to Marseilles and then over land to Belgium where it remained for the duration of the European campaign, caring for battle casualties until it was disbanded after VE-Day. Lt Fitzgerald returned to Canada and was demobilized in November 1945.

Joan took advantage of her veteran's credits to return to school, and she enrolled at the University of Ottawa in a program of public health nursing. Soon after graduating in 1948, she enrolled in the Royal Canadian Air Force as a Flying Officer (N/S) and was posted to RCAF Station Rockcliffe near Ottawa.

In 1950, Flying Officer (F/O) Fitzgerald was sent as a candidate to the United States Air Force Flight Nursing Course at Montgomery Air Force Base in Alabama. First, there was classroom and practical training at Montgomery and then actual air evacuation flights on the Tokyo, Japan to Los Angeles,

California route. But first, F/O Fitzgerald had to get from Montgomery to Hawaii and this was accomplished on the first available trans-Pacific aeroplane available – a Boeing B-29 Superfortress bomber. Accompanied by a USAF nursing officer on her way home on furlough, Joan sat in a cramped area at the rear of the aircraft, seldom seeing the outside world except when the plane stopped for refuelling before heading across the Pacific.

The actual air evacuation flights originated in Tokyo where the aeromedevac team picked up a plane load of casualties from the Korean conflict. The aircraft in use at that time was the Douglas C-54 Skymaster, a four-engine passenger-cargo plane that could take twenty-eight patients, and the Douglas C-57[1]

F/O Fitzgerald, sitting right front, with USAF Nurses on High Altitude Indoctrination Training in the decompression chamber at Gunter Air Force Base in Alabama.

Liftmaster, a larger four-engine troop-cargo carrier that could accommodate as many as sixty-nine patients. Patients were accommodated on canvas stretchers stacked along the side walls of the fuselage and five high along the centre of the cargo bay. The centre stacks were two deep, requiring nursing staff on both sides. The stretchers were held separated on stanchions and litter straps with less than twenty-four inches of space between litters. Regardless of their degree of mobility, all casualties had to be on litters because of the duration of the flight and the limited walking space around the plane's interior. Neither of these aircraft was pressurized, that is to say, it had to fly below 10,000 or, if a higher altitude was necessary, crew members had to provide oxygen from portable bottles to the patients. There was limited seating, even for the aeromedevac crew, but there was little time to sit with the constant need to check and care for patients, especially if they were in need of oxygen.

The flights from Tokyo to Hickam Air Force Base in Hawaii were never direct. Limited range and weather conditions made stops necessary to refuel, restock the dietary and medical supplies and to give the crews and patients a respite from the gruelling flight. Stops were made at various islands, including Kwajalein Atoll in the Marshall Islands, Wake Island and Midway before reaching Hawaii. On arrival, patients were deplaned and rested in hospital before embarking on the next leg of their journey to Los Angeles, where other crews would take them, most by air, to hospitals in the US and Canada. As a result of F/O Fitzgerald's aeromedevac experiences and recommendations, more nurses were trained and Medical Assistants were added to the training program.

On her return to Canada, F/O Fitzgerald went to RCAF Station Rockcliffe Hospital where she was placed in charge of Medical Assistant (MedA) training. Shortly thereafter, the trades training functions of the Air Force were centralized at RCAF Station Aylmer, Ontario, so F/O Fitzgerald organized a new staff and, in December 1951, moved the entire MedA training operation to its new location. The school was assigned a barrack block to use for its classrooms, but F/O Fitzgerald was told that she couldn't start renovating it until the Santa Claus Shop, a Christmas gift shop, moved out. Santa finally moved out and the carpenters added dividers to this great expanse of floor space to make classrooms. These part-walls had the predictable result that the students at the back of the class could hear the lecturer in the next classroom better than the one at the front. This made question periods most interesting. The Air Force had re-opened its ranks to women, so the MedA school was co-ed.

F/L Fitzgerald was selected to be part of the RCAF contingent sent to England in 1953 to celebrate the coronation of Queen Elizabeth II. There was a good deal of training for the fourteen mile trek of the coronation procession for its march through London. When she talks about walking the fourteen miles on the Coronation Parade she says it was relatively easy for a 33 year old, but to this day, Joan is an active walker.

In 1954-1955, F/L Fitzgerald attended the University of Toronto, completing the Nursing Administration Course. This was followed by posting to Air Force Headquarters (AFHQ) where she was appointed Assistant to the Matron-in-Chief. Simultaneously, Fitzgerald conducted the Military Nursing Courses at the RCAF Institute of Aviation Medicine in Toronto for Royal Canadian Navy, Royal Canadian Army Medical Corps and RCAF nursing officers.

Squadron Leader (S/L) Fitzgerald was then assigned to Air Defence Command (ADC) at St-Hubert, Québec as Command Matron on the staff of the Staff Officer Medical Services. ADC units were spread right across Canada and into remote locations of the Pine Tree Line of radar sites. Joan's staff visits to these sites, often alone and by car, on at least a yearly basis were difficult, but necessary. The radar stations were always located on a hilltop, but road directions to the station were not publicized, making it a bit difficult for one to get there, especially by car. S/L Fitzgerald had an easy solution for this. She simply scanned the skyline, looking for the big white geodesic domes that covered the radar receiving antennas. With these in sight, she drove in their general direction until she found the entrance to the station.

A posting as Director of Nursing of the Canadian Forces Hospital Kingston located at CFB Kingston Ontario must have been a relief after the years of travelling, but it also had its moments. Joan was the first Air Force Director of Nurses posted to this Army hospital. There was, understandably, some anxiety on the part of the Army staff at her arrival. In typical fashion, Joan soon dispelled these anxieties and she was quickly accepted by nurses and medical staff alike. This 125-bed hospital provided full care to the military in the region as well as to penitentiary inmates who required surgery or special medical care.

The hospital was built with these Correctional Service patients in mind and special secure wards were included. However, the demand for service exceeded the designed space, so some had to be accommodated in four-bed wards designated for their use, but without the special security features. The nursing staff was instructed not to interfere with any escape attempt, but to inform the authorities after the fact.

Squadron Leader Fitzgerald was next assigned to Canadian Forces Headquarters (CFHQ) in Ottawa on the staff of the Surgeon General as Assistant to the Matron-in-Chief. In 1968, Joan Fitzgerald was promoted to Wing Commander, subsequently re-ranked to Lieutenant-Colonel, and became

Matron-in-Chief, Canadian Forces Medical Service.

The year 1972 was a year of firsts. Joan was promoted to Colonel, the first women to achieve this rank in peace-time. She was selected to attended the National Defence College, the first nursing officer to attend this course. Colonel Fitzgerald returned to CFHQ in 1973 as Director of Nursing, an appointment she held until her retirement in 1976. In 1975, in recognition of her distinguished service, Colonel Fitzgerald was named an Officer of the Order of Military Merit.

Summary of Achievements

Order of Military Merit (OMM)
Officer of the Most Venerable Order of the Hospital of St. John of Jerusalem (OStJ)
Canadian Forces Decoration (CD)
1939 – 1945 Star
Italy Star
France and Germany Star
Defence Medal
Canadian Volunteer Service Medal
War Medal – 1939 – 1945
Queen Elizabeth II – Coronation Medal
United Nations Service Medal – Korea
Silver Jubilee Medal
Registered Nurse (RN)
National Defence College

Note 1.
C-57 Liftmaster aircraft were given the USAF designation C-118 and specifically those configured for aeromedical evacuation were designated M-118 and marked with a large red cross on the tailplane.

MARIELLE S. GAGNÉ
OSTJ, CD, RN
COLONEL

Marielle S. Gagné was born in the region of Rimouski, Québec. She enrolled in the Royal Canadian Air Force in 1966 shortly after completing her nursing training. During her career, Gagné's appointments included employment as a staff nurse at Canadian Forces Hospital, Cold Lake, Alberta (1967-1969); 1 Canadian Brigade Medical Units, Germany (1969-1971), and at the National Defence Medical Centre (NDMC), Ottawa, Ontario (1971-1973). From June 1973 to July 1977, she served as head nurse of the intensive care unit at the National Defence Medical Centre (NDMC) in Ottawa, Ontario.

Following her promotion to Major and on completion of a Baccalaureate Degree in Nursing, she returned to NDMC where she was first appointed Nursing Education Coordinator and then Assistant Director of Nursing.

In August 1982, Major Gagné was posted to Maritime Command Headquarters in Halifax, Nova Scotia as Staff Officer Nursing on the staff of the Command Surgeon. She was promoted to the rank of Lieutenant-Colonel in 1983 and was subsequently posted to Canadian Forces Hospital Halifax where she served as the Director of Nursing until 1985 when she was recalled to NDMC assume the responsibilities of Director of Nursing of this larger facility.

In 1986, LCol Gagné was appointed Staff Officer to the Director Women Personnel at National Defence Headquarters

Col Marielle S. Gagné

222

(NDHQ) in Ottawa and a year later, in July 1987, she was promoted to the rank of Colonel.

With this latest promotion, Col Gagné assumed the appointment of Director of Nursing for the Canadian Forces Medical Service on the staff of the Surgeon General at NDHQ. In August 1991, the position Director of Nursing was restructured and given added responsibilities as well as a name change to Director Health Care Personnel Training and Development.

Colonel Gagné holds a diploma in nursing, a nursing certificate in intensive care, a Baccalaureate Degree in Nursing and a Baccalaureate Degree in Arts. Colonel Gagné is the only serving nursing officer included in this work.

Summary of Achievements

Officer of the Most Venerable Order of the Hospital of St. John of Jerusalem (OStJ)
Canadian Forces Decoration (CD)
QHNS - Queens Honorary Nursing Sister
Baccalaureate Degree in Nursing
Baccalaureate Degree in Arts
NATO Defence College, Rome

Jessie E. Lawson
OStJ, CD, RN
Colonel

Jessie Lawson was born in Campbellton and was raised in Saint John, New Brunswick. She attended school there where she excelled in mathematics. While in high school, she wrote, but did not publish, adventure stories for girls. As she grew up, she developed a hobby of painting, mostly old barns. As a young woman, she golfed, skied and skated. Jessie graduated in nursing from Soldiers' Memorial Hospital in Campbellton and subsequently worked in Saint John, New Brunswick before continuing her nursing studies in Public Health Nursing. In 1947, her nursing career took her to New York where she nursed at the Presbyterian Medical Centre. Here, with a nursing colleague from Saint John, she specialized in obstetrical nursing.

In 1952, after returning to Canada and working for a period in public health, Jessie, at age 31, joined the Royal Canadian Air Force as a Flying Officer (F/O). The usual basic training courses followed and F/O Lawson, along with another young Flying Officer, Peggy Brown, were sent off to take Flight Nursing training with the United States Air Force at Montgomery Air Force Base in Alabama. The training at Montgomery was followed by actual flights with Korean War casualties being brought back from Tokyo Japan over the Pacific to continental United States.

Col Jessie E. Lawson

These arduous trips in unpressurized, propeller driven aircraft required stops and lay-overs. From Tokyo, the flights would stop in Guam, Midway, and Hawaii, before heading out on the last leg to San Francisco. Casualties numbered fifty or more, many in serious condition with battle wounds, requiring a great deal of care in flight along with the full range of nursing care, they sometimes had casualties in portable respirator equipment comparable to an iron lung.

As senior nurse in the 1960's, Flight Lieutenant (F/L) Lawson was Matron of the Hospital at 4 (Fighter) Wing at Baden-Soellingen, Germany. This hospital looked after the Air Force members as well as their families, but the facilities did not provide special

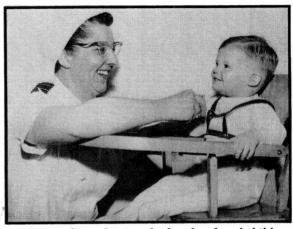

Nursing Sister Lawson feeding her found child.

pediatric wards, so the little ones were often in adult size beds. Despite a shortage of nursing staff, the care of patients was always first. An incident may serve to illustrate her dedication. Before going off duty one evening after a long hard day, she went to check on all her "little charges" to find one missing from his bed. She immediately instituted a search with all available staff and kept a calm outer appearance despite her growing feelings of panic. It was some time before the toddler was found, all curled up and sound asleep in the bottom half of an open bedside table.

Squadron Leader Lawson headed up Medical Assistant Training at the Canadian Forces Medical Service School at Borden, Ontario in the late sixties before going on to the National Defence Medical Centre as Director of Nursing with the rank of Lieutenant-Colonel. She served a tour of duty as Career Manager for the Nursing Classification, an office that required the patience of Job and the wisdom of Solomon to keep nurses and their employers reasonably happy.

Colonel Lawson finished her 28-year career in 1978 at the top of her profession as Director of Nursing Services for the Canadian Forces on the staff of the Surgeon General. Career oriented, she never married. Her old friend and nursing colleague, Doreen Plummer, speculates that if she had married she would have had a dozen or more children, she was so fond of children. Following her retirement, Jessie nursed her aging mother and two maiden aunts in her home in Ottawa.

Jessie Lawson died on 12 June 1998 at age 76 at her home in Ottawa, following a long battle with cancer. Her life-long friend, Mary Trecartin of New Brunswick, said, "Jess was the most caring person. Despite her illness, she arranged to have a very personal gift sent to me on my birthday."

Her brother Frank, who also had a full military career, remembers how she was always careful and caring of her younger brother. At age 14 she would haul Frank, age six, on his sled in winter and engaged in snowball fights, but always with great care.

Summary of Achievements

Officer of the Most Venerable Order of the Hospital of St. John of Jerusalem (OStJ)
Canadian Forces Decoration (CD)
UN Service Medal Korea, 1950 - 1954
Queen Elizabeth II Jubilee Medal, 1977
Special Service Medal - NATO
Registered Nurse

MURIEL CATHERINE MCARTHUR
OSTJ, CD, RN
WING COMMANDER

Muriel McArthur was born on 31 August 1913 at Oro Station, Ontario, a village on the shores of Lake Simcoe, just north of Barrie. Muriel went to public school there and graduated from Barrie Collegiate Institute. Nursing was her chosen profession, and she was enrolled in the Toronto General Hospital School of Nursing, graduating in 1937.

On 29 December 1941, Muriel joined the Royal Canadian Air Force as a Nursing Sister with the rank of Pilot Officer (P/O) and was sent directly to No. 1 Technical Training School (No. 1TTS) at St. Thomas, Ontario. No. 1 TTS was housed in a large complex of buildings designed as a psychiatric hospital. This huge complex provided barrack accommodation, mess halls, training classrooms and recreational and sports facilities. Buildings were connected by underground tunnels to facilitate movement of patients from one area to another in

W/C Muriel C. McArthur

inclement weather. The Royal Canadian Air Force commandeered these buildings as soon as they were completed for use as a training centre. Newly enrolled officers were outfitted in uniforms, taught foot drill and were introduced to RCAF rules, regulations and service etiquette.

New Air Force recruits, coming from all across Canada, who were housed in congested open barrack accommodation, quickly passed on every form of communicable respiratory disease. There were numerous cases of diphtheria, scarlet fever, measles, whooping cough, etc. Immediately after completing basic training, P/O McArthur was sent on temporary duty to the Isolation Hospital in Toronto for five months to help care for these recruits, many who had been living in the Horse Palace at the Exhibition grounds in Toronto and had contracted scarlet fever.

From August 1943 to January 1944, P/O McArthur was the senior Nursing Sister at No. 2 Wireless School in Calgary, Alberta. This school was housed in a permanent building that had been a community school. There was an infirmary where minor illnesses were treated and where preventive care was practiced. Airmen and airwomen with more serious illnesses were sent to Calgary hospitals, principally the Colonel Belcher, a hospital operated by the Department of Veterans' Affairs. Many units in the area were part of the British Commonwealth Air Training Plan, so as well as Canadians there were British, Australian and New Zealand airmen attending these medical facilities.

In January 1944, Muriel began her journey overseas, first to an Embarkation Depot in Montreal and then to Halifax to board a French liner named Pasteur. There were six women on this troop ship full of men, three Nursing Sisters and three Women Division personnel officers. They were told that the ship's stabilizers had been removed for greater speed and that they would not be sailing in a convoy. January on the Atlantic can be quite rough, especially when a ship is travelling at top speed and without stabilizers. Most of the passengers were indeed happy to reach England, but on arrival at Liverpool there was so much traffic that they could not dock. Fortunately, the ship had sufficient supplies, so the Pasteur sat outside the port for three days until a pier became available for it to dock.

During that three-day period, one of the Canadian Army soldiers developed acute appendicitis. McArthur was quickly pressed into service, assisting the ship's doctor with an emergency appendectomy. The appendix had ruptured but the doctor filled the abdomen with sulphathiazole. The soldier survived the operation and wrote to McArthur to thank her and to let her know how he was faring. It is not known whether he survived the war.

From the ship, the Nursing Sisters were sent to the Canadian Reception Depot at Bournemouth in the south of England and a short time later they went on to Yorkshire to the Conversion Unit at Wombleton. The Conversion Unit was a part of No. 6 Bomber Group RCAF where aircrews were trained to fly the Handley-Page Halifax bomber in preparation for operational flying. This was a wartime station, so the buildings were Nissen huts. These huts, named after their designer, LCol Peter N. Nissen, were prefabricated, semicylindrical, corrugated iron shelters set on a cement base. Three of these units had been joined at a common central point to be used as an infirmary. Patient beds were lined up in each of the huts and the centre space at the point of juncture was used for a nursing station and service area. This facility only provided care for minor illnesses; patients with serious illnesses were sent to the Royal Air Force hospital in North Allerton, to Canadian Army hospitals or to the plastic surgery hospital in East Grinstead *(see S/L Frances Oakes in this chapter.)*

From October 1944 to May 1945, F/O McArthur was the Nursing Sister at the RCAF Station at Leeming, an operational station. Squadrons on the station were flying Handley Page Halifax bombers and later Avro Lancaster bombers were introduced.

From May 1945, after VE Day (Victory in Europe Day) to February 1946 F/O McArthur was at the RCAF Station at Bournemouth, which was then a Repatriation Depot for Air Force personnel returning to Canada. When Bournemouth closed in February 1946, McArthur went to RCAF Station Odiham where transport squadrons of Douglas DC-3 Dakotas were flying back and forth to Europe to service the occupational forces. In August 1946 the RCAF left the station and the Dakotas were flown home to Canada.

Muriel McArthur's return trip to Canada in 1946 was in sharp contrast to her outbound sea journey. The troops were going home, there was no longer any anxiety about submarines, the sun shone every day and the sea was smooth. It was a glorious crossing.

On return to Canada on 12 August 1946, F/O McArthur went to RCAF Station Rockcliffe, just outside of Ottawa. Rockcliffe was an active flying base and the Hospital also cared for personnel from Air Force Headquarters. Although on strength of RCAF Station Rockcliffe, McArthur was, for a three-month period, on temporary duty at the Imperial Oil Hospital in Norman Wells, Northwest Territories. There was a number of Air Force personnel working out of Norman Wells on 414 Photo Squadron. The Squadron flew DC-3 Dakotas on aerial-photo missions to map the North. If they were ill or needed care, it was provided by F/O McArthur at the Imperial Oil Hospital.

Following her tour of duty at Rockcliffe, McArthur went to 1 Supply Depot at Weston, Ontario in September 1949. This was the principal supply depot for the RCAF and the nursing care provided to the depot staff would have been what is called industrial nursing today. This short tour came to an end in December 1950, but was followed by a more interesting job.

In 1950, Flight Lieutenant (F/L) McArthur was appointed Matron at the RCAF Hospital at Goose Bay, Labrador. Goose Bay was considered an isolated post and the Station provided full medical care to its Air Force personnel as well as to their wives and children. In addition, some civilian patients were flown in from remote sites in Labrador for medical care. This provided McArthur's first experience with obstetrics since joining the service. This was another short tour and, in August 1951, she was brought back from Goose Bay to work at RCAF Station Borden, Ontario for a four-month stint, before returning to RCAF Station Hospital Rockcliffe as Matron, as the senior nursing officer was then called.

F/L McArthur left this last post to undertake studies at the University of Toronto in Nursing Administration for the period 1953-1954. This prepared her for her next appointment, that of Command Matron at 1 Air Division Headquarters at Metz, France - a three year tour from August 1954 to August 1957.

1 Air Division Headquarters was housed in the Chateau de Mercy and other buildings that had been constructed by the Canadian Government on the grounds of the Chateau. The Air Division was made up of four fighter wings, two in France and two in Germany, a supply depot in England and, of course, the headquarters staff at Metz. It was a part of the North Atlantic Treaty Organization in Europe to prevent a further outbreak of war with the Soviet Union. The Command Matron, who was part of the Staff Officer Medical Services' team, was responsible for supervising the nursing services throughout the Division. There were lighter moments during this tour and Muriel delighted in travelling to neighboring European countries and the British Isles on her time off duty.

Squadron Leader McArthur returned from Europe in August 1959 to

230

assume the duties of Principal Matron of the RCAF on the staff of the Director General Medical Services (Air) at Air Force Headquarters in Ottawa. Canadian Forces integration was in process at this time and on 20 May 1960 the DGMS(Air) staff was integrated with that of the newly appointed Surgeon General when the Canadian Forces Medical Service (CFMS) was formed. S/L McArthur continued to be involved primarily with the RCAF Nursing Service. In September 1960, Muriel McArthur was appointed Matron-in-Chief of the CFMS and was promoted to Wing Commander (W/C) on 16 June 1961. W/C McArthur held this appointment until her retirement 29 March 1965, after a long and dedicated career devoted to the well being of airmen, airwomen and to family members who, from time to time, came under her care. She was always grateful to the RCAF, she said, for the opportunities she was afforded and for a most interesting career and happy memories of Air Force life. There is little doubt that Muriel McArthur gave much of herself in this distinguished career, far more than the value of the rewards she received.

Summary of Achievements

Officer of the Venerable Order of the Hospital of St. John of Jerusalem (OStJ)
Canadian Forces Decoration (CD)
Defence Medal
Canadian Volunteer Service Medal and Clasp
War Medal, 1939 - 1945
Queen Elizabeth II Coronation Medal
Special Service Medal - NATO
Queen's Honorary Nursing Sister

DOROTHY McCLELLAND
CD, RN
LIEUTENANT-COLONEL

Dorothy McClelland was born in Toronto, Ontario on 4 March 1937 where she obtained her early schooling. Shortly after graduating high school, Dorothy entered the nursing training programme at the Ontario Hospital in Whitby, graduating in 1958 with a Nursing Diploma. Dorothy came from an Air Force family, her father having served in the RCAF in wartime. It is not surprising that one year after graduation, Dorothy enrolled in the Royal Canadian Air Force in March 1959 as a Pilot Officer (P/O) Nursing Sister.

The RCAF Officers' Indoctrination Course was conducted at RCAF Station Centralia, a small station just north of London, Ontario. P/O McClelland completed her basic training there in May 1959 and was posted just a few miles further north to RCAF Station Clinton. Clinton was the principal training station for armament and electronics engineering and trades. During McClelland's tour at Clinton, she was promoted to Flying Officer (F/O).

LCol Dorothy McClelland

As soon as a Tri-Service Nursing Officer's Course became available in April 1960, McClelland went sent to RCAF Station Downsview, Ontario to complete this program. F/O McClelland, now a qualified nursing officer, reported to RCAF Station Rockcliffe Hospital near Ottawa in March 1961. This Hospital closed and the staff opened a new facility just completed in Ottawa called the National Defence Medical Centre. McLelland joined the Operating Room staff

232

of this new facility as Head Nurse of Central Sterile Supply in August 1961. During this tour, she completed the extension course in Nursing Unit Administration given at the University of Toronto under the aegis of the Canadian Hospital Association, a diploma program at St. Michael's Hospital in Toronto in operating room procedures and techniques and a diploma program in Central Sterile Supply at Kitchener-Waterloo, Ontario.

Two years later, in August 1963, F/O McClelland assumed the duties of the Nursing Officer in-charge of the Operating Room at RCAF Station Hospital Goose Bay, Labrador. Goose Bay was, and still is an active flying station. There were many Air Force members and their families living in the area for whom the Station Hospital provided full medical care. It was a busy and exciting time.

The Goose Bay posting was rather brief and one year later in August 1964, F/O McClelland was on her way to the opposite end of the country for duties at British Columbia Area Headquarters Medical Inspection Room (MIR) in Vancouver. The term MIR described the out-patient facilities at military units. This last posting was also short-lived and, in February 1965, Dorothy was needed further north on Vancouver Island at RCAF Station Comox. In addition to the squadrons of all-weather jet interceptors, flying aerial defence patrols of the northwest, Comox was also the principal air search and rescue station in the area and conducted numerous air evacuations of patients to larger medical centres in Victoria and Vancouver. Now a Flight Lieutenant (F/L), McClelland accompanied many of these patients and for this reason was sent off for formal training as a Flight Nurse in May 1965.

F/L McClelland's first overseas posting took her to 3 (Fighter) Wing Hospital at Zweibrucken in Germany in November 1965. 3 (F) Wing was one of three fighter wings based in Europe at that time, comprising 1 Air Division. The hospital had full surgical and specialist services to look after Air Force personnel and their families for the entire Air Division. These were busy years, but it also afforded the opportunity to travel on holidays and time off duty.

The end of the European tour in December 1967 brought F/L McClelland back to Ottawa to manage the Central Sterile Supply section of the Operating Room at the National Defence Medical Centre. Her potential for further training was recognized and Dorothy was enrolled at the University of Ottawa's baccalaureate program in nursing sciences. Canadian Forces integration brought a change in rank from Flight Lieutenant to its equivalent rank of Captain (Capt). McClelland was, at various times, starting in 1968, assigned to the staff of No. 1 Canadian Field Hospital augmentation staff for deployment should the unit be sent to an operation or called out for training and exercises. The Field Hospital is a 200-bed, air transportable facility that can provide medical and surgical services to forces deployed in a combat or humanitarian role.

Capt McClelland graduated BScN in May 1972 and was sent to Germany to take charge of the Operating Room at the new Canadian Forces location at Canadian Forces Base Lahr for a two-year tour.

Returning to Canada in 1974, McClelland again crossed the country to assume the duties of the Operating Room Supervisor of Canadian Forces Hospital Esquimalt on Vancouver Island. These were changing times and one of the requirements for career progression was a knowledge of the French language, so in August 1975, Captain McClelland returned to Ottawa to take a one-year program in French.

She remained in Ottawa following French language training and took charge of the Out-patient Department and Emergency Room of the National Defence Medical Centre, taking time out to complete the Middle Management Course in 1977. Captain McClelland remained at NDMC until September 1978 when she was appointed Senior Nursing Officer at Canadian Forces Base Borden, Ontario. CFB Borden was and still is the principal training base of the Canadian Forces where all basic trades training and some arms field training is conducted. While at Borden, Dorothy was promoted to Major (Maj) and re-assigned to the NDMC in Ottawa.

Maj McClelland became the Operating Room Supervisor of NDMC in June 1979 and remained in this role for two years until she joined the staff of the Surgeon General at National Defence Headquarters (NDHQ) as assistant to the Director of Nursing Services for the Canadian Forces Medical Service in June 1981. During this tour, Maj McClelland completed the military course in Instructional Techniques. It was during this period that Maj McClelland was Acting Chair of the NATO Nuclear Planning Group "Montebello 83."

Four years later, Maj McClelland served a short term as Career Manager for the Nursing Classification. This one-year tour brought another promotion to Lieutenant-Colonel (LCol) and a new assignment as the Director of Nursing at the NDMC in September 1986.

In June 1990, LCol McClelland was assigned to an "out-of-classification" job with the Director General Ceremonial as Chair of the NATO Nuclear Planning Group "Kananaskis 90."

Dorothy McClelland retired from the Regular Force, after a thirty-two year career that included two European tours and numerous postings in Canada, both with the RCAF and with the CFMS. On retirement, LCol McClelland was placed on the Supplementary Reserve list until a final release in March 1997.

Summary of Achievements

Canadian Forces Decoration (CD)
Special Service Medal - NATO
Registered Nurse - Ontario Hospital Whitby, 1958

Veronika Agnes "Roni" McKee
née Loewe
SSStJ, CD, RN
Colonel

Veronika Loewe, known to all her friends as "Roni" was born in Hohndorf, Germany on 17 April 1932. She attended elementary and high school in Germany, following which she entered the Elisabeth Hospital School of Nursing in Bochum, Germany, graduating with a diploma in Nursing in 1953. In November of that same year, Roni immigrated to Canada and took up employment at the Municipal Hospital in Medicine Hat, Alberta as general duty nurse and then as night supervisor.

Four years later, in 1957, Roni enrolled in the Royal Canadian Air Force as a Pilot Officer Nursing Sister. Basic officer training was conducted at RCAF Station London, after which Loewe was promoted to Flying Officer (F/O) and posted to RCAF Station Greenwood, Nova Scotia. Roni was keenly interested in aviation and took training on the job as a flight nurse, learning aeromedevac procedures and techniques for transporting patients by air. She also took flying training and obtained a private pilot's license.

Col V.A. "Roni" McKee

It seemed almost perverse that with her love of flying, Roni was transferred from Greenwood to the Royal Canadian Navy Hospital HMCS Stadacona in Halifax, Nova Scotia in 1958. The two years in Halifax went quickly and almost as a reward, her next posting, in 1960, was to Germany.

During this three-year posting at 3 (Fighter) Wing Hospital in

Zweibrucken, she held positions as head nurse and Out-Patient Department supervisor. She met her future husband, Flight Lieutenant W.A. "Bill" McKee an RCAF fighter pilot, during this posting.

F/O Lowe returned to Canada in January 1964 and was appointed head nurse at the National Defence Medical Centre in Ottawa, Ontario. She was promoted to Flight Lieutenant a month later. In January 1965, Roni and Bill were married at the RCAF Chapel at Uplands in Ottawa. They have been married for thirty-five years.

In October 1966, Roni was back in a flying milieu when she was posted to RCAF Station Gimli, Manitoba where she was the senior nursing officer at the Station Hospital. While at Gimli, Roni was permitted to fly second seat in the Lockheed T-33 "T-Bird." She had to go through the High Altitude Indoctrination and Ejection training and was equipped with her own flying suit and helmet. Roni's outfit had one minor difference – the helmet was painted a shocking pink so that the flight line boys would see her coming and modify their language accordingly. T-33 long range training flights onto U.S. Air Force Bases provoked some interesting reactions and comments. Air controllers sat up and paid attention when an RCAF jet crew member gave her position and requested weather, wind, altimeter settings and runways in use in a soprano female voice. There was, at times, consternation when the occupant of that jet removed her helmet and let her long hair come cascading down.

The four years at Gimli must have passed too quickly and in July 1970 she returned to the National Defence Medical Centre in Ottawa as Nursing Supervisor. This experience served her well as she began undergraduate studies in 1973 at the University of Ottawa. A Baccalaureate in Nursing Sciences was conferred on Major McKee on successful completion of these studies in 1976. Following university training she was appointed staff officer with the Specialist Officers Career Development Program Research Study Group at National Defence Headquarters in Ottawa.

With another promotion to Lieutenant-Colonel in 1979, Roni was appointed Director of Nursing at the National Defence Medical Centre. LCol McKee's talents in personnel management resulted in a transfer in 1981 to National Defence Headquarters in the Directorate of Personnel Careers Officers, as career manager for the nursing classification.

There was one more promotion in store and in 1983 Colonel McKee moved to the staff of the Surgeon General at National Defence Headquarters as Director of Nursing Service, the most senior nursing officer in the CFMS. At that time, she was appointed the Queen's Honorary Nursing Sister. Col McKee also served as a consultant to the Canadian Forces Medical Council and nursing advisor to St. John Ambulance of Canada.

Col McKee retired from the Canadian Forces on 1988, but remained on the Supplementary Ready Reserve list for several years.

Colonel McKee prepares for a field hospital inspection.

Summary of Achievements

Serving Sister of the Most Venerable Order of the Hospital of St. John of Jerusalem (SSStJ)
Canadian Forces Decoration (CD)
Special Services Medal - NATO
Queen's Honorary Nursing Sister
RN - Elisabeth Hospital School of Nursing Bochum, Germany
BSc - Baccalaureate in Nursing Science - University of Ottawa, 1976

FRANCES M. "FRAN" OAKES
ARRC, CD, RN
SQUADRON LEADER

Frances Oakes, known to everyone as "Fran" was born 5 May 1906 in Rockwood, Ontario where she graduated from high school. She enrolled in the Kitchener-Waterloo School of Nursing and graduated in 1930. In the years following graduation, Fran did postgraduate work in Operating Room at the Montreal General Hospital and the Toronto General Hospital. This led to her work at the Kitchener-Waterloo Hospital as the Operating Room Supervisor.

With the outbreak of war, Fran enrolled in the Royal Canadian Air Force in October 1940 as a Pilot Officer (P/O) Nursing Sister. Her first assignment was to No. 1 Technical Training School at St. Thomas, Ontario. The infirmary of No. 1 TTS was in a new medical facility of 250 beds, which had a capacity of 700. The huge complex of buildings that housed No. 1 TTS was originally intended to be a mental institution, but before it could be used for this purpose, the RCAF commandeered it as a training school for what was termed

S/L Frances M. "Fran" Oakes

"ground" or non-flying trades training . The staff of the infirmary included nurses of the Royal Canadian Army Medical Corps (RCAMC) and a senior nurse called the Matron. There were several army medical doctors and Medical Assistants, as well as clerical help. Some were on loan from the RCAMC while others were awaiting transfer to the new Air Force Medical Branch.

Personnel of the RCAMC provided medical care for the RCAF at the beginning of World War II and Army nursing sisters were posted to RCAF stations. As the RCAF expanded, and the British Commonwealth Air Training

Plan was organized, the need for a separate medical organization was apparent. The Medical Branch of the RCAF was established by Order-in-Council, September, 1940 and on 28 November 1940 the RCAF Nursing Service was authorized. Colonel Elizabeth Smellie organized the new nursing service and acted as its Matron-In-Chief until June 1943 when Flight Lieutenant J.E.C. Porteous assumed the appointment of matron. In 1944 she became Principal Matron. The first twelve RCAF nursing sisters had re-mustered from the RCAMC. In all, 481 joined the RCAF, 68 of them served overseas.

Not so well known is the fact that two Air Force nursing sisters landed in Normandy with an RCAF mobile field hospital thirteen days after D-Day. These first Canadian service women to cross the channel after D-Day were Flying Officer Dabina "Wyn" Pitkithly of Ottawa and Flying Officer Dorothy Mulholland of Georgetown, Ontario.

Most of the patients at No. 1 TTS were new recruits, many of whom had travelled by rail across the country, had been housed in close quarters and exposed to upper respiratory and other communicable diseases. As well, there were a few emergencies and accidental injuries brought in from the three nearby flying stations where aircrew were being trained under the British Common-wealth Air Training Plan. P/O Oakes was assigned to the operating room primarily, but was expected to perform her share of staff nursing duties as well. P/O Oakes' work at No. 1 Technical Training School was recognized by the Royal Red Cross in January of 1943 when they she was made an Associate (second class) of the Royal Red Cross. The citation read:

"This nursing sister has been in charge of the operating room at TTS since 1940. She has been in charge of a 250-bed hospital. Squadron Leader Oakes has carried out her duties in an exceptional manner and, as a direct result of her initiative, a very high standard efficiency has been maintained. She set a very high example at all times."

S/L Oakes was one of twenty of in a total of 481 RCAF nurses to receive this award.

In April 1942, P/O Oakes was posted overseas along with Nursing Sister Lenora Lloyst, a Kingston General Hospital graduate - the first RCAF nurses sent to England. They were posted to the East Grinstead, Sussex Plastic Unit. The hospital had 146 beds to accommodate Navy, Army, and Air Force

240

personnel casualties from the retreat from Dunkirk and from the Battle of Britain as well as burned civilians. Following surgery in the main hospital, the patients were housed in Nissen huts adjoining the hospital for follow-up care. Nissen huts were temporary shelters constructed from semicylindrical sheets of corrugated iron and set on a cement slab[1]. They were used as workshops, for barrack accommodation and as temporary hospital facilities.

In September 1939, the British Ministry of Health selected the Queen Victoria Cottage Hospital to be one of the specialty centres to deal with plastic surgery required to repair burns and jaw injuries. The Ministry appointed Mr. A.H. McIndoe[2], Consultant to the RAF in plastic surgery and Mr. W. Kelsey-Fry[2], consultant in dental surgery, to be in charge of these respective fields.

From the earliest days of the war, Canadian airmen requiring this form of specialized treatment were sent here as well as other injured Allied air force personnel. The injuries suffered by Aircrews while parachuting from burning planes were devastating.

In January 1942, a Canadian surgeon, Group Captain Ross Tilly, was posted to East Grinstead. The number of casualties needing care soon exceeded all available beds and the Canadian government authorized the construction and equipping of a special Air Force wing designed to accommodate 50 patients. The Royal Canadian Engineers carried out construction. It opened in July 1944 with an all RCAF staff.

The very highest degree of co-operation and friendship existed between the staff of the Queen Victoria Hospital and the RCAF unit. All the various facilities were always mutually available. This helped immeasurably in the efficient functioning of the unit as concerned both patients and staff. The work done at this hospital was unique, innovative and extraordinary. The repairing and rebuilding of disfigured hands and faces were important, but equally important was the restoration of personal morale and self-assurance, which almost inevitably were burned away simultaneously with the normal features. The patients considered their disfigurements at best a social disability - at worst a tragedy.

Tilley, who was in charge of the Canadian airmen, would sit down and discuss their problems. He would invite them to watch the surgeons doing skin grafts so they would realize they were in competent hands before they

241

themselves underwent these procedures. There were four different types of skin grafts. Tilley requested that nurses become familiar with these techniques as well as hospital regulations, surgical skills and the psychological ability to assist in restoring self-confidence to the patients. Along with the opportunity to observe the operations, Tilley stressed to the patients that "it is great to be alive, and that the real joy is the gift of life regardless of handicap."

The types of problem handled at East Grinstead were thus both broad and specific. It required highly specialized surgical skill to restore the physical appearance, as well as the psychological ability to restore mental ease and self-confidence. One of the greatest problems lay in preventing the patient from becoming a physical and mental recluse.

Consequently the hospital was conducted on an entirely different basis than other military hospitals. Discipline and regimentation were kept to a minimum. There were neither ranks nor separate rooms for officers. The "boys" were allowed and encouraged to go to the pubs and mix with other people. Theatre parties to London were arranged three times a week. The residents of East Grinstead dined and danced with the patients ignoring burnt hands or faces. The people of East Grinstead had been warned by Tilley that they would see all sorts of disfigurements and sometimes the repairs taking place looked more grotesque than the actual injury.

Among the unusual facilities for rehabilitation available at Queen Victoria Hospital was a factory which turned out aircraft instruments, specifically "directional gyros" and "turn and bank" indicators. A small staff of trained operators was maintained to teach patients how the work should be done. In addition to this useful industrial therapy, the participating patients received regular hourly rates of pay, regardless of the volume of output. Strange as it may seem, the services of a psychiatrist were never required. Approximately 80 per cent of patients recovered sufficiently to return to flying duties.

An organization called the Guinea Pig Club was founded in 1941. The membership consisted of allied Aircrew patients who had been or were being treated at East Grinstead following severe burn injuries on "ops." One of the purposes was and is to keep track of the hospital alumni and lend a hand to those in need. There is a reunion every year in Britain and every five years in Canada with a newsletter to help keep in touch. A special sterling pin, a winged guinea pig, was devised and issued to these patients and to some staff members who were considered to be associate members of the club. Fran Oakes is one of these.

The Guinea Pig Wing

In five years, the hospital did not send a single man to an institution - all went back into service or returned to civilian life. Some very senior officers were among those hospitalized and they too liked the policy of no rank distinction. This is apparent in the wording of the plaque which hangs inside the Canadian Wing's main entrance. It is dedicated "To the gallant young men of the Royal Canadian Air Force whose wounds have brought them here and to the doctors and nurses who cared for them; this building has been erected by the people of the Dominion of Canada". On 5 September 1945, the wing was officially handed over to the board of management of the Queen Victoria Hospital, East Grinstead.

During their nursing service at East Grinstead, Lenora Lloyst and Fran Oakes were billeted at "Herontyne" the home of Lord and Lady Glendyne. This was originally the estate of the Earl, John Rushworth Jellico, British Admiral of WWI fame for his battle with the German navy at Jutland in 1916. Their billet was four miles from the hospital and as petrol was scarce they walked morning and night to and from work. They were issued ration cards as were their hosts, who treated them royally as war guests and shared what they had with them. Lloyst and Oakes were expected to take their turns along with their hosts in night duty putting out incendiary bombs while keeping watch. In addition, they shared the air raid shelters with the entire household. Their stay with nobility did much to allay their previous misconceptions regarding the "upper class."

Oakes returned to Canada in June 1944 and was posted to RCAF Station Trenton, then to the Technical Training School in St. Thomas to close out that facility. This was followed by a short stay at Trenton before moving to Ottawa.

After the war ended in 1945, the RCAF was required to supply medical staff to a number of radar stations, called the Pine Tree Line, situated roughly along the 50th parallel. This was the most southerly of three lines of radar sites. The other two, further north were the Mid-Canada Line along the 55th parallel and the Distant Early Warning or DEW Line north of the Arctic Circle. Air force personnel and their dependents were based on Pine Tree Line sites, which were some great distance from urban centres and where civilian health services were minimal or non-existent. Therefore, the RCAF was responsible for providing whatever care was needed by the Air Force members, their dependents and emergency care to some local inhabitants . In her position as Principal Matron she regularly visited these sites. As well, other areas with RCAF nursing staff such as the stations in Germany, France and Belgium were visited. Oakes flew in "butter and eggs" (supply planes) and commercial aircraft, rode in jeeps, canoes, trucks or whatever was available.

During these years S/L Oakes spent much of her time in administration. Immediately after the war, the recruitment quota for nurses for the three services was very small - a quota of thirty for the RCAF. The military was cut to a minimum in the defence planners' hopes that collaboration and negotiation would replace war. However, the rise of Communist aggression made it obvious that an increase in the services and thus an expansion of the RCAF nursing service was needed. Oakes was involved in the recruiting program and later in preliminary work on the integration of the medical services of the three branches of the armed forces. The Canadian Force Medical Service came into being 1 January 1959.

S/L Oakes retired in 1958 and has, from time to time, looked back on her career as an RCAF Nursing Sister. Many changes took place during those years of which she is proud to be have been a part - assisting in the early days of plastic surgery, observing the effects of the first usage of penicillin, transportation of casualties by air, organizing and ordering supplies suitable for outlying posts and the advent of the Para-Rescue training for nurses to name a few. The variety of experiences, the chance to visit many places, the cross-section of people she met has all combined to make many unforgettable memories.

Fran Oakes donated her medals and miniatures to the RCAF Memorial Air Museum along with her Guinea Pig Wing awarded to her as an associate of the

Guinea Pig Club. This year she contributed to a memorial stone to the RCAF Memorial Museum. Squadron Leader Oakes lives in a retirement home in Guelph and maintains contact with many of her nursing friends.

Summary of Achievements

Canadian Forces Decoration (CD)
ARRC - Associate Royal Red Cross (Second Class)
Defence Medal
Canadian Volunteer Service Medal and Clasp
War Medal 1939 - 1945
Coronation Medal
RN - Kitchener Waterloo School of Nursing - 1930

Notes:
1. Named after their designer, LCol Peter N. Nissen and similar to a later design called Quonset huts, named after Quonset, Rhode Island, the place of their origin.

2. The honorific Mister is used in Britain to address surgeons. Physicians are called Doctor.

SHIRLEY M. ROBINSON
CD, RN
LIEUTENANT-COLONEL

Shirley Robinson is a native of Lucknow, Ontario where she graduated from high school. Shirley trained in nursing at the General and Marine Hospital School of Nursing in Owen Sound, Ontario and graduated as a a registered nurse in 1953. A year later, Shirley enrolled in the Royal Canadian Air Force as a Pilot Officer and underwent basic officer training RCAF Station London, Ontario.

During a 30-year career with the Canadian Armed Forces, she served in numerous senior military nursing and administrative positions in Canada and overseas, including those of staff officer to the Surgeon General at National Defence Headquarters, Ottawa, and Director of Nursing at the National Defence Medical Centre, Ottawa.

LCol Shirley M. Robinson

Robinson completed courses in military nursing, medical nursing, nursing unit and nursing service administration. She is a graduate of both the junior and senior staff courses from the Canadian Forces Command and Staff College in Toronto, Ontario. Additionally, she completed French language training and advanced management courses at St- Jean, Québec.

Prior to her retirement in 1984, Robinson was the Deputy Director of Women Personnel at National Defence Headquarters and, as such, was intimately involved with all aspects of women's employment and conditions of service within the armed forces. Throughout her career, she endeavoured to improve and advance the military nursing service and the role and employment opportunities for Canadian Forces women.

Since retirement, she has been politically active in efforts to gain career equity for service women by:

- co-founding the Association for Women's Equity in the Canadian Forces (AWECF);
- presenting written and verbal briefs to federal ministers and other parliamentarians;
- acting as consultant to the Canadian Human Rights Commission, and the Status of Women of Canada on the role of military women;
- assisting the legal profession in the preparation of discrimination cases against the armed forces; and,
- appearing before the media to publicize the importance of equity for military women.

Robinson is a founding member of the AWECF, a past vice-president of the Nursing Sisters' Association of Canada, and a past president of the Ottawa Unit of the Nursing Sisters' Association of Canada. She is a member of:

- the Council of Canadians;
- the Human Rights Institute of Canada; and
- the College of Nurses of Ontario

For devoting a significant part of her life to improving and enhancing the role and opportunities of Canadian Forces women while a member of the armed forces, and since her retirement, Robinson received the Governor General's award in commemoration of the Person's Case in October, 1992.

Publications and Articles
- *The Canadian Forces Policy on the Employment of Women: Time for Change* - brief presented to the Parliamentary Committee on Equality Rights, 15 July, 1985.
- *Women in Combat: The Last Bastion* - published by Canadian Woman Studies, Winter 1985, Vol. 6, No. 4.
- Response of the AWECF to the Department of Justice Canada's Report:

Toward Equality, concerning Women in the Armed Forces, May 1986. (Co-authored).

- *The Right to Serve: Women and the 'Combat Issue'* - published by Forum (sponsored by the Conference of Defence Associations), 1989.
- *Canadian Military Women: The Struggle for Equity* - paper presented to the Learned Society, Queen's University, June 1991.

Summary of Achievements

Canadian Forces Decoration (CD)

Registered Nurse - General and Marine Hospital School of Nursing, Owen Sound - 1953 (R.N.)

Governor General's Award in Commemoration of the Person's Case in October 1992

CHAPTER 7
THE INNKEEPERS*

MEDICAL ASSOCIATE OFFICERS
(Health Care Administration)

- **Colonel Roger A. Cunningham**

    A Technical Assistant Medical, and a talented administrator, who went from an Aircraftman Class 2 (AC2) to Colonel, the first Medical Associate Officer in that rank; he was awarded the Order of Military Merit.

- **Squadron Leader C. Nelson Evoy**

    A medical administrative officer with wide field, command and headquarters experience.

*Luke 10, 35   *"And the next day he took out two denarii and gave them to the innkeeper and said, "Take care of him; and whatever more thou spendest, I, on my way back, will repay thee."*

- **Squadron Leader Ted Gerein**
  Originally in the Royal Canadian Army Medical Corps, he transferred to the RCAF when its Medical Branch was formed in November 1940.

- **Major A.C. "Chuck" King**
  A boy soldier, artillery gunner, airman, officer who progressed through the military ranks and three grades in the Most Venerable Order of the Hospital of St. John of Jerusalem.

- **Lieutenant-Colonel D. G. "Doug" Manderson**
  The first RCAF medical administrative officer of that rank; he served as the first Senior Medical Administrative Officer at the National Defence Medical Centre, which he helped design.

- **Lieutenant-Colonel H. M. "Hal" Wright**
  A Technical Assistant Medical and health care administrator who worked with various medical organizations for over 50 years .

ROGER A. CUNNINGHAM
OMM, SBStJ, CD
COLONEL

Roger Cunningham, born in Pubnico, Nova Scotia in 1926. He attended Acadia University for three years with the intention of going to medical school. Instead, he went to the Nova Scotia Teachers College and, after teaching for only two years, joined the Royal Canadian Air Force, attracted by the opportunity to work in a research environment.

He enjoyed a career spanning 39 years with postings that took him to Toronto and Ottawa in Ontario, Cold Lake in Alberta, and Halifax, Nova Scotia. His employment during that period was in the areas of aviation medicine, research and development, materiel management, teaching, personnel administration, financial management, and health care administration.

Throughout his career he welcomed opportunities to advance his education. The Air Force sent him to the mandatory training courses, and to the USAF School of Aerospace Medicine in San Antonio, Texas and sponsored him for the Canadian Hospital Association's two year course in hospital administration. At night, he took university courses while in Toronto, Ottawa and Halifax.

Col Roger A. Cunningham

Cunningham reflected that his career highlights included the opportunity to work with fine scientists at the RCAF Institute of Aviation Medicine as a technician, and later as Chief Instructor of the School of Aviation Medicine. These included Group Captain W.R. Franks *(see Aviation Medicine Pioneers)*, whose contributions to aviation medicine during

251

WW II earned him the OBE and other honors, and who continued his research in the post-war years, and Major-General W.G. Leach *(see The Leaders)* who won the McKee trophy for his contributions to aviation while at the Institute of Aviation Medicine, and went on to become Surgeon General.

During his tour at RCAF Station Cold Lake, Alberta, Roger was instrumental in establishing survival training for aircrew and a ground search and rescue team. He enjoyed his posting to Canadian Forces Hospital Halifax, which provided an opportunity to make major renovations and to improve the health care facilities. His work in finance brought about the development of agreements with provincial ministries of health for military involvement in health care delivery to civilians. Later, as Director of Medical Administration and Resources on the staff of the Surgeon General, he enjoyed overseeing and becoming actively involved in planning the construction and staffing of military health care facilities in Canada and Europe.

Roger Cunningham, who had been commissioned from the ranks, was promoted to full Colonel while serving with the Surgeon General. He became the first Medical Associate Officer (Administration) to hold this rank.

Colonel Cunningham's last major project before retiring was the designing of a new state-of-the-art hospital in Lahr[1], Germany for the Canadian Forces and their dependents based there.

Shortly after retirement, he conducted a study of the need for a surgical medical capability on the West Coast and another on the need for two military hospitals in the Atlantic Provinces. He then was employed by the RCMP as a consultant to study and report on its health services across Canada.

Colonel Cunningham was a founder and charter member of the Canadian College of Health Service Executives and an honourary member of the Association of Military Surgeons of the United States. His work was recognized by his appointment as a Serving Brother of the Most Venerable Order of the Hospital of St. John of Jerusalem, and his later appointment as an Officer of the Order of Military Merit on 30 June 1985.

Roger Cunningham continues his long-time association with military medicine through his membership in the Defence Medical Association. He has made Windsor, Ontario, his retirement home where he is involved in community affairs. He winters in Naples, Florida and in both locations

252

indulges in his hobbies of genealogy and water-colour painting, as well as working on his golf game.

Summary of Achievements

Officer of the Order of Military Merit (OMM)
Serving Brother of the Most Venerable Order of the Hospital of St. John of Jerusalem (SBStJ)
Canadian Forces Decoration (CD)
Member of the Defence Medical Association of Canada
Honorary Member of the Association of Military Surgeons of the United States

Note: *1. This hospital was no sooner officially opened when it was announced that Canada would withdraw its forces from Europe. The new facility was handed over to the German government for use by the city of Lahr.*

Nelson C. Evoy
CD
Squadron Leader

Nelson Evoy, usually known as "Nels" joined the Royal Canadian Army Medical Corps as a Private in January 1940. The Royal Canadian Air Force did not have its own medical branch at that time, but the RCAF recruiting centre in Ottawa informed him that he would be transferred to the RCAF as soon as its own medical branch was formed. Therefore, Nelson was duly enrolled with Regimental Number C93040 as a Private (Pte) in the RCAMC/RCAF/Canadian Army Special Force.

RCAF Station Rockcliffe. Pte Evoy was sent to Rockcliffe, a few miles out of Ottawa, to RCAF Station Rockcliffe Hospital where he served until August 1940. Nels was put to work in the Orderly Room as a clerk. There were thousands of men on the station, getting ready to go overseas or to training stations across Canada. The hospital had fifty beds and a large Medical Inspection Room (MIR) to handle outpatients and inoculations. The facility was open twenty-four hours a day, so everyone was kept very busy.

S/L Nelson C. Evoy

Along with medical duties, Evoy learned how to parade, to participate in war games, to transport casualties on a field stretcher and how to render first aid. However, there were some demeaning chores, such as taking the rug from the Senior Medical Officer's office and beating it on the clothes line behind the hospital, once a week. For some of these "joe-jobs", Nels said, you had to swallow your pride. In fact he got reprimanded for stating he felt these were demeaning. An inspector general from headquarters visited frequently to ensure the premises were clean and tidy. Everyone cleaned his area a little better just in case "the old man" chose it for closer inspection.

He applied himself to his new duties, attended weekly Wing Parade and studied the Canadian Air Publication (CAP) 90 to learn as much as he could about RCAF drill. His diligence was duly noted and he was sent on an administrative course for non-commissioned officers and promoted to Acting Corporal (Cpl) in May 1940.

School of English, Hospice St. Charles in Québec City. English was the working language of the Air Force during wartime and the RCAF operated a School of English for French speaking servicemen at Hospice St. Charles in Québec City. Cpl Evoy was sent to work at this school in August 1940. While there, he was promoted to Sergeant (Sgt) and transferred to the RCAF Medical Branch with RCAF Special Reserve Regimental Number R55809 in November 1940.

Hospice St. Charles was a convent that was being used by the RCAF as a school. During the early days, everyone had to enter and leave the building through a cellar-way with low-hanging steam pipes during renovations to the main part of the building. With inadequate lighting and the low pipes in the passageway, it was inevitable that someone would get hurt. Evoy was on duty one night when they brought in a young serviceman who had hit his head on a steam pipe while going down the basement stairway. Within a few hours the poor lad was paralyzed from the neck down and was transferred to a DVA hospital in Québec City .

Sgt Evoy, who was married and had one daughter, was allowed to move his family if he could find accommodations, but without any financial help from the government. He moved the family to Québec City and rented three rooms from a French family on Rue Artillerie Their landlady was most accommodating during their stay.

No. 9 Service Flying Training School. These were busy years as Canada undertook to train aircrew from Commonwealth countries. In January 1941, Sgt Evoy was on his way to No. 9 Service Flying Training School at Summerside, Prince Edward Island. A month later in February 1941, Evoy was promoted to Flight Sergeant (F/S) and was appointed NCO in-charge of the Medical Orderly Room. He was required also to take charge of a "Flight" on parades. A flight is a formation similar to an army platoon, comprising about twenty-five airmen and or airwomen.

Commanding Officer's inspections on Friday mornings required every part of the station to be spick and span, including the medical facilities. As Senior NCO, Evoy was responsible to see that this was done. Finding the pharmacy area, waiting room and adjacent washroom in a somewhat untidy state, he assigned Leading Aircraftman McCarten to clean it up. An indignant McCarten quickly informed F/S Evoy that he was the pharmacist and he was not about to take on the work of the cleaning crew. Do it or else, he was told and he reluctantly did so, but years later, Flight Lieutenant McCarten, still a pharmacist and Evoy's boss got the last laugh.

No. 2 SFTS - Uplands. When F/S Evoy arrived at Uplands in May 1941, No. 2 Service Flying Training School, a part of the British Commonwealth Air Training Plan (BCATP), was at its height of operations, turning out fighter pilots. Amongst his many duties at the Station Hospital, Evoy was responsible for the "diet account" of the hospital which necessitated many meetings with the army ordinance to make sure that the hospital got the best cuts of beef, fresh vegetables, especially good potatoes etc. One of his secondary duties was secretary of the Sergeants' Mess. This included collecting one day's pay from each successful pilot, who was promoted to Sergeant on graduation and became a member of the Mess. To ensure that Mess dues were paid, Evoy would sit with the paymaster on pay days to ensure these dues were collected.

Everyone had to keep physically fit and periodic route marches were laid on to keep the airmen in shape. The medical staff took their march to Mooney's Bay, a local swimming hole, so that they could have a swim before returning. F/S Evoy could never convince the Medical Officers to join them on the march nor the swim. By January 1942, Evoy was on the move again.

No. 9 Bombing & Gunnery School, Mount-Joli, Québec. The bombing and gunnery school used single-engine Fairy Battle, Westland Lysanders, and Northrup Nomads, as well as multi-engine Avro Ansons and Bristol Bolingbrokes. The Nomads were used to tow target drogues at which the air gunners fired. There was great potential for accidents and the Station Hospital received its share of casualties resulting from crashes and other injuries.

BCATP trainees came from many countries and Evoy's room-mate was a

New Zealander, whose name was Wally Osborne. He was one of the crash casualties, bringing his Fairy Battle down on the airfield. He survived, but required a good deal of plastic surgery at the Montreal Neurological Hospital. His flying career was ended due to his injuries. An Australian Flight Sergeant, who had become a good friend of Evoy and his family, was flying a Nomad, towing a drogue when the aircraft came down on the railroad line just outside Mont-Joli. F/S Evoy was on ambulance duty that day. They managed to stop the oncoming train and went to remove the bodies from the aircraft. It was quite a shock for Evoy to find his friend dead in the plane, but they had to carry on. The Flight Sergeant was buried at Priceville, a little town outside Mont-Joli.

F/S Evoy's work at 9 B&G School earned him two more promotions– to Warrant Officer 2nd Class in August 1942 and to Warrant Officer 1st Class (WO1) in February 1944.

The war was winding down as WO1 Evoy was posted to No. 1 "Y" Depot in Lachine, Québec in April 1944. A "Y" depot's functions were to process airmen to go overseas. An "X" depot would process them on their return from overseas. Although known as a "Y" depot, the unit at Lachine performed both functions. Large numbers of air force members were returning from overseas to be demobilized while others had to be processed to go overseas. He remained here until May 1945 and the end of the war in Europe. The station hospital had seventy-five beds, mainly for returning airmen who required specialized care and surgery. The hospital employed psychiatrists to look after those patients who needed counselling.

There was a heavy workload generated by in-patient care, processing those leaving the service, and preparing others to go to England and Europe, that kept the hospital records and orderly room busy. The staff had over 5,000 medical files at any given time and these had a high turn-over rate.

Streetcar Hijinks. Although the station was generally busy, there were periods of inactivity that led to boredom and then to hijinks. On one such night, one of the NCOs, a hefty fellow, mentioned he had always wished to drive a Montreal streetcar. The cars came all the way out to Lachine, so wouldn't it be a great prank to commandeer one and drive it into Montreal. About six Mess members trundled off to the Lachine streetcar terminal and waited for a car to appear. The elderly conductor was more than a little perturbed when he heard what the boys had in mind, and tried to resist the take-over. He was physically, but gently, removed from his seat to join the rest of the merry band as a passenger as the Flight Sergeant conductor took over the controls. The ride into Montreal was "non-stop" leaving confounded passengers at stations along the way. There were six police cars waiting at the Montreal terminal to escort the pirate crew back to the Station and into the hands of the Service Police. Although there were no civilian charges laid, the Commanding Officer was not amused and confined the lot to barracks for a week to repent their sins.

Putative Father Parade. Although not a common occurrence, there were a number of instances where an unwed lady of the community complained that one of the station members had fathered her child. On such occasions, the whole station might be called out on parade while the lady in question walked along the ranks to see if she could identify the putative father. In the Lachine incident, no one was identified, producing a mass sigh of relief and the incident was closed.

Reversion Day. Nels decided to remain in the RCAF Regular, even though this meant dropping down two ranks from that held at the end of hostilities. Evoy went back to the rank of F/S in the RCAF Regular in October 1946. However, his work and responsibilities did not diminish, but this was accepted as normal by the majority of those who continued with the Regular Force. F/S Evoy had, by this time been posted back to RCAF Station Rockcliffe.

RCAF Station Rockcliffe. F/S Evoy was able to live off the station with his wife and family during this second tour at Rockliffe, making life a bit more pleasant. His Senior Medical Officer at the thirty-five bed hospital was Wing Commander (W/C) "Don" G.M. Nelson *(see The Leaders).* It was a rather unusual work situation as W/C Nelson was double-hatted as the Command Staff Officer Medical Services (SOMS) and as the Station Senior Medical Officer (SMO), in effect his own boss. This resulted in some unusual two-way correspondence between Nelson the SOMS and Nelson the SMO, which Evoy had to keep straight in files in both offices.

A Mop In The Face. On one occasion, F/S Evoy was directed to find a well-trained Medical Assistant quickly to be posted to Resolute Bay on Cornwallis Island, located north of the 70° parallel. The need for haste was that changing weather would soon prevent the aircraft from flying in. The Corporal in question was just moving into Emergency Married Quarters on the Station, so he wouldn't be hard to find, even on this Saturday morning. These quarters had just previously been used as barracks and there was a good deal of cleaning to be done to make them livable. Evoy faced a rather large woman at the Corporal's door who wanted to know his business. No, she said, she wouldn't call her husband, just state your business. When told that her husband was needed for duties at Resolute Bay, she grabbed a long-handled mop, pushed it into Evoy's face and said her husband wasn't going anywhere until he had finished mopping up their new quarters. Evoy beat a hasty retreat and got the Service Police to make sure the Corporal was in the aircraft at 1430 hrs for Resolute Bay. He and the aircraft landed safely at Resolute where he remained for three weeks or so.

Commissioned From The Ranks. During this second posting to Rockcliffe, Evoy was promoted back to Warrant Officer Class 2 in October, 1950, and less than a year later, in April 1951, he was commissioned from the ranks. His rank on commissioning was Pilot Officer, but he was simultaneously promoted to Flying Officer. The immediate promotion was normal for those commissioned from the ranks when their previous rank was F/S or higher and who had a minimum of ten years continuous service. Promotion to Flight Lieutenant (F/L), which came in January 1955, required officers to write and pass qualifying examinations. Similar examinations were successfully passed to qualify for promotion to Squadron Leader (S/L), and that promotion was effected in July 1962.

RCAF Station Trenton. On commissioning, F/O Evoy, a Medical Secretarial Officer, joined the staff of the the Director General Medical Services (Air) at Air Force Headquarters (AFHQ) in Ottawa for a short one-month tour, before going to RCAF Station Trenton, Ontario. His appointment at Trenton was administrative officer of the Station Hospital under the command of Wing Commander T.J. Powell *(see Aviation Medicine Pioneers).* Evoy held this appointment until September 1952. In addition to health care for the Station, the Hospital also had a decompression chamber that was used for High Altitude Indoctrination. There was also a night vision trainer. Consequently, there was a good deal of attractive equipment about and Evoy was responsible for keeping track of all this on a Hospital Inventory.

There was a "Sgt Bilkoe type" on the staff at Trenton at this time and F/O Evoy discovered that he was operating a private business during working hours and using station telephones to do it. This NCO, a senior laboratory technician was acting as an agent, buying and selling potatoes and arranging shipment between supplier and client by long-distance phone from one end of the country to the other. The phone service was discontinued immediately and the NCO made to pay the long-distance charges. Shortly thereafter, in September 1952, Flight Lieutenant Evoy returned to AFHQ on the staff of DGMS(Air) for a one-year tour of duty with the Director of Administration.

Westminster DVA Hospital London. During the 1950s, a number of military patients were hospitalized in the Department of Veterans Affairs hospitals and it was found necessary to establish liaison officers in the larger of these institutions. For this reason, F/L Evoy was assigned to Westminster DVA Hospital in London, Ontario in November 1953. He had a staff of two NCOs and was responsible for all the administration of patients in hospital or sent to this facility as outpatients. The hospital had 1500 beds, of which 600 were devoted to psychiatry. Although Evoy and his staff were held on strength of RCAF Station London, they worked quite independently under the direction of a medical officer appointed as Senior Medical Officer.

Air Defence Command. F/L Evoy moved to Air Defence Command (ADC) Headquarters at St-Hubert, Québec in April 1956. Air Defence Command was then tasked with the aerial defence of the north and had nation wide stations from Gander, Newfoundland to Holberg, British Columbia and as far north as the Arctic Circle. Evoy was appointed the administrative officer to the Staff Officer Medical Services in the Command Headquarters. The SOMS during his tour of duty were Group Captain T.J. Powell, mentioned earlier, and Group Captain Bonar Coles *(see Aviation Medicine Pioneers)*.

Annual visits were supposed to be made to each of the ADC units to check on equipment, supplies and administrative procedures. The problems of scheduling and getting transportation to many of these remote sites made this an impossible schedule. Completing the visits in eighteen months was considered a a job well done. Evoy's family lived in Permanent Married Quarters on this tour, making his long absences from home a little more tolerable. Eventually, two additional officers, Flight Lieutenant Briant Elliott and Flight Lieutenant Lloyd Flewelling joined the staff and shared the load.

Air Vice Marshal "Wild Bill" O'Brien was the Air Officer Commanding ADC at this time. He was an officer who got to know your name immediately you joined his staff. A fitness "nut," you might find yourself being overtaken on the stairs leading up to the Headquarters building as he bounded up them at a running pace, two steps at a time, but offering you a greeting by name as he went by. It was rumoured that anyone in his command overweight by as much as twelve pounds would find himself packing his bags to move on elsewhere.

Air Force Headquarters. In July 1962, Evoy was promoted to Squadron Leader and returned to Air Force Headquarters for a third time. These were the years of planning for the integration of the Forces and the Medical Branch was in the forefront of this planning. Medical equipment scales, widely different in the Navy, the Army and the RCAF, had to be rationalized and normalized into a single scale. This was the work that occupied S/L Evoy during this tour with the Directorate of Medical Supplies Scales of Issue for Static Canadian Forces Medical Services Facilities. It was a joint effort with officers of the other two services to reconcile differences in both equipment scales and operating procedures. Common field operating manuals had to be developed and Evoy worked on this project as well.

Squadron Leader Evoy continued with the work of unification for the formation of the Canadian Forces Medical Services until his retirement in February 1968. He did not see many of his projects reach completion, but was satisfied that he had helped get them underway before he retired.

After retirement, Nelson Evoy went to work for the Department of National Health and Welfare where he remained for fifteen years. He was a project officer for the Health Manpower Program in the Federal/Provincial arrangements on the construction of Health Science Centres.

Summary of Achievements

Canadian Forces Decoration (CD)
Canadian Volunteer Service Medal
War Medal 1939 - 1945

TED GEREIN
CD
SQUADRON LEADER

Ted Gerein's service career began on 14 October 1940 at a Calgary, Alberta recruiting centre with enrolment in the Royal Canadian Army Medical Corps for later transfer to the Royal Canadian Air Force Medical Branch. The year involved big career decisions for him. After Dunkirk and the fall of France in June 1940, he entertained serious thoughts about military service. He was employed in hospital laboratory technology and, that summer, he had an opportunity to work his way through a two-year advanced course at a St. Louis University or to take over the laboratory services for a large clinic in Calgary. Procrastination paid off in the end. For Gerein, the only military service of choice was the RCAF and word finally got around that the Air Force would have its own medical service.

Actual service began at No. 2 Initial Training School at Regina, Saskatchewan where he joined nineteen others to don army uniforms, which appeared to be leftovers from World War I. They were the most uncomfortable clothes he had ever worn. His boss was a regular force Regimental Sergeant-Major named Jimmy Duncan, who would later also transfer to the air force and serve on the staff of the Director Medical Services (Air).

At Regina, Gerein learned how to make a military bed, how to shine brass buttons and shoes, how to

S/L Ted Gerien

march and halt properly, as well as how to salute. This skill was practiced by marching up to a post and smartly bringing the open right hand up to the forehead. Two weeks later, most of the group were transferred to the Manning Depot in Toronto where they joined other recruits for the RCAF Medical Branch. There, they donned air force blues and spent all their time on drill.

262

One of the chaps left behind at Regina mustered as a nursing orderly, would remuster to aircrew a year or so later and end the war in Burma flying the "hump." This term referred to the transport pilots who flew supplies over the Himalayas to Burma, a treacherous and often fatal operation. After the war, he wrote and published a book entitled *How Papa Won The War.*

After two weeks in Toronto, Gerien's group of forty was transferred to the No. 2 Service Flying Training School at RCAF Station Uplands in Ottawa for a month-long course in medical administrative services required by the new RCAF Medical Branch. There, Ted was selected for training in medical statistics and posted to Ottawa to work in the statistics section of the Director General Medical Services (Army). This training period lasted until about 1 March 1941, when he moved to DMS (Air) in the Jackson Building. There he had to remuster from laboratory technician (Group 3) to Clerk Medical (Group 2), a loss in pay of twenty-five cents a day. What to do - since promotion to corporal rank would still entail a loss of five cents a day? The answer was to boost him to the rank of Sergeant.

Organization of the statistics section and determination of objectives involved some hectic periods and a lot of night duty in 1941. Early in 1943, because of manpower shortage in the forces, a project began to locate all personnel previously rejected at recruiting centres because of hernia. If these people could be enticed to enlist, they would be given free hernia repair surgery at a special hospital in Calgary and undergo intensive rehabilitation program devised by the two physical training experts on the directorate staff at the time.

In 1943, for some unknown reason, Gerien was selected by G/C Wilbur Franks *(see Aviation Medicine Pioneers)* to take an aero-medical exhibit to a conference of aero-medical specialists in St. Louis. The exhibit was produced at the RCAF Institute of Aviation Medicine in Toronto. The exhibit crew was trained to operate the exhibit which ran for three days.

In 1944, Gerien left the statistics section to take over the management of the directorate orderly room, a job he would retain until 1951. The job brought a promotion to Warrant Officer 1st Class (WO1), a rank that would be held until reversion day on 1 October 1946. On "R" or reversion day, all those who chose to remain in the RCAF Regular Force were required to revert in rank. At the end of the war there were some excellent opportunities to leave the service for good jobs on civvy street but Gerien opted to stay, in spite of dropping three ranks. The years up to 1951 were rather quiet, the only big job involved the purging of central registry files of all paper not having historical significance.

Air Marshal C.R. Dunlap bids farewell to S/L Gerien's on his retirement.

In 1951, he was commissioned and transferred to Air Materiel Command Headquarters, along with the very able Flying Officer Charlie Richer. There, he and Richer got into the business of purchasing medical equipment to a level required by the mobilization plan then in effect because of the Korean war. They also drafted contracts for the army to stock central medical stores with supplies and equipment to a level required by the plan and had the National Research Council develop specifications.

In 1954, Gerien was transferred to RCAF Station Rockcliffe Hospital in Ottawa. This hospital was undergoing extensive renovations under the direction of the Commanding Officer, Group Captain J.A. Mahoney. While there, he took the two-year Kellogg Foundation course in hospital organization and management. In July 1957, he was transferred to 3 (Fighter) Wing at

Zweibrucken in Germany, which turned out to be the highlight of his service career. Administrative duties at the hospital entailed jobs entirely different from anything in Canada and brought a promotion to Squadron Leader rank in 1959. Travelling in Europe with a family of five children was a priceless experience.

In 1960, he was transferred back to Ottawa where duties at the Surgeon General's office entailed mostly budgets and financial administration. Because of the geographical overlapping of military commands at the time, regional medical officer positions were established and he and his colleagues managed to devise a system that enabled them to pay directly for all medical expenses incurred in their regions.

Living in Ottawa with a young family during the war, and for a few years after, was a stressful experience. Shortage of adequate accommodation involved frequent moves. One winter was spent in a summer cottage, another entailed commuting from a farm house six miles beyond Kemptville, and still another in emergency quarters at Station Rockcliffe barracks, until finally new apartments became available in Ottawa. However, he never had any regrets about his decision to remain in the service because the RCAF provided ample opportunities for initiative and enterprise, and the four-year tour in Europe alone more than made up for all the hardships.

Summary of Achievements

Canadian Forces Decoration (CD)
War Medal - 1939 - 1945
Canadian Volunteer Service Medal
Special Service Medal - NATO

AMEDEUS CHARLES KING
CSTJ, CD
MAJOR

Charles King better known as "Chuck" was born in Moncton, New Brunswick on 22 April 1927 as the country was going into the years of the Great Depression. As a result early schooling was cut short after one year of high school and King joined the workforce. Work was in a newly opened aircraft war plant that did major overhauls on airplanes from Coastal Command. These airplanes had either run out of safe operating hours or had had a mishap in operations. The planes in question included Consolidated PBY-5A Cansos, Lockheed Hudsons, Lockheed Venturas and Avro Ansons. After an initial training period, Chuck became an airframe mechanic. After his introduction to the RCAF from his one year in the Air Cadets in high school, he found his work on airplanes an exciting experience.

The Air Force Beckons. In 1943, with two brothers in the Army overseas, there was only one place for this seventeen year old to be and that was the Royal Canadian Air Force. His wartime training as an airframe mechanic should have made him so attractive to the RCAF that they would not have noticed his age. Unfortunately, he faced a sharp-eyed sergeant whose only concern was a birth certificate. This document would have revealed a barely 17-year old youth unacceptable for military service. Determined, Chuck turned from one office, walked across the hall to the Army recruiting office and was promptly enrolled.

Maj A. Charles "Chuck" King

The Army Wins. However, he got his comeuppance after reporting to the recruit training depot in Fredericton, New Brunswick where a birth certificate was demanded and the truth was eventually bared. However, all was not lost and options were given; an outright discharge or remain in the army as a Boy Soldier. The latter option would entail a reduction in pay of fifty percent – from a dollar fifty cents a day to seventy cents a day. And this after having earned a salary of over $150 a month as an airframe technician in a war plant! The desire for glory was greater than that for gold, so the decision was made to remain in the army in an organization called the Canadian Technical Training Corps. This corps was formed to provide preparatory training to under-aged soldiers for future service in the artillery, engineers or signals corps. There were 5,000 or more of these young Canadians in this situation. Remaining in the army was a good decision . It gained for Boy Soldier King some knowledge of drafting and surveying, gained him veterans' credits that made possible further education at a Commercial College after demobilization in 1945 and gave him a leg up on his subsequent enrolment. As with many young men of this period, the war ended before they were old enough to be sent to a theatre of operations. Now a Gunner in 1 Canadian Horse Artillery, but with the war ended in Europe, he rushed to volunteer for service as part of the 6th Division being organized for service in the Pacific. Again, fate intervened and the atom bomb attacks on Japan brought that war to an end before training could even begin.

A Temporary Civvy. Demobilization in late 1945, back to school and on to a civilian job with CN Express did not fill the void left by the loss of camaraderie of service life. Application and acceptance as Aircraftman Class 1 (AC1) by the RCAF in 1949 not only filled this void, but it was yet another turn in life's course. Back to basic training at RCAF Station Aylmer, Ontario, followed by trades training as a Clerk Administration at 2 KTS Trenton, Ontario brought yet another turn in life's course. KTS was the acronym given to ground trades training schools – the meaning or origin of the K is not known.

Air Force Medical Branch. The policy of the School was to give the top student on each course the choice of postings on graduation. Naturally there was stiff competition for this privilege and this determined young airman wanted the pick of the postings. As a result, his consistently high grades brought AC1 King to the attention of the instructors and, when the Station

267

Hospital asked the School to recommend one of their students for their medical records department, he was picked out of the class and sent for an interview. The interview went so well that he was graduated early and sent off to a job that determined the direction of the rest of his military career.

At about this time, he met his future wife Cecile Hello, a nurse at the Belleville General Hospital. Wedding plans were soon being formed when near catastrophe struck. He was posted away from Trenton to a non-medical unit where it would be difficult to travel to complete his marriage plans and he would be out of the Medical Branch. The Senior Medical Officer, Squadron Leader T.J. Powell *(see Aviation Medicine Pioneers)*, was also reluctant to lose his medical records clerk and suggested that King search the Station for someone who might like to take this posting. If that failed, Powell said, he would admit him to hospital and keep him there under any pretext until such time as they got tired of waiting and posted someone else. Fortunately, this was not necessary so that wedding plans and the medical records job went on uninterrupted for the remainder of 1950.

Instructor/NCO. Later in 1950, a posting came in that could not be refused. The Medical Assistant School, then located at RCAF Hospital Rockcliffe, was being moved to 2 KTS at RCAF Station Aylmer, Ontario and the entire staff of the MedA school, including newly appointed Leading Aircraftman (LAC) King, was scheduled on an instructor's course at the School of Instructional Technique at Trenton. LAC King had more than a few anxious moments as he joined the group of officers and senior non-commissioned officers on this course, people who would subsequently be his bosses. However, he overcame his fear of public speaking and found that his new colleagues were most supportive. Furthermore, he found the visual aids portion of the course much to his liking. The experience of teaching at the MedA School built up his self-confidence and prepared him for his first promotion to Corporal *(Acting Whilst So Employed)* as an instructor. This rank was to be confirmed only if he passed his Group 3 trades test or withdrawn if he failed. The relief at getting a pass mark was palpable and Cpl King went on to complete five years with the school and to the next turning point.

Headquarters Tour #1. The posting to the staff of the Director General Medical Services (Air) [DGMS(Air)] in Ottawa came at a critical family time.

A third child was expected and complications in the delivery were predicted by the attending physician. Hence the family was temporarily located with extended family members in Montreal pending a surgical delivery. However, the new job with DGMS(Air) proved challenging and rewarding, bringing a promotion to Sergeant (Sgt) and, after four years in this appointment(1955-1959), a posting to 4(Fighter) Wing at Baden-Soellingen, Germany.

The NATO Tour. The four-years in Baden-Soellingen (1959-1963) were the most stressful, yet the most enjoyable of Sgt King's career. The stress of having a family living in a German village, without telephone communication, of having to live on the base in isolation during "exercises" *(one was never quite certain whether or not they were exercises)*, the workload of providing medical care for the military members as well as their families at a Station Hospital staffed only on the basis of the military population, all contributed to a high stress level. The camaraderie of colleagues *(the difference between officers and non-commissioned members was virtually non-existent after work hours)* resulted in a mutually supportive and collaborative social atmosphere that made life relatively enjoyable. Further, it was a learning experience without parallel. Situations arose, in the absences of the hospital administrative officer, that required a junior Sergeant chief clerk to search through the books to find the appropriate answers. Unwittingly, a store of knowledge was being built up that would be invaluable later on.

Instructor Tour #2. Ironically, after having previously served five years in training, the choice of postings on return to Canada was training – namely the Canadian Forces Medical Training Centre at Camp Borden, Ontario. Here, the Commandant, an RCAF Group Captain, G/C Ian Barclay, insisted that this new RCAF member of his school staff rotate through the Orderly Room to learn how the army functioned in each administrative area. After a period of this rotation, he insisted that his RCAF Sergeant could teach anything that was required of him, and promptly assigned him to teach on the staff of the First Aid Instructors Course. Whether this was luck or chance, it worked out well, leading to a promotion to Flight Sergeant (F/S). As you will see later, it also led directly to a post-retirement second career with St. John Ambulance. The added task of setting up and running a medical records course during this time also added greatly to the store of administrative knowledge. There is no better way to learn a subject than to teach it.

The tools added to F/S King's kit-box during this tour were of immense value; a good grounding in first aid, casualty simulation taught by masters in the art, an in-depth knowledge of medical records and statistical analysis, as well as personnel management in an army milieu, were of inestimable value. But F/S King had other ambitions and their achievement, even though he had been completing his high school education by night courses, seemed in doubt.

Civvy Street An Option. Promotion policy of the time precluded commissioning from the ranks beyond the age of 39. That age, for F/S King, was fast approaching in 1966 and there were no signs of a commission offer on the horizon. It was decided that the best option was to plan for a civilian career in health care administration and that the route to this was to enrol in a degree program at Waterloo University. But first there was the hurdle of writing and passing the entrance examinations required of mature students who could not produce sufficient high school credits for university entrance. University entrance examination study books were quickly obtained and studied throughout the spring and summer of 1966 in preparation for the exams in late summer. Successful completion of the exams brought a university enrolment offer from Waterloo that coincided with an order to appear before an officer candidate examining board sitting in Toronto!

A Commission is Offered. The officer candidate examinations, spanning three days, included written tests in math, English, chemistry and physics – and what a coincidence – these were at the university entrance level, very much like the ones just written at Waterloo University. The degree of success on these exams raised eyebrows and the examiners wanted to know if the records of his previous formal education were accurate. A commission as a Flying Officer Medical Associate Officer followed, and with it a more interesting job as Air Transport Command's Aeromedical Evacuation Coordinating Officer (AMECO) and relocation to Canadian Forces Base Trenton, Ontario. The task of reviewing and revising the policies and procedures for air evacuation of medical patients in Air Transport Command aircraft was undertaken and recommended changes were accepted by the Surgeon General and Air Transport Command. Unification brought a rank change to Lieutenant (Lt) in 1968.

270

Health Care Administration Training. Formal health care administration training still eluded Lieutenant King and once more he took things into his own hands by making application to the Canadian Hospital Association(CHA) to be enrolled in their University of Manitoba program as a private student. This would have entailed paying a fairly stiff tuition and foregoing two years of annual leave to attend the intra-mural sessions at the University of Manitoba in Winnipeg. Travel and accommodation costs would have added to this burden. Unbeknownst to Lt King, the CHA routinely communicated with the Department of National Defence on the selection of military officers for training in health care administration. Only two candidates from DND were admitted each year, and they wanted to know who this maverick was who wanted to enroll as a private student? The coincidences are hard to believe, but at that very moment, DND was pondering the dilemma of a last minute withdrawal of a candidate who had been groomed to attend a master's degree program in health care administration at Baylor University of Waco Texas, given by the U.S. Army at the Fort Sam Houston campus in San Antonio, Texas. Here, although he did not have an undergraduate degree, was a candidate who appeared to be keenly interested. And so off the family went to San Antonio for an academic year 1969-1970.

Headquarters Tour #2. The lack of an undergraduate degree meant that a master degree could not be conferred for the Baylor program. However, a diploma was issued and even more interesting appointments resulted. First as assistant administrative officer at Canadian Forces Hospital Kingston and then to the staff of the Surgeon General in Medical Plans and Requirements. This latter eight-year appointment was perhaps the most interesting, involving work on the On Site Manpower Evaluation Team, the re-writing of the manpower/workload indicators for these reviews and assisting Base Surgeons in preparing their reports on which these reviews were based. It was also during this tour of duty that Captain King suffered a myocardial infarct (MI), but made a good recovery after a lengthy hospital stay. MIs are usually career enders and King was prepared to see his career end as a Captain, but fate intervened again and his recovery was such that he would not be precluded from holding almost any of the appointments at the major rank. His next promotion was therefore granted.

271

Retirement Planning. At CRA (compulsory retirement age) minus four years, it was time to get back into the hospital administration field and Major King's request for a posting to the National Defence Medical Centre was granted in 1980. During this short tour of duty, he learned of a job opportunity with St. John Ambulance, writing first aid manuals and preparing visual aids for first aid training. Harking back to his days on the staff of the First Aid Instructor's Course, his dissatisfaction with the training manuals then in use and of his efforts then to have them amended, this job looked most interesting. Although two years from compulsory retirement, and the prospects of a dramatic drop in salary, he weighed the prospects of doing something he had always wanted to do as an alternative to the more stressful field of hospital administration. In 1981, King voluntarily retired to take on this new appointment of Publications Officer for St. John Ambulance, a position he held for the next eight years. During this tenure, he produced two editions each of the *Standard First Aid* manual and of the *Emergency First Aid* manual along with a number of pocket references, industrial safety and first aid booklets and fourteen hours of first aid videos to complement first aid training. This contribution to first aid training was considered to be of sufficient value that Charles King was admitted to the Most Venerable Order of St. John of Jerasulem and subsequently promoted through the grades to Officer and Commander.

A Happy Ending. Through the thirty-four years of service, through the ranks of Boy Soldier, Private, Gunner, AC1, LAC, Cpl, Sgt, F/S, F/O, Captain, and Major, there was never a posting or an appointment that did not provide a challenge and good deal of satisfaction. There was never a job that did not provide a learning experience and added to the font of knowledge needed for a future appointment. With the devoted and determined support of his wife, "Cec" and with his family of two boys and a girl, it has been a totally satisfying experience.

Summary of Achievements
Commander The Most Venerable Order of the Hospital St. John of Jerusalem (CStJ)
Canadian Forces Decoration (CD)
Canadian Voluntary Service Medal
War Medal 1939-1945
Special Service Medal - NATO
Queen's Jubilee Medal
Diploma - Health Care Administration - Baylor University/Fort Sam Houston Texas

G. Douglas Manderson
SBStJ, CD
Wing Commander

Douglas **Manderson** was born on 26 April 1919 in Haywarden, Saskatchewan. Following high school, Doug worked in his father's business and then attended business college in Regina. It was during this period in 1940 that he decided to join the military and enlisted in the Royal Canadian Army Medical Corps (RCAMC). After basic training with the RCAMC in Regina, the new recruits were informed of the formation of the Royal Canadian Air Force Medical Branch. Private Manderson and a number of others of his group transferred to the RCAF as Aircraftmen 2nd Class (AC2) on 16 November 1940.

As Doug progressed through the Non-Commissioned Officer ranks he worked for the Director General Medical Services (Air) in Medical Statistics at Air Force Headquarters in Ottawa. When that section was moved to Toronto to be part of the RCAF Institute of Aviation Medicine (IAM) in 1946, Doug moved with it..

Manderson was commissioned as a Flying Officer (F/O), Medical Secretarial Officer in 1951 while serving at the IAM. This promotion took him to Air Transport Command Headquarters in Lachine, Québec where he worked

W/C G. Douglas Manderson

with the Staff Officer Medical Services (SOMS) for two years. F/O Manderson took on much of the administrative and financial work involved in ensuring adequate supplies and services for stations to operate their medical facilities.

The RCAF was planning to build its own definitive care hospital in Ottawa and Flight Lieutenant Manderson, who was later promoted to Squadron Leader,

273

was called to join the staff of the Director General Medical Services (Air) to help develop these plans. This facility, which was planned as a joint venture by DND-DVA, was called the National Defence Medical Centre (NDMC). It opened in October 1961 with a combined staff of Navy, Army and RCAF.

Manderson was promoted to Wing Commander (W/C) in 1961 and was appointed the Senior Medical Administrative Officer when NDMC opened, the first RCAF Medical Administrative Officer in the combined medical staff of the hospital.

Following his tour of duty at the NDMC, W/C Manderson was recalled to the staff of the Surgeon General and appointed Director of Medical Finance in the combined Canadian Forces Medical Service. He retained this appointment until his retirement in 1974. W/C Manderson was highly respected in provincial and federal health departments, enabling him to negotiate numerous agreements on shared services and access to specialized services.

On retirement in 1974, Doug continued his work in health care management with the Ottawa-Carleton District Health Council. Even after final retirement from the Council, he continued to serve as a member of one of their planning committees.

He was an outstanding curler and competed in many bonspiels. He then became a dedicated golfer until his health limited his physical activities. He was married to Hazel Stewart who died in 1997.

Summary of Achievements

Serving Brother of the Most Venerable Order of the Hospital St. John of Jerusalem (SBStJ)
Canadian Forces Decoration (CD)
Canadian Volunteer Service Medal
War Medal, 1939-1945

HAROLD M. WRIGHT, CD
LIEUTENANT-COLONEL

Harold M. Wright was born in Glanworth, Ontario, a small community which is now part of London, Ontario. He attended London Central Collegiate, getting to school every day on an electric rail line running between London and Port Stanley. It was named, appropriately, the London and Port Stanley Railway or L&PS, but was called, unaffectionately, "late and poor service."

In March 1942, Wright joined the Royal Canadian Air Force, starting his career at #1 Manning Depot in Toronto. The Depot was situated in one of the buildings of the Central Canada Exhibition, referred to as the cow palace. More than 2,000 men were housed here and slept in two-tiered bunks lined up row upon row in one large area. When one of the airman complained about the lack of privacy, the sergeant replied, ``Just close your eyes if you want privacy.''

LCol Harold M. Wright

The once-a-month pay parades took all day. The airmen lined up in the morning in alphabetical order and if they were not paid before lunch, they came back in the afternoon. Wright, whose name came only a little before Zavitz, was always paid in the afternoon, but nonetheless had to stand there all morning, shuffling forward one payee at a time. This is probably where the story originated about the marginally literate NCO who was lining up the lads who called out their names as he checked them off on a list. Coming to the Ps, one lad called out "Phillips!" "What are you doing back here in the Ps" said the NCO, "Get up in the Fs where you belong."

It was a common occurrence to have new recruits arrive in large groups. Often one wag would yell out, "anybody here from the west" and another wag would reply "fuddle duddle the west," or something similar. And so the bantering went on as they went through their daily routine. They were documented, inoculated and outfitted with uniforms. There was a lot of truth to the jest that military uniforms come in two sizes -- too big or too small, so there was tailoring as well. And last but not least, they were drilled – and boy were they drilled. They came out of that program looking much less like civilians and a lot more like soldiers – albeit in blue. Now it was time to start doing something useful.

Off they went in all directions, Wright went to # 2 Clinical Investigation Unit Regina, Saskatchewan to learn how to operate a decompression chamber used to train pilots and other aircrew on the use of oxygen in flight and the hazards of anoxia. Wright also served as a guinea pig for medical research. Having acquired the basic skills of a Technical Assistant Medical and survived the rigors of high altitude training and medical research, he was transferred to # 1 Y Depot in Halifax Nova Scotia to work in the Flying Personnel Medical Section. A "Y" depot was a station that prepared airmen for overseas duty. This unit had twelve decompression chambers to train and process British Commonwealth Air Training Plan aircrew members before they were sent to England to join a fighter or bomber squadron.

A decompression chamber is a steel tank, large enough to accommodate ten or twelve adults and made up of two compartments, one smaller than the other. The tank-like structure, positioned on its side, had access doors on one end, one into the smaller chamber or lock, leading to another into the larger chamber where training took place. Each compartment door had a small observation window and airtight seals to prevent air entry. The two chambers could have oxygen removed from them separately to simulate high altitude atmosphere. Each chamber had a four-man crew consisting of an observer, a chamber operator, a lock operator and a float who looked after oxygen cylinders. There was always a physician on standby when the chambers were in operation. Groups of aircrew trainees were taken into the chamber and exposed to an atmosphere of 12,000 feet. Those who tolerated the first run were then taken up on three additional runs to 35,000 feet. In the training run, the observer was in charge and demonstrated the oxygen system. One trainee was selected to remove his oxygen mask at 10,000 feet. The observer pointed out the physical changes taking place due to anoxia -- the trainee's blue lips, blue fingernails, loss of concentration and inability to write legibly were meant to show the effects of lack of oxygen at altitudes of 10,000 and higher, and the resulting loss of coordination and judgement.

Three regular runs were given to assess and give further training. It took thirty minutes to reduce the oxygen level in the chamber to approximate the rarified atmosphere of 35,000 feet. The chamber was held at that level for two hours to familiarize the students with supplemental oxygen equipment, to acclimatize them to demand oxygen breathing and to assess their ability to function at this altitude. Then it would take a further half hour to return to ground level.

If a trainee experienced decompression sickness, the supervising physician would enter the lock, have it brought up to the main compartment altitude, open the passageway into the main chamber and bring the distressed student back through the lock. Once in the secured lock, this smaller room was re-pressurized to ground level while the physician examined and cared for the trainee. Each trainee's log-book was annotated to show his suitability for high altitude flying. Those with a lesser category were assigned to coastal flying duties where aircraft were operated at lower altitudes.

At the end of 1943, the demand for high altitude training was reduced, so the unit was relocated to Lachine, Québec. Wright, now a fully qualified Technical Assistant Medical, remained with the unit for an additional six months before moving to the RCAF Institute of Aviation Medicine in Toronto. On "R" day in 1946, all those holding temporary wartime ranks reverted to a lesser rank if they were selected to remain in the service. Flight Sergeant Wright reverted to Sergeant and stayed in the peacetime Regular Force.

In 1951, after regaining the rank of Flight Sergeant, Wright was commissioned as a Flying Officer and transferred to # 1 Manning Depot as the administrator of the Station Hospital. The Depot, now located at St-Jean Québec, had been moved from its post-war location at Aylmer, Ontario.

The Korean War was in full swing and the RCAF was on a recruiting drive. Compounding the problems of the large number of recruits coming into the Manning Depot, an epidemic of influenza broke out. The illness raged through the barracks and the spread of the virus was increased by the open sleeping quarters and proximity of the two-tiered bunks. Airmen and airwomen reported sick at the hospital in droves.

Having determined that treatment was mainly the relief of symptoms in one of two categories, the doctors and pharmacists arrived at a simple solution. Medication was pre-packaged in paper bags numbered #1 and #2 to deal with each category. After patients had their temperature taken, they were formed in a line at the pharmacy wicket. A doctor examined each patient's throat and, based on his examination, he would simply say #1 or #2 and the pharmacist would issue a paper bag containing the appropriate treatment items. It was a form of mass treatment that worked well for the majority of cases. More serious cases were hospitalized.

In 1953, Flight Lieutenant Wright returned to the Institute of Aviation Medicine in an administrative post he held for eighteen months. A posting to Air Materiel Command in Ottawa followed and he was appointed Procurement Officer. During this six years stint, he was responsible for the purchasing of a wide range of medical equipment, including optical contracts for spectacles for the RCAF. This led to a one- year tour of duty with the Surgeon General's staff on medical equipment related duties. It was during this period that Wright completed a two-year extension course of studies given under the auspices of the Canadian Hospital Association at the University of Manitoba. He graduated with a diploma in Hospital Administration and Organization and became a charter member of the Canadian College of Health Services Executives..

In 1961 he was transferred to 3 (Fighter) Wing Zweibrucken, Germany as the Senior Hospital Administrative Officer. Trans-Atlantic air travel was not well established yet, so the journey was by train to Montreal, by ship to Le Havre, France and again by rail to Paris for an overnight stay and rail again to Zweibrucken. The ocean crossing was a tremendous experience for the family with sitings of an iceberg and foreign fishing ships off the coast of Newfoundland. The overnight stay in Paris provided the opportunity to see some of the sights, including the Eiffel Tower looming over the city. To add to the excitement, it was the day the Russians barricaded East Berlin by putting up the famous Berlin Wall and there was also an uprising in Algeria against the French government. There were armed guards with submachine guns all over the city, particularly at the railroad station.

The years at Zweibrucken were enjoyable, giving one the opportunity to travel, even on week-ends, but they were also extremely busy. The family travelled as often and as widely as time and money would permit. Wright's sons remember visiting interesting places that had once only been names on the school map.

The hospital provided all the care for the serving members and almost all of the care for their families. 3(F) Wing Hospital was the referral hospital for the other three bases, comprising Air Division, and for the Air Division Headquarters personnel. The hospital had specialists in aviation medicine, surgery, anaesthesiology, obstetrics and gynecology, psychiatry and radiology. Major changes in operational equipment created its own workload as new squadron personnel arrived with the Lockheed CF-104 Starfighter and others left with the decommissioning of Avro CF-100 Canuck and Canadair F-86 Sabre squadrons.

The return journey to Canada in 1965 was much faster than the outgoing trip. Air Transport Command was, by this time, operating Canadair CC-106 Yukon aircraft in sufficient numbers that they were able to accommodate all returning families in reasonable comfort. The Wrights were soon settled into their new home in Halifax as Squadron Leader Wright assumed his new duties, first at the Canadian Forces Hospital as Senior Administrative Officer and the second year on the staff of the Regional Surgeon Atlantic Region. With a promotion to Lieutenant-Colonel an appointment as Section Head in the office of the Directorate of Medical Plans and Requirements on the Surgeon General's staff beckoned in 1967. He held this appointment until 1975 when he was retired from the Canadian Forces Medical Service.

On retirement, he took a job with the Correctional Service of Canada as health care facilities co-ordinator, an appointment he held for eleven years. Following a second retirement, Wright accepted the voluntary appointment of National Secretary to the Defence Medical Association of Canada. He held this appointment for an unprecedented eleven-year tenure until 1997.

In 1998, he offered to assist the Air Museum in Trenton to recognize the contributions made by medical personnel to aviation in Canada and began preparing this book.

He married Dorothy Fraser in Halifax in 1945 while he was stationed at the IAM in Toronto. They recall leaving Halifax by train to return to Toronto with one trunk, two suitcases and $100. They raised two sons Kevin and Keith. Kevin married Margaret Faircloth and they have a son Fraser. Kevin is the assistant-principal of a school in Calgary. Keith died in 1982.

Harold Wright served for 34 years in the RCAF and Canadian Forces Medical Services, progressing through the ranks of aircraftman to lieutenant-colonel as a Technical Assistant Medical and Medical Associate Officer (Administration).

Summary of Achievements

Canadian Forces Decoration (CD)
Canadian Volunteer Service Medal
War Medal, 1939 - 1945
Special Service Medal - NATO
Canadian Centennial Medal
Diploma - Canadian Hospital Organization and Management

CHAPTER 8

THE APOTHECARIES

MEDICAL ASSOCIATE OFFICERS (PHARMACY)

- **Lieutenant-Colonel "Ken" Commons**
  The first RCAF pharmacist to obtain a Masters of Science degree in Pharmacy.

- **Squadron Leader W.A. "Bill" Curtis**
  A war-time navigator awarded the Distinguished Flying Cross; post-war pharmacist in the RCAF who helped in the design of the National Defence Medical Center.

- **Squadron Leader John L. Fachnie**
  War-time pilot, son of a WWI pilot/pharmacist, he became a pharmacist in the RCAF. Commanded medical equipment depots in Debert Nova Scotia, and North Luffenham England.

- **Flight Lieutenant D.F. "Don" McGourlick**
  A war-time air-gunner awarded a Distinguished Flying Cross; shot down over France, but escaped the Germans with the help of the French underground and returned to Britain across the English Channel. Post-war pharmacist in the RCAF.

KENNETH COMMONS
CD, MSc
LIEUTENANT COLONEL

Ken Commons was born in Fernie, B.C. and received his early education in Vancouver. He attended the University of British Columbia, graduating in 1952 with a Bachelor of Science Degree in Pharmacy. During his final year at UBC, he joined the RCAF under the University Training Program.

After graduation, he served at several airforce stations including RCAF Station Clinton, 3 (Fighter) Wing Zweibrucken, Germany, RCAF Station Moose Jaw, Saskatchewan, RCAF Station Cold Lake, Alberta and RCAF Station St- Hubert, Québec.

In 1965, he attended graduate school at the University of Toronto where he received a Master of Science degree in Pharmacy. He was subsequently posted to National Defence Medical Centre in Ottawa as Director of Pharmaceutical Services and then

LCol Kenneth Commons

to National Defence Headquarters on the staff of the Surgeon General in its Directorate of Pharmaceutical Services.

In 1973, he was appointed Commanding Officer of Central Medical Equipment Depot in Petawawa, and in 1976 became Director of Pharmaceutical Services at NDHQ.

He retired from the Canadian Forces Medical Service in 1979 and worked for several years with the Health and Welfare Canada. In 1987, he retired and returned to his home province where he and his wife Vicki enjoy their West Coast lifestyle. They have two married sons and three grandchildren.

Summary of Achievements

Canadian Forces Decoration and Clasp CD -
Special Services Medal - NATO
University of British Columbia, 1952 B Sc -
University of Toronto, 1965 M Sc Pharm -

WILLIAM A. "BILL" CURTIS
DFC, CD, BSc
SQUADRON LEADER

William A. Curtis, known to everyone as "Bill," hails from Melfort, Saskatchewan. He joined the Royal Canadian Air Force in 1941 as a "P" or "O" (pilot or observer), and was trained at No. 9 Air Observer School at St-Jean, Quebec, graduating as a Sergeant Navigator in December 1942. He served as a Navigator from 18 September 1941 until 3 October 1945. His Operational Flying tour was with 433 "Porcupine" (named after Porcupine, Ont.) Squadron in 6 Group of Bomber Command. The Squadron was based at Skipton-on-Swale in Yorkshire, England. During its war-time service, 433 Squadron operated first with Handley Page Halifax Mk III aircraft and later with Avro Lancasters. Bill took part in thirty operational raids over occupied Europe in Halifax's. He was awarded the Distinguished Flying Cross and the citation in the London Gazette of 17 October 1944 read:

"Has completed, in various capacities, numerous operations against the enemy in the course of which he has invariably displayed the utmost fortitude, courage and devotion to duty"

Bill credits his survival of WWII in Bomber Command to two main things. First, he was fortunate to be a member of a very good crew that lived, played and worked together. His pilot, Jimmy Monahan was not only a very skilled flyer, but as an ex-aeroengine mechanic who knew a lot about aircraft and in

S/L William A. Curtis

285

particular aircraft engines. He was always able to coax a bit more altitude out of any aircraft he flew and at the same time optimize fuel consumption and detect minor engine problems that could cause serious trouble later. Jimmy always impressed on his crew the value of reporting any degree of unserviceability with as much detail as possible -- when did it go unserviceable, did it happen suddenly or over a period of time, at what altitude, at what temperature, etc. This information was very important for the ground crew who were generally able to fix the problem quickly and this meant that his aircraft had very few equipment failures throughout the tour. He saved his crew from serious or fatal injuries on two specific occasions, once by making a forced landing in a field after both engines failed on a clumsy old aircraft, an Armstrong Whitworth Whitley, and the second in a three-engine landing of a Halifax Mk III with a blown tire. Certainly, there was a degree of luck, but crew skill played a large part.

On a second flying tour Bill flew with test pilots at RCAF Station Topcliffe during which he made fifty-three test flights in Halifax and Avro Lancaster aircraft.

At the end of the war, Mr. W. Woolett, the General Manager of No. 9 Air Observer School at St-Jean, sent an oak shield to Bill's mother. This shield, along with others, had been displayed at the School to commemorate her son's DFC and distinguished service as a Navigator.

On demobilization, Bill attended the University of Saskatchewan from September 1946 to April 1950, graduating with a Bachelor of Science in Pharmacy. After graduation, he rejoined the RCAF as a Pharmacist, serving from 5 April 1950 to 19 November 1971, a total of twenty-one years -- eleven years with the RCAF and ten years with the Canadian Forces Medical Services. During that time, Bill served at a number of posts, including RCAF Station Goose Bay, Labrador; RCAF Station Rockcliffe, Ontario; on the staff of the Director General Medical Services (Air) [DGMS(Air)]; 4(Fighter) Wing, Baden-Soellingen, Germany; the Central Medical Equipment Depot, Petawawa, Ontario; the National Defence Medical Centre, and on the the Surgeon General's staff at National Defence Headquarters in Ottawa.

The posting at DGMS (Air) is of particular interest, because Flight Lieutenant Curtis was on the design team for the new National Defence

Medical Centre (NDMC), a facility designed and operated by the RCAF until unification in 1968. Bill designed the pharmacy and its associated stores area and fought with great determination for its location at the NDMC.

Also, while on the staff of DGMS(Air) Bill became aware of the need for continuing education for RCAF pharmacists. A graduate of the University of Saskatchewan, Bill negotiated with his alma mater to provide a one-month program for four RCAF pharmacists. This was probably the first such course in continuing education for pharmacists in Canada. On evaluation, this course was reduced to a two-week refresher course that continued for several years and eventually included other government pharmacists.

During Squadron Leader Curtis' tour at NDMC, he worked on The Frozen Blood Bank Program, for which he received commendations for the countless hours of work in the preparation of glycerol and wash solutions used in preparing blood for freezing.

He married Helen Perkins 15 May 1950. She was in the RCAF during the war years serving, as a wireless operator ground. She is also a graduate of the University of Saskatchewan, graduating with degrees in Commerce and Arts.

Summary of Achievements

Distinguished Flying Cross (DFC)
Canadian Forces Decoration (CD)
1939 - 1945 Star
Aircrew Europe Star France and Germany and Clasp
Defence Medal
Canadian Volunteer Service Medal and Clasp
War Medal, 1939 - 1945
Special Service Medal NATO
Operations Wing
Bachelor of Science Pharmacy, University of Saskatchewan BSc - 1950

JOHN LENNOX FACHNIE
CD, BSc
MAJOR

John Fachnie was born in Collingwood, Ontario and grew up in the village of Beeton where his father owned the village drugstore. He attended school there, completing his high school education at Bradford High. During World War I, his father, Alexander, was a pilot in the Royal Flying Corps and served in England, Scotland and France with Ferry Command and became a pharmacist after the war.

On graduation from high school in 1943, John enlisted in the Royal Canadian Air Force. Selected for pilot training, he received his Wings on 2 November 1944 at RCAF Station Brandon, Manitoba.

After being discharged from the RCAF in 1945, Fachnie completed his apprenticeship in pharmacy and subsequently attended the Ontario College of Pharmacy, graduating in 1947. Three years later, John married Sheila MacLean and re-enlisted in the RCAF as a pharmacist. He was immediately transferred to RCAF Station Greenwood, Nova Scotia and started his Air Force career as a hospital pharmacist. During this posting, he and his wife Sheila started their family of two children, Cherry and Ian.

Major John L. Fachnie

In 1955, Flight Lieutenant Fachnie was transferred to the RCAF Station Rockcliffe Hospital in Ottawa, where he served as Chief Pharmacist for the next four years. Then, in 1959, the family sailed overseas to England where John took up a post as a medical supply officer at RCAF Langar and helped supply

288

Canada's NATO Forces in Europe. From 1962-1963, John was stationed at 2 (Fighter) Wing at Grostenquin, France as the pharmacist at the station hospital.

Returning to Canada in 1963, John was posted to No. 1 Central Medical Equipment Depot at Camp Petawawa, Ontario. The Depot supplied all military medical facilities with medical equipment supplies and pharmaceuticals. From Petawawa in 1967, Fachnie headed east as Depot Commander of the Regional Medical Equipment Depot, Camp Debert, Nova Scotia. This Depot supplied all maritime province bases as well as the ships of the Navy. Flight Lieutenant Fachnie held this appointment for five years.

In 1972, Major Fachnie returned to Ottawa where, during the next seven years, he served as Chief of Pharmacy at National Defence Medical Centre (NCMC) during 1972 and 1973, and then at the Directorate of Pharmaceutical Services on the Surgeon General's staff from 1973 to 1977. Major Fachnie returned to NDMC as Chief Pharmacist until he retired in 1979.

John Fachnie retired to White Lake, Ontario where he enjoyed the outdoor life of hunting and fishing and pursued his many hobbies including gardening, carpentry and auto mechanics. He was always busying himself with one project or another and served on various community projects and committees until his health began to decline. He was diagnosed with A.L.S. (Amyotropic Lateral Sclerosis) and passed away on the 14 July 1997 at the Arnprior hospital.

Summary of Achievements

Canadian Forces Medal (CD)
Canadian Volunteer Service Medal
War Medal, 1939 - 1945
Special Service Medal - NATO
Bachelor of Science (Pharmacy)

DONALD F. MCGOURLICK
DFC, CD, BSc
FLIGHT LIEUTENANT

Donald McGourlick was born in Gull Lake, Saskatchewan and was educated as a teacher. He was teaching school in April 1941 when he decided to join the Royal Canadian Air Force in Calgary.

Aircraftman 2nd Class McGourlick went through the initial phases of aircrew selection and training quickly, completing initial training selection at No. 1 Initial Training School on 11 April 1942, elementary flying training at No. 7 Elementary Flying Training School on 25 May 1942, bombing and gunnery training at No 2. Bombing and Gunnery School on 14 August 1942.

F/L Donald F. McGourlick

McGourlick's first preference was to take pilot training, but this was not to be and he was commissioned a Pilot Officer as an Air Gunner.

Arriving overseas, P/O McGourlick went through a whole series of operational training programs in bombing and gunnery to prepare him for flying duties on heavy bombers. His first squadron posting was to 106 Squadron RAF, based at Syerston in the Midlands, flying in Avro Lancaster aircraft. On McGourlick's fourteenth operational flight, in August 1943, his aircraft was badly damaged by night fighters and caught fire. Not all the crew was able to get out of the burning airplane, but McGourlick managed to bail out over France.

The French underground dressed him up as a farm worker and hid him out in the open amongst field hands. The Germans seldom if ever questioned field workers and he continued to hide out for four months until he was able to arrange his escape back to England. Flying Officer McGourlick eventually made his way across the English Channel in a motorized sail boat, accompanied by a member of the underground. Their boat landed in a mine field, but fortunately they were not blown up. The French partisan was taken in for questioning and McGourlick was returned to his Squadron.

Four months after his return, Flight Lieutenant McGourlick was assigned to 405 Squadron, the first RCAF bomber squadron to be formed in England. The Squadron, now assigned Pathfinder duties, was flying Avro Lancaster Mk III aircraft, leading the main bomber force in operations over Europe. Pathfinders preceded the main bomber force, using the best navigational skills available to locate the intended target and mark it with incendiary bombs. The bomber main force tried to locate the fires set by the incendiary bombs over which to release their bomb loads. The tactic was recognized by the Germans, who made every effort to destroy these Pathfinder aircraft. McGourlick flew twenty-four operational flights with 405 Squadron for which he was awarded the Distinguished Flying Cross. The London Gazette of 14 November 1944 published this award, noting in the citation:

"Flight Lieutenant McGourlick completed OPS with courage and devotion to duty."

McGourlick was returned to Canada on furlough and was returning to England when the war ended.

After demobilization, Don McGourlick took advantage of his Veterans credits to complete a degree in pharmacy. He then re-enrolled in the RCAF in 1951.

Flight Lieutenant McGourlick served on several RCAF stations including a tour of duty at 1 (Fighter) Wing at Marville, France between 1958-1960. It was during this tour that he made contact with the French family who had sheltered him during his escape from the Germans during WWII. He and his wife Jean were warmly welcomed and invited to stay, occupying the same quarters and using the same bed McGourlick had used for the four months of his undercover visit.

Don McGourlick retired to British Columbia and served as replacement pharmacist for outpost hospitals. He is now enjoying retirement on Vancouver Island.

Summary of Achievements

Distinguished Flying Cross (DFC)
Canadian Forces Decoration (CD)
1939 - 1945 Star
Aircrew Europe Star, 1939 - 1944 with Bar
Defence Medal, 1939 - 1945
Canadian Volunteer Service Medal
War Medal 1939 - 1945
Special Service Medal-NATO
Bachelor of Science (Pharmacy)

AFTERWORD

. . . . and on it goes, with the many Air Force Medical Doctors, Nurses, Pharmacists, Medical Associates and Technicians who continue to support the Canadian Air Force in its commitments in peace and war. This is not the end of the story, indeed is it not even the beginning. It is rather a slice of time that tries to capture moments through the biographical sketches of some of the early contributors to aviation through medical discoveries and medical support.

I am reminded of something a mentor once said. "If a thing is worth doing," he said, "it's worth doing badly." What he meant was that if events are recorded, even though imperfectly, there will be someone who will come along someday to improve it. However, if one hesitates, for whatever reason, it may never be done, leaving nothing for improvement by some more skilled person later.

I must confess that this is probably the case with this collection of stories. Although done to the best of my abilities, I am certain the collection can be vastly improved upon by someone more skilled as an author and historian. I sincerely hope that this book will inspire future historians to add some of the missing biographies from the early days, to improve on the ones here presented, and to augment the collection with biographies of future generations of aviation medicine scientists, researchers and practitioners, as well as supporting members of the Air Force medical team.

Harold M. Wright

293

Index

Text prepared with Corel Word Perfect 8.0

Typeset:

    - Times Roman 10 point

Display Fonts :

    - Title Page: Algerian 30 pts and Unicorn 20 pts

    - Chapter Titles: Algerian 30 and 20 pts

    - Section Titles: Copperplate Gothic Heavy Bold 18 Pts

Layout, design and cover art concept by Charles King

Cover Art:

    Central graphic element, comprising a stylized pilot, formed by Air Force wings, and a flight surgeon, formed by a caduceus, was taken from *The Journal of the Canadian Medical Services*, Vol 4, No 1, November, 1946, p. 112 captioned *"A handshake in the clouds embodies the natural bond of friendship and cooperation that exists between the "Flying Type" and the "Doc."* Original artist is not known. The F-18 aerobatics frame was created with Corel Draw and superimposed on the RCAF Tartan.

    Final art assembly by Hangar 13 Art and Design of Ottawa, Ontario

Printing and Binding:

    - DocuLink International of Kanata, Ontario, Canada